‖‖‖ ‖‖ ‖‖‖‖‖ ‖‖‖ ‖ ‖ ‖‖‖ ‖‖‖‖‖‖‖‖‖‖‖‖‖ ‖‖
⚹ **W9-CBM-860**

Nutshell Series

of

WEST PUBLISHING COMPANY

P.O. Box 3526

St. Paul, Minnesota 55165

August, 1981

Administrative Law and Process, 2nd Ed., 1981, approx. 440 pages, by Ernest Gellhorn, Professor of Law, University of Virginia and Barry B. Boyer, Professor of Law, SUNY, Buffalo.

Agency-Partnership, 1977, 364 pages, by Roscoe T. Steffen, Late Professor of Law, University of Chicago.

American Indian Law, 1981, 288 pages, by William C. Canby, Jr., former Professor of Law, Arizona State University.

Antitrust Law and Economics, 2nd Ed., 1981, 425 pages, by Ernest Gellhorn, Professor of Law, University of Virginia.

Church-State Relations—Law of 1981, 305 pages, by Leonard F. Manning, Professor of Law, Fordham University.

Civil Procedure, 1979, 271 pages, by Mary Kay Kane, Professor of Law, University of California, Hastings College of the Law.

Civil Rights, 1978, 279 pages, by Norman Vieira, Professor of Law, University of Idaho.

Commercial Paper, 2nd Ed., 1975, 361 pages, by Charles M. Weber, Professor of Business Law, University of Arizona.

Conflicts, 3rd Ed., 1974, 432 pages, by Albert A. Ehrenzweig, Late Professor of Law, University of California, Berkeley.

I

NUTSHELL SERIES

Constitutional Analysis, 1979, 388 pages, by Jerre S. Williams, former Professor of Law, University of Texas.

Constitutional Power—Federal and State, 1974, 411 pages, by David E. Engdahl, former Professor of Law, University of Denver.

Consumer Law, 2nd Ed., 1981, 418 pages, by David G. Epstein, Dean and Professor of Law, University of Arkansas and Steve H. Nickles, Professor of Law, University of Arkansas.

Contracts, 1975, 307 pages, by Gordon D. Schaber, Dean and Professor of Law, McGeorge School of Law and Claude D. Rohwer, Professor of Law, McGeorge School of Law.

Contract Remedies, 1981, approx. 325 pages, by Jane M. Friedman, Professor of Law, Wayne State University.

Corporations—Law of, 1980, 379 pages, by Robert W. Hamilton, Professor of Law, University of Texas.

Corrections and Prisoners' Rights—Law of, 1976, 353 pages, by Sheldon Krantz, Professor of Law, Boston University.

Criminal Law, 1975, 302 pages, by Arnold H. Loewy, Professor of Law, University of North Carolina.

Criminal Procedure—Constitutional Limitations, 3rd Ed., 1980, 438 pages, by Jerold H. Israel, Professor of Law, University of Michigan and Wayne R. LaFave, Professor of Law, University of Illinois.

Debtor-Creditor Law, 2nd Ed., 1980, 324 pages, by David G. Epstein, Dean and Professor of Law, University of Arkansas.

Employment Discrimination—Federal Law of, 2nd Ed., 1981, 402 pages, by Mack A. Player, Professor of Law, University of Georgia.

II

NUTSHELL SERIES

Energy Law, 1981, approx. 330 pages, by Joseph P. Tomain, Professor of Law, Drake University.

Estate Planning—Introduction to, 2nd Ed., 1978, 378 pages, by Robert J. Lynn, Professor of Law, Ohio State University.

Evidence, Federal Rules of, 1981, 428 pages, by Michael H. Graham, Professor of Law, University of Illinois.

Evidence, State and Federal Rules, 2nd Ed., 1981, 514 pages, by Paul F. Rothstein, Professor of Law, Georgetown University.

Family Law, 1977, 400 pages, by Harry D. Krause, Professor of Law, University of Illinois.

Federal Estate and Gift Taxation, 2nd Ed., 1979, 488 pages, by John K. McNulty, Professor of Law, University of California, Berkeley.

Federal Income Taxation of Individuals, 2nd Ed., 1978, 422 pages, by John K. McNulty, Professor of Law, University of California, Berkeley.

Federal Income Taxation of Corporations and Stockholders, 2nd Ed., 1981, 362 pages, by Jonathan Sobeloff, Late Professor of Law, Georgetown University and Peter P. Weidenbruch, Jr., Professor of Law, Georgetown University.

Federal Jurisdiction, 2nd Ed., 1981, 258 pages, by David P. Currie, Professor of Law, University of Chicago.

Future Interests, 1981, 361 pages, by Lawrence W. Waggoner, Professor of Law, University of Michigan.

Government Contracts, 1979, 423 pages, by W. Noel Keyes, Professor of Law, Pepperdine University.

Historical Introduction to Anglo-American Law, 2nd Ed., 1973, 280 pages, by Frederick G. Kempin, Jr., Professor of Business Law, Wharton School of Finance and Commerce, University of Pennsylvania.

Injunctions, 1974, 264 pages, by John F. Dobbyn, Professor of Law, Villanova University.

Insurance Law, 1981, 281 pages, by John F. Dobbyn, Professor of Law, Villanova University.

International Business Transactions, 1981, 393 pages, by Donald T. Wilson, Professor of Law, Loyola University, Los Angeles.

Judicial Process, 1980, 292 pages, by William L. Reynolds, Professor of Law, University of Maryland.

Jurisdiction, 4th Ed., 1980, 232 pages, by Albert A. Ehrenzweig, Late Professor of Law, University of California, Berkeley, David W. Louisell, Late Professor of Law, University of California, Berkeley and Geoffrey C. Hazard, Jr., Professor of Law, Yale Law School.

Juvenile Courts, 2nd Ed., 1977, 275 pages, by Sanford J. Fox, Professor of Law, Boston College.

Labor Arbitration Law and Practice, 1979, 358 pages, by Dennis R. Nolan, Professor of Law, University of South Carolina.

Labor Law, 1979, 403 pages, by Douglas L. Leslie, Professor of Law, University of Virginia.

Land Use, 1978, 316 pages, by Robert R. Wright, Professor of Law, University of Arkansas, Little Rock and Susan Webber, Professor of Law, University of Arkansas, Little Rock.

Landlord and Tenant Law, 1979, 319 pages, by David S. Hill, Professor of Law, University of Colorado.

Law Study and Law Examinations—Introduction to, 1971, 389 pages, by Stanley V. Kinyon, Late Professor of Law, University of Minnesota.

Legal Interviewing and Counseling, 1976, 353 pages, by Thomas L. Shaffer, Professor of Law, Washington and Lee University.

NUTSHELL SERIES

Legal Research, 3rd Ed., 1978, 415 pages, by Morris L. Cohen, Professor of Law and Law Librarian, Yale University.

Legislative Law and Process, 1975, 279 pages, by Jack Davies, Professor of Law, William Mitchell College of Law.

Local Government Law, 1975, 386 pages, by David J. McCarthy, Jr., Dean and Professor of Law, Georgetown University.

Mass Communications Law, 1977, 431 pages, by Harvey L. Zuckman, Professor of Law, Catholic University and Martin J. Gaynes, Lecturer in Law, Temple University.

Medical Malpractice—The Law of, 1977, 340 pages, by Joseph H. King, Professor of Law, University of Tennessee.

Military Law, 1980, 378 pages, by Charles A. Shanor, Professor of Law, Emory University and Timothy P. Terrell, Professor of Law, Emory University.

Post-Conviction Remedies, 1978, 360 pages, by Robert Popper, Professor of Law, University of Missouri, Kansas City.

Presidential Power, 1977, 328 pages, by Arthur Selwyn Miller, Professor of Law Emeritus, George Washington University.

Procedure Before Trial, 1972, 258 pages, by Delmar Karlen, Professor of Law, College of William and Mary.

Products Liability, 2nd Ed., 1981, 341 pages, by Dix W. Noel, Late Professor of Law, University of Tennessee and Jerry J. Phillips, Professor of Law, University of Tennessee.

NUTSHELL SERIES

Professional Responsibility, 1980, 399 pages, by Robert H. Aronson, Professor of Law, University of Washington, and Donald T. Weckstein, Professor of Law, University of San Diego.

Real Estate Finance, 1979, 292 pages, by Jon W. Bruce, Professor of Law, Stetson University.

Real Property, 2nd Ed., 1981, approx. 440 pages, by Roger H. Bernhardt, Professor of Law, Golden Gate University.

Remedies, 1977, 364 pages, by John F. O'Connell, Professor of Law, Western State University College of Law, Fullerton.

Res Judicata, 1976, 310 pages, by Robert C. Casad, Professor of Law, University of Kansas.

Sales, 2nd Ed., 1981, 370 pages, by John M. Stockton, Professor of Business Law, Wharton School of Finance and Commerce, University of Pennsylvania.

Secured Transactions, 2nd Ed., 1981, 391 pages, by Henry J. Bailey, Professor of Law, Willamette University.

Securities Regulation, 1978, 300 pages, by David L. Ratner, Professor of Law, Cornell University.

Titles—The Calculus of Interests, 1968, 277 pages, by Oval A. Phipps, Late Professor of Law, St. Louis University.

Torts—Injuries to Persons and Property, 1977, 434 pages by Edward J. Kionka, Professor of Law, Southern Illinois University.

Torts—Injuries to Family, Social and Trade Relations, 1979, 358 pages, by Wex S. Malone, Professor of Law Emeritus, Louisiana State University.

Hornbook Series
and
Basic Legal Texts
of
WEST PUBLISHING COMPANY

P.O. Box 3526

St. Paul, Minnesota 55165

August, 1981

———

Administrative Law, Davis' Text on, 3rd Ed., 1972, 617 pages, by Kenneth Culp Davis, Professor of Law, University of San Diego.

Agency, Seavey's Hornbook on, 1964, 329 pages, by Warren A. Seavey, Late Professor of Law, Harvard University.

Agency and Partnership, Reuschlein & Gregory's Hornbook on the Law of, 1979 with 1981 Pocket Part, 625 pages, by Harold Gill Reuschlein, Professor of Law, St. Mary's University and William A. Gregory, Professor of Law, Southern Illinois University.

Antitrust, Sullivan's Handbook of the Law of, 1977, 886 pages, by Lawrence A. Sullivan, Professor of Law, University of California, Berkeley.

Common Law Pleading, Koffler and Reppy's Hornbook on, 1969, 663 pages, by Joseph H. Koffler, Professor of Law, New York Law School and Alison Reppy, Late Dean and Professor of Law, New York Law School.

Common Law Pleading, Shipman's Hornbook on, 3rd Ed., 1923, 644 pages, by Henry W. Ballantine, Late Professor of Law, University of California, Berkeley.

Constitutional Law, Nowak, Rotunda and Young's Hornbook on, 1978 with 1979 Pocket Part, 974 pages, by John E. Nowak, Professor of Law, University of Illinois, Ronald D. Rotunda, Professor of Law, University of Illinois, and J. Nelson Young, Professor of Law, University of Illinois.

Contracts, Calamari and Perillo's Hornbook on, 2nd Ed., 1977, 878 pages, by John D. Calamari, Professor of Law, Fordham University and Joseph M. Perillo, Professor of Law, Fordham University.

Contracts, Corbin's One Volume Student Ed., 1952, 1224 pages, by Arthur L. Corbin, Late Professor of Law, Yale University.

Contracts, Simpson's Hornbook on, 2nd Ed., 1965, 510 pages, by Laurence P. Simpson, Late Professor of Law, New York University.

Corporate Taxation, Kahn's Handbook on, 3rd Ed., Student Ed., Soft cover, 1981, 614 pages, by Douglas A. Kahn, Professor of Law, University of Michigan.

Corporations, Henn's Hornbook on, 2nd Ed., 1970, 956 pages, by Harry G. Henn, Professor of Law, Cornell University.

Criminal Law, LaFave and Scott's Hornbook on, 1972, 763 pages, by Wayne R. LaFave, Professor of Law, University of Illinois, and Austin Scott, Jr., Late Professor of Law, University of Colorado.

Damages, McCormick's Hornbook on, 1935, 811 pages, by Charles T. McCormick, Late Dean and Professor of Law, University of Texas.

Domestic Relations, Clark's Hornbook on, 1968, 754 pages, by Homer H. Clark, Jr., Professor of Law, University of Colorado.

Environmental Law, Rodgers' Hornbook on, 1977, 956 pages, by William H. Rodgers, Jr., Professor of Law, University of Washington.

Equity, McClintock's Hornbook on, 2nd Ed., 1948, 643 pages, by Henry L. McClintock, Late Professor of Law, University of Minnesota.

Estate and Gift Taxes, Lowndes, Kramer and McCord's Hornbook on, 3rd Ed., 1974, 1099 pages, by Charles L. B. Lowndes, Late Professor of Law, Duke University, Robert Kramer, Professor of Law Emeritus, George Washington University, and John H. McCord, Professor of Law, University of Illinois.

Evidence, Lilly's Introduction to, 1978, 486 pages, by Graham C. Lilly, Professor of Law, University of Virginia.

Evidence, McCormick's Hornbook on, 2nd Ed., 1972 with 1978 Pocket Part, 938 pages, General Editor, Edward W. Cleary, Professor of Law Emeritus, Arizona State University.

Federal Courts, Wright's Hornbook on, 3rd Ed., 1976, 818 pages, including Federal Rules Appendix, by Charles Alan Wright, Professor of Law, University of Texas.

Future Interest, Simes' Hornbook on, 2nd Ed., 1966, 355 pages, by Lewis M. Simes, Late Professor of Law, University of Michigan.

HORNBOOKS & BASIC TEXTS

Income Taxation, Chommie's Hornbook on, 2nd Ed., 1973, 1051 pages, by John C. Chommie, Late Professor of Law, University of Miami.

Insurance, Keeton's Basic Text on, 1971, 712 pages, by Robert E. Keeton, former Professor of Law, Harvard University.

Labor Law, Gorman's Basic Text on, 1976, 914 pages, by Robert A. Gorman, Professor of Law, University of Pennsylvania.

Law Problems, Ballentine's, 5th Ed., 1975, 767 pages, General Editor, William E. Burby, Professor of Law Emeritus, University of Southern California.

Legal Writing Style, Weihofen's, 2nd Ed., 1980, 332 pages, by Henry Weihofen, Professor of Law Emeritus, University of New Mexico.

New York Practice, Siegel's Hornbook on, 1978, with 1979-80 Pocket Part, 1011 pages, by David D. Siegel, Professor of Law, Albany Law School of Union University.

Oil and Gas, Hemingway's Hornbook on, 1971 with 1979 Pocket Part, 486 pages, by Richard W. Hemingway, Professor of Law, University of Oklahoma.

Partnership, Crane and Bromberg's Hornbook on, 1968, 695 pages, by Alan R. Bromberg, Professor of Law, Southern Methodist University.

Poor, Law of the, LaFrance, Schroeder, Bennett and Boyd's Hornbook on, 1973, 558 pages, by Arthur B. LaFrance, Professor of Law, University of Maine, Milton R. Schroeder, Professor of Law, Arizona State University, Robert W. Bennett, Professor of Law, Northwestern University and William E. Boyd, Professor of Law, University of Arizona.

HORNBOOKS & BASIC TEXTS

Property, Boyer's Survey of, 3rd Ed., 1981, 766 pages, by Ralph E. Boyer, Professor of Law, University of Miami.

Real Estate Finance Law, Osborne, Nelson and Whitman's Hornbook on, (successor to Hornbook on Mortgages), 1979, 885 pages, by George E. Osborne, Late Professor of Law, Stanford University, Grant S. Nelson, Professor of Law, University of Missouri, Columbia and Dale A. Whitman, Professor of Law, University of Washington.

Real Property, Burby's Hornbook on, 3rd Ed., 1965, 490 pages, by William E. Burby, Professor of Law Emeritus, University of Southern California.

Real Property, Moynihan's Introduction to, 1962, 254 pages, by Cornelius J. Moynihan, Professor of Law, Suffolk University.

Remedies, Dobbs' Hornbook on, 1973, 1067 pages, by Dan B. Dobbs, Professor of Law, University of Arizona.

Sales, Nordstrom's Hornbook on, 1970, 600 pages, by Robert J. Nordstrom, former Professor of Law, Ohio State University.

Secured Transactions under the U.C.C., Henson's Hornbook on, 2nd Ed., 1979, with 1979 Pocket Part, 504 pages, by Ray D. Henson, Professor of Law, University of California, Hastings College of the Law.

Torts, Prosser's Hornbook on, 4th Ed., 1971, 1208 pages, by William L. Prosser, Late Dean and Professor of Law, University of California, Berkeley.

Trial Advocacy, Jeans' Handbook on, Student Ed., Soft cover, 1975, by James W. Jeans, Professor of Law, University of Missouri, Kansas City.

HORNBOOKS & BASIC TEXTS

Trusts, Bogert's Hornbook on, 5th Ed., 1973, 726 pages, by George G. Bogert, Late Professor of Law, University of Chicago and George T. Bogert, Attorney, Chicago, Illinois.

Urban Planning and Land Development Control, Hagman's Hornbook on, 1971, 706 pages, by Donald G. Hagman, Professor of Law, University of California, Los Angeles.

Uniform Commercial Code, White and Summers' Hornbook on, 2nd Ed., 1980, 1250 pages, by James J. White, Professor of Law, University of Michigan and Robert S. Summers, Professor of Law, Cornell University.

Wills, Atkinson's Hornbook on, 2nd Ed., 1953, 975 pages, by Thomas E. Atkinson, Late Professor of Law, New York University.

Advisory Board

Professor JESSE H. CHOPER
University of California School of Law, Berkeley

Professor DAVID P. CURRIE
University of Chicago Law School

Dean DAVID G. EPSTEIN
University of Arkansas School of Law

Professor ERNEST GELLHORN
University of Virginia School of Law

Professor YALE KAMISAR
University of Michigan Law School

Professor WAYNE R. LaFAVE
University of Illinois College of Law

Professor RICHARD C. MAXWELL
Duke University School of Law

Professor ARTHUR R. MILLER
Harvard University Law School

Professor JAMES J. WHITE
University of Michigan Law School

Professor CHARLES ALAN WRIGHT
University of Texas School of Law

ADMINISTRATIVE LAW AND PROCESS

IN A NUTSHELL

SECOND EDITION

By

ERNEST GELLHORN

T. Munford Boyd Professor of Law,
University of Virginia

and

BARRY B. BOYER

Professor of Law, State University of
New York at Buffalo

ST. PAUL, MINN.
WEST PUBLISHING CO.
1981

COPYRIGHT © 1972 By WEST PUBLISHING CO.
COPYRIGHT © 1981 By WEST PUBLISHING CO.
           50 West Kellogg Boulevard
           P.O. Box 3526
           St. Paul, Minnesota 55165

All rights reserved
Printed in the United States of America

Library of Congress Cataloging in Publication Data

Gellhorn, Ernest.
  Administrative law in a nutshell.

  (Nutshell series)
  Previously published as: Administrative law and proc-
ess in a nutshell. 1972.
  Includes index.
  1. Administrative law—United States. I. Boyer, Barry
B. II. Title. III. Series.
KF402.Z9G4   1981   342.73'06   81–10289
                     347.3026   AACR2

ISBN 0-314-59978-9

KF
5402
.Z9
G4
1981

OUTLINE

327715

TABLE OF CASES

_____

References are to Pages

_____

TABLE OF CASES

TABLE OF CASES

TABLE OF CASES

TABLE OF CASES

TABLE OF CASES

TABLE OF CASES

TABLE OF CASES

TABLE OF CASES

TABLE OF CASES

TABLE OF CASES

TABLE OF CASES

TABLE OF CASES

TABLE OF CASES

TABLE OF STATUTES

References are to Pages

TABLE OF STATUTES

TABLE OF STATUTES

*

TABLE OF AGENCIES

References are to Pages

TABLE OF AGENCIES

ADMINISTRATIVE LAW
AND PROCESS
IN A NUTSHELL

INTRODUCTION

Administrative agencies usually are created to deal with current crises or to redress serious social problems. Throughout the modern era of administrative regulation, which began approximately a century ago, the government's response to a public demand for action has often been to establish a new agency, or to grant new powers to an existing bureaucracy. Near the turn of the century, agencies like the Interstate Commerce Commission and the Federal Trade Commission were created in an attempt to control the anticompetitive conduct of monopolies and powerful corporations. The economic depression of the 1930's was followed by a proliferation of agencies during the New Deal which were designed to stabilize the economy, temper the excesses of unregulated markets, and provide some financial security for individuals. Agencies were also established or enlarged in wartime to mobilize manpower and production, and to administer price controls and rationing. The development of new technologies, ranging from radio broadcasting to air transportation to nuclear energy, often led to creation of new government bureaus to promote and supervise

[1]

these emerging industries. In the 1960's when the injustices of poverty and racial discrimination became an urgent national concern, the development of programs designed to redress these grievances expanded the scope of government administration. More recently, increased public awareness of risks to human health and safety and threats to the natural environment have resulted in new agencies and new regulatory programs.

The primary reason why administrative agencies have so frequently been called upon to deal with such diverse social problems is the great flexibility of the regulatory process. In comparison to courts or legislatures or elected executive officials, administrative agencies have several institutional strengths that equip them to deal with complex problems. Perhaps the most important of these strengths is specialized staffing: an agency is authorized to hire people with whatever mix of talents, skills and experience it needs to get the job done. Moreover, because the agency has responsibility for a limited area of public policy, it can develop the expertise that comes from continued exposure to a problem area. Agencies also may have broad flexibility in the standards of decision they apply; often an agency will be free to evolve rules and policies under a general delegation of discretionary authority. An agency's regulatory techniques and decisionmaking procedures can also be tailored to meet the problem at hand. Agencies can control entry into a field by requiring a license to undertake specified activities; they can set standards, adjudicate violations, and impose penalties; they can dispense grants, subsidies or other incentives; they can set maximum or minimum rates; and they can influence conduct through a wide variety of informal methods.

However, these potential strengths of the administrative process can also be viewed as a threat to other important values. Administrative "flexibility" may simply be a mask for unchecked power, and in our society unrestrained government power has traditionally been viewed with great and justifiable suspicion. Thus, the fundamental policy problem of the administrative process is how to design a system of checks which will minimize the risks of bureaucratic arbitrariness and overreaching, while preserving for the agencies the flexibility they need to act effectively. Administrative law concerns the legal checks—mostly procedural in nature—that are used to control and limit the powers of government agencies.

Moreover, continued exposure to the same issues may lead not only to agency experience but also to insensitivity and ineffectiveness. One constant concern reflected in Congressional oversight of regulatory administration is whether agencies such as the Interstate Commerce Commission have developed expertise to solve problems or instead have become impediments to their resolution. By their nature and assignment, agencies and their regulations interfere with private decisions. As the deregulation of air transportation illustrates, the need for regulation is being reexamined, and where possible less intrusive measures are being considered. In other cases, for example the Nuclear Regulatory Commission's oversight of nuclear power facilities, the need for government regulation is not questioned. Here the debate focuses on how much nuclear power should be generated (if any) and whether the agency has paid sufficient attention to safety. In either situation, however, the central questions involve interrelated issues of substantive law, procedure and agency structure. This text nonetheless treats the administrative process as if it were a separate, self-contained body of law, much like Property or Contracts. There is admittedly artificiality and oversimplification in this approach. Administrative law as applied by the agencies and the courts cannot be separated from the particular mix of factors that make each agency unique— factors such as the nature of the agency's legislative mandate, its structure and traditions, the values and personalities of the people who work in the agency or deal with it regularly, and, most importantly, its substantive law. Even the procedural uniformity imposed on the federal agencies by the Administrative Procedure Act, 5 U.S.C.A. §§ 551–706 (statutory appendix), seems to be weakening, as the Congress has become increasingly willing to prescribe detailed codes of procedure in enabling leglislation. Thus, it is an open question whether the differences among agencies are more important than the similarities.

Still, there is something useful to be gained from the effort to view the administrative process as a whole. The student, the lawyer or the citizen who is trying to penetrate the workings of an unfamiliar bureaucracy needs a general framework of principles and doctrines in order to understand—much less to criticize or try to change—the particular agency decisionmaking process confronting him. It is also important to remember that, despite their many differences, agency decisionmaking procedures must deal with a common problem: how to strike a workable compromise among important and potentially conflicting public values. These values can be grouped into four categories.

(1) *Fairness.* Concern with the fairness of government decisionmaking procedures is a primary feature of Anglo-American legal systems. The basic elements of fairness, embodied in the concept of due process, are assurances that the individual will receive adequate notice and a meaningful opportunity to be heard before an official tribunal makes a decision that may substantially affect his interests.

(2) *Accuracy.* The administrative decisionmaking process should also attempt to minimize the risk of wrong decisions. The real difficulty, however, is in defining and measuring accuracy. Since the goals of many regulatory programs are not simple or clearly stated, and the consequences of agency decisions may be difficult to identify, there will often be differences of opinion as to whether a particular decision was accurate or wise—and how the procedures may have influenced the result. Nevertheless, there is widespread agreement that different procedures are more suitable for some kinds of decisions than for others. For example, trial procedures are generally considered most useful for resolving disputes over specific facts concerning past events, and least useful for making general predictions or policy judgments about the future.

(3) *Efficiency.* Efforts to increase the fairness of an administrative decision by expanding opportunities to participate, or to improve accuracy by gathering and evaluating additional information, can be very costly in time,

money and missed opportunities. Since agency resources are always limited and usually insufficient to accomplish the full range of duties imposed by statute, it becomes necessary to consider the efficiency of decision-making procedures. Typically, this takes the form of an inquiry into whether additional procedural safeguards are likely to increase the fairness or accuracy of decisions enough to warrant the costs and delays they will create.

(4) *Acceptability.* Because the legitimate exercise of official power ultimately depends upon the consent of the governed, it is necessary to consider the attitudes of constituency groups and the general public toward the regulatory process. That is, administrative procedures should be judged not only on their actual effects, but also on the ways they will be perceived by affected interest groups. There are probably few situations in which public attitudes toward agency procedures play a determinative role in shaping beliefs about the basic legitimacy of the regulatory decision or program. Still, it seems clear that a widespread feeling that a government bureaucracy makes decisions arbitrarily or unfairly can undermine the public's confidence in the agency and the regulated industry's willingness to comply with its decisions.

While administrative procedures are a significant component of the modern regulatory system, it is well to remember that matters of process, structure and organization are only a part of the picture. A considerable body of scholarship and popular criticism has identified a wide variety of causes for regulatory failures: the basic theory of the regulatory program may be wrong, or the state of knowledge not adequate to support wise decisions; there may be a mismatch between the regulatory objective and the technique chosen to achieve it; the agency may be unduly influenced or "captured" by a powerful constituency group; agency officials may be incompetent or corrupt or lack incentives to produce quality work; and regulatory programs may simply be politically unacceptable in a particular time and place.

These substantive problems of administrative regulation are important and interesting, but they are largely beyond the scope of this text. This explanation of the administrative process will concentrate on how it operates, on "the rules of the game". The primary focus is on federal administrative agencies, although there are some discussions of state administrative practice. There are several reasons for this approach. As a practical matter, the numerous variations in state law make it impossible to cover the subject adequately in a brief survey. Moreover, the standard teaching materials in the field deal primarily with the federal system. Thus, the basic objective of this book is to help the student of the administrative process develop a framework of general principles, policy considerations and methods of analysis that will be useful in understanding a wide variety of administrative agency procedures, regardless of whether they are found at the federal, state or local level.

CHAPTER I

JUDICIAL CONTROL: THE DELE-GATION DOCTRINE

The study of Administrative Law can be viewed as an analysis of the limits placed on the powers and actions of administrative agencies. These limits are imposed in many ways, and it is important to remember that legal controls may be supplemented or replaced by political checks on agency decisions. One set of legal controls which we will examine at length is the procedures which reviewing courts have required the agencies to use. Another is the rules specified by Congress in the Administrative Procedure Act (APA). Conceptually, however, the first question relates to the amount of legislative or judicial power which can be delegated initially to the agency by the legislature—the governmental body creating it. This is the question which first concerned the courts.

A. THE REASONS FOR BROAD DELEGATIONS

Throughout the modern era of administrative regulation, agencies have been delegated broad powers which are characteristic of each of the three branches of government. Many agencies operate under statutes that give them *legislative power* to issue rules which control private behavior, and which carry heavy civil or criminal penalties for violations; *executive power* to investigate potential violations of rules or statutes and to prosecute offenders; and *judicial power* to adjudicate particular disputes over whether an individual or a company has failed to comply with the governing standards.

For example, the Securities Exchange Commission (SEC) formulates law by writing rules which spell out what disclosures must be made in a stock prospectus; these rules may have the same effect as a law passed by the legislature. The SEC then enforces these rules by prosecuting those who violate its regulations through disciplinary actions against broker-dealers or through stop order proceedings against corporate issuers. Finally, the SEC also acts as judge and jury in deciding whether its rules have been violated by conducting adjudicatory hearings to determine guilt and mete out punishment. In addition, administrative agencies are often unattached to any of the three branches of government (executive, legislative or judiciary). Although the Commissioners— agency members—of the SEC are presidential appointees (subject to Senate approval), the SEC is an independent agency; it is not attached to the Congress nor is it a part of any executive department.

The reasons for these broad delegations of combined powers can be found in the institutional advantages of the administrative agency. Particularly in novel or rapidly changing fields of activity, the legislature may be unwilling or unable to specify detailed rules of conduct. An agency, armed with flexible decision-making procedures and charged with continuing responsibility for a limited subject matter, may be better equipped to develop sound and coherent policies. Moreover, effective development and implementation of regulatory policy may require the exercise of all three kinds of power. A rule or a policy decision can be quickly nullified in practice if investigations and prosecutions are not vigorously pursued, or if adjudications are decided by tribunals which do not understand or support the regulatory goals. When the subject matter of a regulatory program is technical or complex, or when detailed knowledge of the regulated industry is essential to the formulation of sound policy, administrative agencies can bring to bear their superior experience and expertise. Uniformity and predictability are also important in many areas of economic regulation. Businesses need to plan their operations and make their investment decisions with some assurance that the ground rules will not be changed abruptly or applied inconsistently—problems which might well arise if decisionmaking power were dispersed among the three branches of government.

It should also be noted, however, that a substantial number of administrators, Congressmen and commentators are unpersuaded by these arguments. They feel that little real justification exists for continued sweeping delegations or for the combination of prosecutorial, rulemaking and adjudicative powers within one agency. Thus there is pressure to separate such functions, to establish an administrative court, or otherwise to limit the delegation of broad authority to the agencies.

B. BASIC POLITICAL (CONSTITU-TIONAL) THEORY

While there are some very practical reasons for granting broad, combined powers to regulatory agencies, these delegations raise fundamental questions concerning the constitutional distribution of authority in our system of government. The federal Constitution, and most state constitutions as well, are based on the principle of separation of powers. Generally, law-making power is assigned to the legislature, law-enforcing power to the executive, and law-deciding power to the judiciary. With responsibility divided in this fashion, each branch theoretically provides checks and balances on the exercise of power by the other two branches.

The rise of administrative agencies as a "fourth branch" has strained, if not destroyed, this three-part paradigm of government. But it is important to remember that the separations among the three traditional branches were never airtight. Government functions are not readily distinguishable or mutually exclusive; they tend to blend and overlap, and from the beginnings of our national government there are many examples of courts or executive officials exercising what amounts to legislative power. Perhaps the most familiar of these is the rulemaking authority of the federal courts to issue codes of procedure and evidence, such as the Federal Rules of Civil Procedure. Statutes which establish broad general standards of liability may also have the effect of delegating lawmaking power to those who must interpret and apply the legislation. The Sherman Antitrust Act, passed near the end of the nineteenth century, prohibits in general terms any "restraint of trade" which tends to reduce competition substantially. It does not specify whether a particular type of conduct, such as an agreement between two steel companies to fix the price at which they will sell their products, is an unlawful restraint. The executive branch—acting through the Justice Department—may answer this question by issuing rules which interpret the statute as prohibiting price fixing, and then by prosecuting the two steel companies in our example who violate these rules. If the steel companies dispute this interpretation, a court will "make the law" just as the common law courts created much of the law of Torts or Contracts. At each level—the legislature, the executive and the judiciary—the governmental body has announced a "rule" which involves law making. Thus, it is incorrect to say that this function is the exclusive domain of the legislature.

This does not suggest, however, that the principle of separation of powers is irrelevant in modern administrative and constitutional law. The underlying objective of the system of checks and balances is to assure that governmental power is properly confined, and that public officials can be held to account for their decisions. Providing this control and accountability is a primary goal of Administrative Law. In this chapter, we consider one of the most basic questions concerning the relationship between agencies and the other branches of government: what are the constitutional limits on the nature and scope of the powers that can be delegated to an administrative agency? Later, we will consider the procedural requirements that have been imposed to minimize the risk of unfairness resulting from the combination of legislative, executive and judicial powers in a single agency.

In practice, the principal issue in the debates over the constitutional limits on delegation has been the propriety of granting legislative powers to agencies. Despite some early doubts, it has long been established that the Constitution does not prohibit the Congress from empowering the agencies to adjudicate particular types of disputes, subject to limited judicial review of the final agency decision.[1] In theory, objections might also be raised about the practice of conferring executive powers on the "independent" agencies which are not directly accountable to the Chief Executive. As a practical matter, however, this latter sort of delegation has not been seriously challenged, and the constitutionality of it seems to be generally accepted.

C. DEVELOPMENT OF DOCTRINE

The language of the Constitution suggests that the delegation doctrine should not be regarded as an absolute or unqualified principle. While Article I, Section 1 provides that "All legislative Powers herein granted shall be vested in a Congress of the United States," Section 8, paragraph 18 of the same Article empowers the Congress "To make all Laws which shall be necessary and proper." These two provisions suggest that the delegation doctrine's objective of dividing the responsibilities of government to provide checks on abuses of power must be counterbalanced by the need for effective government. How-

---

1. A few of the older Supreme Court decisions state that "constitutional facts" or "jurisdictional facts" must be determined *de novo* by a reviewing court. Ohio Val. Water Co. v. Ben Avon Borough, 253 U.S. 287 (1920); Ng Fung Ho v. White, 259 U.S. 276 (1922); Crowell v. Benson, 285 U.S. 22 (1932). While these decisions have never been explicitly overruled, they have been ignored for decades and their current vitality seems questionable.

Another constitutional principle which is sometimes applied to invalidate delegations of adjudicative power is the void-for-vagueness doctrine derived from the due process clause. If the standard defining illegal conduct is very broad, and the sanctions for violations are severe, the delegation may not satisfy the requirements of due process. See, e. g., Schware v. Board of Bar Examiners, 353 U.S. 232 (1957).

ever, judicial decisions interpreting the delegation doctrine have frequently contained broad, uncompromising statements.

Typical is the Supreme Court's statement in Field v. Clark, 143 U.S. 649, 692 (1892): "That Congress cannot delegate legislative power . . . is a principle universally recognized as vital to the integrity and maintenance of the system of government ordained by the Constitution." The delegation was nevertheless upheld in *Field* because the Congress had only given the President power to "ascertain and declare the event upon which . . . [the legislative] will was to take effect." A similar standard had been applied in the earlier case of The Brig Aurora, 11 U.S. (7 Cranch) 382 (1813), where the Court concluded that a delegation of authority to the President was permissible if it merely authorized him to act when he found that a specified future event had occurred. In both instances, the delegations upheld by the Court were broader than this language would suggest. The *Field* case involved a congressional authorization for the President to impose retaliatory tariffs when foreign nations raised their duties on agricultural products; *The Brig Aurora* dealt with the President's decision to lift trade embargoes when France and England ended their refusal to honor the neutrality of American shipping. Both of these determinations involved not only "findings" of particular fact, but also a substantial measure of policy judgment about the alternative courses of action then available, and the consequences of different approaches in the sensitive field of international relations.

Around the turn of the century, the Supreme Court continued to seek a simple verbal formula which could serve as a benchmark to measure the constitutionality of legislative delegations. In United States v. Grimaud, 220 U.S. 506 (1911), the Court upheld the power of the Secretary of Agriculture to issue regulations backed by criminal penalties governing the use and preservation of the national forests. The rationale was that the Congress had defined the crime, and the Secretary was not really legislating but only exercising a " 'power to fill up the details.' " However, as the modern industrial economy developed and demands for regulation grew, it became apparent that these narrow formulas were too restrictive, even with a liberal interpretation. Gradually the focus of judicial inquiry shifted to whether the legislature had provided sufficient standards to limit the scope of agency discretion. The Supreme Court's decision in Buttfield v. Stranahan, 192 U.S. 470 (1904), was the first case to articulate this modern version of the delegation doctrine. Later cases adopted this line of analysis, and in J. W. Hampton, Jr. & Co. v. United States, 276 U.S. 394, 409 (1928), the Court refined it in the often-quoted statement that a permissible delegation must contain an "intelligible principle to which the [agency must] . . . conform."

Throughout this early evolution of the doctrine, the Supreme Court had never invalidated a Congressional grant of authority to an administrative agency on delegation grounds. However, the Great Depression of the 1930's brought a wave of new regulatory agencies, armed with broad statutory delegations of authority, to control the economy. In the rush to find solutions for this overwhelming economic crisis, some regulatory statutes were poorly designed, poorly drafted, and poorly implemented as well. One of the most visible and controversial of these New Deal regulatory agencies, the National Recovery Administration, provided the Supreme Court with an opportunity to demonstrate that the delegation doctrine was still a very real constraint on the powers of administrative agencies.

The first major test came in the "Hot Oil" case, Panama Refining Co. v. Ryan, 293 U.S. 388 (1935). The National Industrial Recovery Act (NIRA) had authorized the President to prohibit interstate shipments of "contraband" oil. The purpose of this provision was to reduce economic disruptions in the oil industry, which was faced with falling demand and an increasing supply from newly discovered oil fields. However, the regulation that was challenged in *Panama Refining* had both procedural and substantive defects. The "code" in question had been issued without prior notice or opportunity for public participation. Just before the case was argued in the Supreme Court, it was discovered that the code had accidentally been amended out of existence. In considering the substantive requirements of the statute, the Court could find no real limitation on the President's power; in the majority's view, the statute "declare[d] no policy." Thus, for the first time in its history, the Supreme Court struck down an Act of Congress as an overly broad delegation of legislative power.

One beneficial side effect of the *Panama Refining* decision was the passage of legislation requiring the federal agencies to publish official texts of their regulations in the Federal Register. See L. Jaffe, *Judicial Control of Administrative Action* 62 (1965); 5 U.S.C.A. § 552(2)(1). However, the opinion did not resolve the central questions about the constitutionality of the system of regulation created by the National Industrial Recovery Act.

Those questions arose a few months later in the decision that is usually referred to as the "Sick Chicken" case. It involved a criminal prosecution for violations of the Live Poultry Code issued under another section of the NIRA. Schechter Poultry Corp. v. United States, 295 U.S. 495 (1935). As in the Hot Oil case, the Court was concerned by the lack of both substantive and procedural standards. The statute had empowered the agency (acting on behalf of the President) to issue "codes of fair competition" for particular industries if the code "tend[ed] to effectuate the policy of this title." However, the Court could not find a clear policy directive in the legislation; indeed, the congressional statements of policy seemed to pull in several different directions. The Act adopted the policies of preventing monopolies while promoting cooperative actions among trade groups, and of encouraging increased production while improving the wages and conditions of labor; it gave no indication of how these potentially conflicting values should be weighed or reconciled. The Court also gave considerable emphasis to the procedural deficiencies in the Act. In contrast to prior delegations of authority to the Interstate Commerce Commission or the Federal Trade Commission, the NIRA did not require the agency to hold trial-type hearings, or even to provide interested persons with notice and a right to participate in the challenged decision. Nor did it provide an opportunity for judicial review to those who might be adversely affected. Thus, the Court concluded that the delegation was unconstitutionally broad.

[*17*]

A third Supreme Court decision invalidating a delegation on constitutional grounds was also decided in the 1930's. Carter v. Carter Coal Co., 298 U.S. 238 (1936), involved a system of industry "codes" for the coal industry, roughly similar to the "codes of fair competition" that were at issue in the *Schechter* case. In *Carter Coal*, however, the Court noted an additional factor which made the delegation suspect: decision-making power had effectively been granted to committees of industry representatives rather than to government officials. Because these private parties had "interests [which] may be and often are adverse to the interests of others in the same business," the statute was "legislative delegation in its most obnoxious form."

In retrospect, these three decisions were the high-water mark for the delegation doctrine. While the Congress has continued to grant sweeping, vaguely defined powers to administrative agencies in the intervening decades, the Supreme Court has not invalidated any other statutes on delegation grounds. This is not to say, however, that the doctrine has become a dead letter; it has continued to evolve, and the underlying issues are as significant today as they were in the 1930's.

D. THE DUE PROCESS DIMENSION

In the *Schechter* and *Panama Refining* decisions, the Court placed considerable emphasis on the fact that the statutes did not require the agency to use fair and open administrative procedures. This suggests that broad delegations of authority without corresponding procedural protections may violate the due process clause of the Constitution. In this context, due process means that an administrative agency may not deprive a person of life, liberty or property without giving him fair warning of the limits of permissible conduct, or providing him a reasonable opportunity to know and challenge the agency's decision before it becomes final. See generally pp. 139–179 infra. In other words, the contemporary delegation doctrine is concerned not only with the existence of adequate *substantive standards* to confine agency power, but also with the provision of *procedural safeguards* to assure fair, informed decisionmaking.

Frequently, due process requires that a party who will be adversely affected must be given the right to a trial-type hearing on crucial factual issues. Thus, it has long been recognized that an agency cannot set railroad rates without allowing the regulated railroad an opportunity to prove to the agency or a court that the proposed rate is not "just and reasonable." This decision involves a variety of specific facts regarding the railroad's costs and revenues, and the risk of an arbitrary or discriminatory decision may be great if the railroad is not permitted to present its own evidence or to challenge the agency's. Basic fairness may also require an impartial decisionmaker. In a situation like the *Carter Coal* case, where governmental power has been delegated to a private group, some members of the industry may attempt to use this grant of authority to harm or exclude their competitors. Thus, the delegation may violate the due process clause.

The importance of the procedural safeguards requirement has grown as the courts have become increasingly lenient in applying the standards test. This contemporary approach approving essentially standardless delegations of lawmaking authority is exemplified by the Supreme Court's decision in Yakus v. United States, 321 U.S. 414 (1944). There the system of wartime price controls was challenged on delegation grounds. The Court upheld the statute, noting that constitutional problems would arise only if the legislation was so lacking in standards "that it would be impossible in a proper proceeding to ascertain whether the will of Congress has been obeyed." This unwillingness to require precise standards in legislative delegations has led some commentators to conclude that this branch of the delegation doctrine is simply unworkable, and ought to be abandoned altogether. See Davis, *A New Approach to Delegation*, 36 U.Chi.L.Rev. 713 (1969); but cf. T. Lowi, *The End of Liberalism* 303 (1969); Wright, *Review—Beyond Discretionary Justice*, 81 Yale L.J. 575, 582–87 (1972).

Due process analysis of delegations has not been limited to consideration of the agency's decisionmaking procedures. In Hampton v. Mow Sun Wong, 426 U.S. 88 (1976), the Supreme Court invalidated a Civil Service Commission rule banning resident aliens from government employment. Although the rule appeared to be within the scope of the Commission's authority and had won the acquiescence of the political branches, the Court concluded that "due process requires that there be a legitimate basis for presuming that the rule was actually intended to serve" a valid governmental interest. Since the Commission was concerned solely with promoting the efficiency of the federal service and the rule had no clear relationship to that purpose, the majority concluded that the rule deprived aliens of due process. *Mow Sun Wong* is a puzzling decision, which has strong overtones not only of equal protection but also of the largely discredited doctrine of substantive due process. (See, e. g., Williamson v. Lee Optical Co., 348 U.S. 483 (1955).) In its emphasis on the institutional competence of the Civil Service Commission to issue such a rule, however, the decision is generally consistent with the modern approach to delegation discussed in the following section.

E. THE DELEGATION DOCTRINE TODAY

While the requirement that delegations of legislative authority must contain substantive standards has been relaxed since the 1930's, courts are still very much concerned with the limits Congress has imposed on agency powers. However, the analysis has become more comprehensive and sophisticated in comparison to the rather mechanical formulas used in some of the early delegation cases. This contemporary approach is best illustrated by Amalgamated Meat Cutters v. Connally, 337 F.Supp. 737 (D.D.C.1971). Like the *Yakus* case, *Meat Cutters* involved a broad grant of discretion to the President to set limits on wages and prices throughout the national economy. The court recognized that the delegation question could not be answered by a simple inquiry into whether the governmental function being exercised was "legislative" in nature, or whether the Congress had enacted an "intelligible" substantive standard. Rather, the policies underlying the delegation doctrine required a careful examination of the total system of controls, both substantive and procedural, which limited agency power. This was necessary because the fundamental objective of the delegation doctrine—assuring adequate control and accountability in the exercise of official power—could be achieved by either substantive or procedural constraints, or by some combination of the two. Starting from this premise, the court had to be concerned with more than the question of whether the Congress had given away too large a share of its legislative authority; it also had to decide whether the statutory scheme provided adequate means by which the public, the Congress, and (perhaps most importantly) reviewing courts could check the agency's exercise of discretion.

In examining the substantive boundaries on the powers conferred by the statute, the *Meat Cutters* opinion looked beyond the text of the statute itself. The court carefully reviewed the legislative history and the experience under previous price control programs to give content to the vague statutory language. This technique of construing ambiguous legislation in such a way as to avoid constitutional defects has frequently been used by the Supreme Court. It was applied to save a questionable delegation in Kent v. Dulles, 357 U.S. 116 (1958), where the Court construed the relevant statutes to prohibit the Secretary of State from denying a passport because of the applicant's political beliefs. Since the administrator's decision curtailed the constitutionally protected freedom to travel, and prior administrative practice had not included similar restraints, the Court would not presume that the agency had been granted the power in question without a clear statement of congressional intention. See also Zemel v. Rusk, 381 U.S. 1 (1965).

More recently, the Court again used this approach to avoid a difficult delegation issue in National Cable

Television Ass'n v. United States, 415 U.S. 336 (1974). The FCC had imposed substantial charges on cable television systems, relying on a broad delegation of authority to regulate the communications industry. The relevant statute could be read narrowly as permitting the agency only to collect "fees" which recouped the costs of regulatory benefits it was conferring, or it could be interpreted broadly as conferring the power to assess "taxes" that were unrelated to the benefits received by the regulated industry. The Court chose the narrow reading, noting that it would be "a sharp break with our traditions to conclude that Congress had bestowed on a federal agency the taxing power."

Both *Meat Cutters* and *National Cable* indicate that functional considerations relating to the institutional competence of the different branches of government are also relevant in deciding whether a particular delegation is constitutionally permissible. In *National Cable*, the Court was apparently concerned that the power to tax implied the authority to make broad policy judgments about whether certain private activities should be encouraged by subsidies, or discouraged by high taxes. These kinds of basic value choices or resource allocation decisions are typically made by the political branches of government, which most closely reflect the preferences and values of the populace. The Treasury Department and the Internal Revenue Service exercise some law-making power in implementing the tax laws, but the delegations of legislative authority in this field are quite narrow in comparison to most areas of economic regulation. By contrast, the *Meat Cutters* court noted that the price control program significantly affected international relations—an area where the President has always been given broad latitude to negotiate with foreign governments and to set national policy. (See also the discussion of *Mow Sun Wong,* p. 20 supra.) [2]

There are probably few areas in which one branch of government has such a clear and absolute institutional superiority that any delegation would be suspect—although the impeachment power may be one such area. Nevertheless, the relative competence of the Congress, the President, and the agencies to deal with particular problems may well influence a reviewing court's decision on whether sufficient substantive limits have been imposed to satisfy the delegation doctrine. Thus, when the subject matter is novel or technical, the court may be willing to sustain a broad delegation because agencies are often better equipped than legislatures to develop policy in these areas. Telecommunications and air transport were new, rapidly evolving technologies when Congress created agencies to regulate them in the 1930's; nuclear power was at a comparable stage of development when the Atomic Energy Commission (predecessor of the current Nuclear Regulatory Commission) was established in the 1950's; and the energy and environmental crises of the 1970's have spawned a variety of new agencies and new delegations of authority. In each of these areas, conditions were changing rapidly and problems were emerging that required some governmental response. The general direction of public policy was established by Congress, but the details could not be anticipated or

2. For a careful discussion of the relationship between the delegation doctrine and institutional competence, see J. Freedman, *Crisis and Legitimacy* 78–94 (1978).

THE DELEGATION DOCTRINE Ch. 1

adequately resolved through the legislative process. Similarly, the courts may be willing to tolerate relatively open-ended delegations when the activity in question is a proprietary or managerial function that requires a continuing series of supervisory decisions which may have to be made quickly and on limited information. The management of national forests in the *Grimaud* case is one example; many areas of personnel policy or government contracting may also fit this description.

The *Meat Cutters* decision also expands the range of procedural safeguards that are considered relevant to the delegation question. While some earlier cases like *Schechter* seem to equate fair procedures with trial-type hearings, the *Meat Cutters* opinion places more emphasis on administrative rulemaking and on the availability of judicial review. The risks of inadequate notice to the regulated, or of inconsistent and arbitrary decisionmaking in particular cases, can be minimized if the statute requires the agency to state its policies in administrative rules. The rulemaking procedures of the Administrative Procedure Act provide those who will be affected with notice and an opportunity to participate in the formulation of regulatory policy. Finally, the availability of judicial review means that administrative rules can be tested for rationality and compliance with the congressional intent, and that the agency's consistency in interpreting and applying those rules in particular cases can be checked.

The *Meat Cutters* approach, in which a reviewing court considers the entire range of procedural and substantive limits on agency authority and construes the statute to minimize delegation problems, is an effort to reconcile a broad range of conflicting concerns. The delegation doctrine raises sensitive questions about the relationships among the three co-equal branches of government. Ever since the Supreme Court asserted the power to declare legislation unconstitutional in Marbury v. Madison, 5 U.S. (1 Cranch) 137 (1803), the exercise of this power has involved at least a potential conflict between the judiciary and the political branches. At times, this potential has escalated into actual confrontations. Perhaps the most familiar example is President Franklin Roosevelt's plan to "pack" the Supreme Court as a means of overcoming the obstacles to the New Deal legislation that were created by decisions like *Schechter* and *Panama Refining*. By contrast, other restraints on administrative action are either cooperative efforts of two branches (e. g., Congress defines the agency's authority and the courts review the agency's decisions to assure consistency with the congressional intent) or the unilateral actions of one branch (e. g., legislative oversight or executive appointment and removal of officers). In addition, a judicial holding that a delegation is unconstitutional may require radical restructuring or even abandonment of the entire program; this result favors statutory interpretations or judicial directives that the agencies improve their procedures since such instructions are less disruptive and more easily correctible if the court has misread the will of the Congress.

The contemporary emphasis on controlling discretion at the agency level rather than striking down entire regulatory programs under the delegation doctrine represents an effort to accommodate the needs of a complex modern economy. Rigid insistence on the legislative specification of detailed standards is thought to be unsound and unworkable. For many regulatory problems, the legislature can neither foresee what actions the agency should take, nor constantly revise the statutory mandate as conditions change. Even when the policy alternatives are reasonably clear, an attempt to write highly detailed standards in the legislature may delay the passage of desired legislation, or jeopardize its chances for enactment. The delegation doctrine remains available to use in truly extreme cases. For the present, however, the more immediate —and more pragmatic—task for Administrative Law is to evaluate and further refine the doctrines and techniques for making bureaucratic power accountable, without destroying the effectiveness of those administrative agencies considered necessary.

F. THE DELEGATION DOCTRINE IN THE STATES

Since many state constitutions are based on the principle of separation of powers and provide for due process of law, delegation questions also arise at the state level. As might be expected, the delegation doctrine that has evolved in the states is more variable than the current federal law on the subject. Some states—a relatively large proportion, judging from the reported cases—still adhere to a relatively stringent version of the doctrine and require that statutes contain detailed standards confining agency discretion. One reason for this divergence between the state and federal approaches may be the fact that the federal government's role in administrative regulation has increased much more rapidly than the state governments' in recent decades. As a result, the federal

courts may be more sensitive to the need for broad
delegations than their state counterparts. Another reason
might be the kinds of regulatory activities undertaken by
the states. A large part of state regulation consists of
occupational licensing. The fairness of these licensing
programs is often suspect, particularly when the regulatory board is dominated by members of the regulated
industry. As in the *Carter Coal* case, due process concerns become more compelling when the administrative
process is controlled by private individuals who may use
government power to protect themselves from competition, rather than to protect the public from incompetent
practitioners.

At the other extreme from the states which still adhere
to the standards doctrine are a few which seem to have
abandoned the requirement of statutory standards altogether. This latter approach is illustrated by Sun Ray
Drive-In Dairy, Inc. v. Oregon Liquor Control Comm'n,
16 Or.App. 63, 517 P.2d 289 (Ct.App.1973). The court in
that case reversed an order of the state Liquor Control
Commission refusing to grant a liquor license, and remanded the case to the agency with a directive not to act
on the petitioner's application until it had adopted general
rules giving content to the vague statutory standard.
The *Sun Ray* decision goes farther than most of the
federal cases in developing a constitutional requirement
that agencies use their rulemaking authority to validate a
broad delegation. A more common judicial technique is
to interpret the statute as mandating the agency to
develop "subsidiary administrative policy" through rulemaking, as the court did in the *Meat Cutters* decision.

However, there are some federal cases which strongly suggest that a constitutional rulemaking requirement might be implied from the due process clause of the Fifth Amendment.

CHAPTER II

NONJUDICIAL CONTROLS: THE POLITICAL PROCESS

In a constitutional democracy, government institutions which set and enforce public policy must be politically accountable to the electorate. When the legislature delegates broad lawmaking powers to an administrative agency, the popular control provided by direct election of decisionmakers is absent. However, this does not mean that administrative agencies are free from political accountability. In many areas, policy oversight by elected officials in the legislature or the executive branch is a more important check on agency power than judicial review.

Formally, agencies are dependent upon the legislature and the executive for their budgets and their operating authority. If an agency loses the support of these bodies or oversteps the bounds of political acceptability, it may be subjected to radical restructuring. During the 1970's the Atomic Energy Commission came under intense criticism for overemphasizing the promotion of nuclear power while underemphasizing safety and environmental protection. The political branches responded by transferring the AEC's promotional functions to the new Department of Energy, and by reconstituting the agency as the Nuclear Regulatory Commission, whose functions are solely regulatory.[1] More recently, when the Federal

---

1. However, the change in structure did not protect the agency from harsh criticism for its handling of the Three Mile Island

Trade Commission instituted a series of sweeping consumer protection proposals which many members of Congress believed were unnecessary or ill conceived, the legislature used its budgetary powers to prohibit the FTC from taking final action on the pending rules until new statutory controls on the agency's authority could be enacted. See FTC Improvements Act of 1980, 94 Stat. 374 (1980), amending 15 U.S.C.A. §§ 41 et seq. Another important form of political control over the agencies is a statutory directive to change their traditional ways of making decisions, either by using different procedures or by taking account of new values and interests. The National Environmental Policy Act of 1969, 42 U.S.C.A. §§ 4321–61, is one of the clearest examples of significant substantive change in the agencies' mandates: for the first time, it forced all federal agencies to consider the environmental impacts of their major decisions.

While there are numerous examples of legislatures and chief executives taking formal action to bring regulatory policy into accord with changing political realities, the network of less formal and less visible political "oversight" mechanisms is probably more important in the day-to-day functioning of the administrative process. There are numerous procedures and practices which bring the activities of the agencies to the attention of elected officials and their staffs, and in most regulatory settings the continuing dialogue which results from this

reactor accident in 1979. See *Report of the President's Commission on the Accident at Three Mile Island* 51–56 (1979); M. Rogovin & G. Frampton, *Three Mile Island: A Report to the Commissioners and to the Public*, vol. 1, at 89–121, 129–52 (1980) (Report of the Nuclear Regulatory Commission Special Inquiry Group).

process is an important determinant of public policy. Here, the role of law and legal rules has been to channel this interaction within limited boundaries—for example, by restricting *ex parte* contacts—rather than to determine final results.

Another significant dimension of agency accountability is the political acceptance of administrative policy among those who will be affected or regulated. Public dissatisfaction not only triggers the oversight of the political branches; it also may determine the practical effectiveness of an entire regulatory program. The Internal Revenue Service would require a much larger staff, and a much different approach to enforcement, if it could not count on a substantial measure of honest self-reporting and voluntary compliance among taxpayers. Thus, an accurate understanding of the methods used to assure the control and accountability of administrative agencies must begin with an appreciation of the political environment within which the agencies function.

In considering the mechanisms for assuring political control over agency policy, it is useful to keep in mind some basic differences between judicial and political methods for making regulatory bureaucracies accountable. Judicial review seeks to assure that agency action is consistent with the will of the political branches, as that will is expressed in constitutional mandates or properly enacted statutes. Political oversight is not limited to these formal directives; a newly elected President, for example, is expected to bring new people and new policies into the regulatory process, even if the basic statutes remain the same. Moreover, judicial review usually is based on the premise that agency actions are reasoned

[*32*]

decisions which result from a process of finding facts and applying generally accepted principles to them. Courts cannot easily review decisions that are the result of bargaining, or compromise, or pure policy choice. Compromise and choice among competing values are the essence of the political process, and for these kinds of issues, political methods for making and legitimizing decisions are essential. Indeed, the "political question doctrine" and other related judicial principles are designed to prevent the courts from making political choices that are conferred upon the other two branches of government. See, e. g., Baker v. Carr, 369 U.S. 186, 277–97 (1962) (Frankfurter, J., dissenting). The difficulty in the administrative process is that agency decisions range across the spectrum, from pure policy choice to reasoned application of settled principles, with most of them falling somewhere in between. Thus, there is often conflict over the proper scope of judicial and political accountability.

A. LEGISLATIVE CONTROLS

Although the modern delegation doctrine puts few limits on the legislature's ability to grant broad powers to administrative agencies, Congress can always revoke or narrow the authority it has granted through subsequent legislation. At times, Congress moves quickly and explicitly to reverse or postpone a controversial agency action. When large numbers of consumers complained to their congressmen about the National Highway Traffic Safety Administration's automobile seat belt "interlock" rule, the legislature promptly amended the agency's organic act to provide that NHTSA safety standards could not require belt systems which prevented the car from starting or sounded a continuous buzzer when seat belts were unfastened. 15 U.S.C.A. § 1410b. Similarly, the Food and Drug Administration's attempts to ban the only approved artificial sweetener, saccharin, aroused such strong popular opposition that the Congress imposed a moratorium on regulatory action, and substituted a warning label for products containing the chemical. 91 Stat. 1451 (1977). More frequently, however, "legislative oversight"—the Congress' supervision of agency performance under existing statutes—uses a variety of other techniques to review and change administrative policy.

1. *The Power of the Purse.* Since administrative agencies are dependent on public funding to support their operations, the legislature's control over government expenditures gives it considerable leverage to influence implementation of regulatory statutes. There are two required stages for Congressional approval of agency funding. First, there must be a legislative *authorization* for appropriations, which is usually contained in the basic delegation of power to the agency. The authorization for a particular program may expire after a fixed period of years, or it may be permanent. Similarly, it may set a ceiling on future appropriations, or permit the appropriation of such sums as are necessary to carry out the purposes of the statute. Regardless of the form of the particular authorization, Congress can always reexamine and amend it if the legislators want to change the scope or direction of a particular program. Congress used this technique in the late 1970's to limit the Federal Trade Commission's consumer protection rulemaking.

More commonly, funding controls are imposed in the annual *appropriations* process. Each year, agencies must submit budget requests which are reviewed by the President (acting through the Office of Management and Budget) and are transmitted to the appropriations committees of the House and Senate. These committees then hold hearings and report bills allocating funds among the various agencies and programs, which must be voted on by both houses of Congress. Generally, the appropriations committees are responsible for "fiscal" oversight of agency spending, while the authorizing committees are primarily concerned with "legislative" oversight or substantive policy. In practice, however, the two functions tend to overlap, and both committees may become involved in reviewing the wisdom or desirability of agency policy.

In some areas of administration, such as disability or welfare benefits programs, the level of annual expenditures may be effectively fixed by formulas or "entitlements" for beneficiaries which are spelled out in the legislation creating the program. In areas where these "uncontrollable" expenditures exist, the appropriations process is a less effective check on agency activities. However, fixed formulas generally are not found in regulatory statutes.

2. *Investigative Oversight.* In addition to its formal legislating and funding powers, Congress has broad authority to investigate implementation of statutory programs and to expose corrupt or ineffective administration. Primary responsibility for investigating the efficiency and effectiveness of the administrative agencies is

lodged in the House and Senate Government Operations committees, but any committee which has jurisdiction over some aspect of the agency's program may conduct investigations. By mobilizing public and political pressure on the agency, and by raising the threat of future legislation, investigative oversight can greatly affect agency behavior.

3. *Appointments.* Under Article II, § 2, clause 2 of the Constitution, the Senate must give its "Advice and Consent" to the appointment of all "Officers of the United States" nominated by the President. However, this provision creates a large exception for "inferior Officers," whose appointments may be made solely by the President or by the heads of the administrative departments, as Congress directs. This exception covers all of the employees who are protected from arbitrary removal or political reprisal by the civil service system.

Although they are relatively few in number, the "political appointees" who are subject to Senate confirmation constitute the primary leadership of the federal bureaucracy. They have considerable discretion to make policy, and the power to approve or reject their appointments is potentially a major means of influencing the content of regulatory programs. However, neither the Congress nor the President has made very effective use of the appointment and confirmation power to shape policy. See generally V. Kramer & J. Graham, *Appointments to the Regulatory Agencies,* Senate Comm. on Commerce, 94th Cong., 2d Sess. (Comm. Print 1976). When Congress does take an active interest in appointments, much of its influence is exerted through informal channels such as "senatorial courtesy" (the practice of allowing senators who are members of the President's party to approve or "veto" nominees from their home state), and not infrequently the nominee to an agency post will have been suggested by an influential Senator. However, constitutional considerations of separation of powers prohibit the Congress from actually appointing administrative officials. Buckley v. Valeo, 424 U.S. 1, 118–43 (1976) (statute requiring that four of six voting members of the Federal Elections Commission be appointed by the Speaker of the House and the President *pro tempore* of the Senate held unconstitutional).

4. *"Casework."* Another method by which the legislature influences agency activities is through the institution of congressional "casework," which is the general name given to legislators' attempts to assist their constituents in dealing with the bureaucracy. Ideally, congressional casework puts the legislator in the role of an "ombudsman" checking up on the quality of administration and helping citizens to obtain fair treatment from the agencies. It can also help the representatives identify problem areas which are appropriate for oversight hearings or statutory correction. In its less-than-ideal manifestations however, casework can become either an attempt by a legislator to pressure the bureaucrats into making an improper decision in favor of his constituent, or a paper shuffle in which the citizen's complaint is simply "bucked" back to the agency topped by a form letter from the congressman. See generally W. Gellhorn, *When Americans Complain* (1966).

5. *Studies by Congressional Support Agencies.* There are several permanent organizations which Congress has created to assist its own legislative and oversight responsi-

bilities. Congressional support agencies like the Congressional Research Service or the Office of Technology Assessment may conduct studies of agency activities which trigger more formal oversight mechanisms, or induce the agencies to modify their practices. The support agency which is most influential in the legislative oversight process is the General Accounting Office. The GAO was originally created to conduct financial audits of the agencies' use of public funds, but in recent years it has taken on considerable responsibility for program review and evaluation.

6. *Reporting Requirements.* Congress may also require the agencies to report back periodically on their activities. Agency reports to the Congress may be limited to a particular function, or they may range more broadly over a variety of activities and programs. Most reports are submitted on an annual basis, but occasionally the Congress will request a special report. Agencies may also submit special reports to Congress on their own initiative, particularly if the agency needs additional legislative authority to deal with a particular problem.

7. *Legislative Veto.* In some regulatory areas, Congress has imposed a "legislative veto" requirement. These provisions take a variety of forms, but most of them direct agencies to transmit final administrative rules to the Congress for review before they become effective. The experience of agencies subjected to legislative veto suggests that one effect of this kind of requirement is to induce the agencies to bargain with the staff members of oversight committees before the agency takes final action, so that the rule ultimately adopted will have a reasonable chance of surviving the veto process.

In recent years, a number of "regulatory reform" proposals have sought to extend the legislative veto to a wider range of agencies and programs, or to make it generally available for all administrative rulemaking. These proposals have been criticized on several grounds, including the possibility that the legislative veto would undercut public participation in the administrative process, or overburden the Congress with the task of reviewing hundreds of rules annually, or threaten the functioning of judicial review as a check on administrative arbitrariness. One variant of the legislative veto, the "one house veto" system which permits either house of Congress to kill an administrative rule simply by passing a resolution, may also be vulnerable to a constitutional challenge. Since this type of provision enables one house of Congress to "legislate" without any opportunity for the President to exercise his own veto power, it may violate separation of powers principles.

8. *"Sunset" Laws.* Another regulatory reform proposal designed to increase the effectiveness of congressional oversight is the "Sunset" law which provides that agencies will go out of existence after a fixed period of time unless the legislature reenacts their statutory charters. "Sunset" provisions differ greatly in their details, but they all share the common assumption that it is useful to compel the Congress to undertake a thorough reexamination of its delegations of authority periodically, and to assess their utility in the light of experience. In this respect, sunset requirements are generally similar to the budget authorization which is limited to a fixed period of time. One variation on the sunset theme, called the "high noon" approach because it seeks to focus the bright

light of public scrutiny on individual agencies rather than forcing a general review of all delegations, would set up a ten-year staggered schedule for complete reviews of the effectiveness of the major federal agencies. See Title III of S. 1291, 96th Cong., 1st Sess. (1979).

Since legislative oversight is basically political in nature, and often operates through pressure or bargaining, it may come into conflict with legal or constitutional requirements for agency decisionmaking. This is particularly true in administrative adjudications when an agency is passing upon the legality of private conduct. In Pillsbury Co. v. FTC, 354 F.2d 952 (5th Cir. 1966), the Commissioners of the Federal Trade Commission were subjected to prolonged and hostile questioning by congressional oversight committees regarding a legal interpretation they had issued in an interlocutory order during a pending adjudication. The court held that this intrusion into the agency's decisionmaking process had deprived the respondent of a fair adjudication. Even when the decision is not adjudicative in nature, however, some kinds of congressional oversight may be improper. The "Three Sisters Bridge" case, D. C. Federation of Civic Ass'ns v. Volpe, 459 F.2d 1231 (D.C. Cir. 1971), cert. denied, 405 U.S. 1030 (1972), is an example of legal limits on political intervention. There, the powerful chairman of a House appropriations committee brought pressure to bear on the Secretary of Transportation to grant approval of a controversial bridge construction project. The court concluded that the Secretary's consideration of this pressure in making his decision was grounds for reversal. In its basic grant of authority to the Secretary, the Congress as a whole had directed him to consider the project "on the merits" and to make a reasoned analysis of the facts. Thus, political pressures were technically irrelevant to that kind of decision; oversight activities by one congressman or one committee could not override the will of the Congress as a whole, as expressed in the underlying legislation.

B. EXECUTIVE CONTROLS

Like the Congress, the President has a variety of powers and techniques he can use to oversee and influence the operations of administrative agencies. Many of these powers find their source directly in the Constitution. When Congress passes legislation affecting the agencies, the President may exercise his veto power to block enactment. Article II also provides for affirmative presidential controls. It vests the executive power of government in the President, and charges him to "take Care that the Laws be faithfully executed." It also contains more specific grants of authority in areas such as military and foreign affairs.

Exercise of these oversight powers often takes the form of an executive order, a formal directive from the President to federal agencies or officials. Depending upon the context, a particular executive order may be based either on an inherent constitutional power of the President, or on an express or implicit delegation from Congress. See generally Fleishman & Aufses, *Law and Orders: The Problem of Presidential Legislation,* 40 L. & Contemp. Prob. 1, 11 (Summer 1976). An example of an express delegation is the price control statute which was challenged in *Amalgamated Meat Cutters,* discussed pp. 21–26, supra. That law authorized the President "to issue such orders and regulations as he may deem appropriate" to stabilize wages and prices, and then permitted him to redelegate that power to any subordinate officials he wished. 84 Stat. 799–800, §§ 202–03 (1970).

Another important executive oversight tool provided in Article II is the President's power to appoint and remove federal officers. Congress may define the terms and conditions of employment for the so-called "inferior officers"—the rank-and-file civil servants who are hired on the merit system of competitive examinations. However, the President's authority to name the high ranking administrative policymakers who are "Officers of the United States" under Article II, Section 2, Clause 2, cannot be taken away by the Congress. Buckley v. Valeo, discussed p. 37, supra. For these "political appointees," the Congressional role is limited to the Senate's power of "advice and consent" in confirming or rejecting the President's nominee for an administrative post.

Since many delegations of authority to administrative agencies are framed in broad or vague language, the policymaking discretion of those who control these agencies is often extensive. As a result, their attitudes, abilities, and political loyalties may become extremely important factors shaping the content of regulatory policy. However, some regulatory policymakers do not serve "at the pleasure of the President." In the so-called independent regulatory agencies like the Securities Exchange Commission or the Interstate Commerce Commission, statutes may provide that commissioners are appointed for a fixed period of years which does not correspond with the President's term of office. There may also be statutory provisions requiring that multimember commissions be politically balanced (for example, no more than three of the five members of the SEC may be members of one political party), and legislation may protect the commissioners from arbitrary removal during their terms of office. On a few occasions, these efforts by the Congress to limit the President's general authority to remove federal officers have given rise to litigation.

One early case, involving the dismissal of a postmaster at a time when the Post Office was still a cabinet department, suggested that Congress could not limit the President's removal power without violating Article II of the Constitution. Myers v. United States, 272 U.S. 52 (1926). However, the decision provided little guidance with respect to the President's power to remove independent agency commissioners. Postmasters had very minimal policymaking or adjudicative powers; moreover, the statute governing their appointment merely said that they were to serve for a period of four years unless "sooner removed or suspended."

The issue of the constitutional status of independent regulatory agencies came to a head a few years later when President Roosevelt sought to remove a chairman of the Federal Trade Commission who was unsympathetic to some of the New Deal programs which the FTC was responsible for administering. The statute provided that FTC commissioners were to serve for a fixed term of years, and it stipulated that they could be removed during their term only for "inefficiency, neglect of duty, or malfeasance in office." The President did not claim that the recalcitrant chairman was guilty of any of these offenses; he simply wanted to change the policy direction of the agency, and he took the position that the *Myers*

[43]

case gave him the power to replace the sitting commissioners with more responsive appointees. When the discharged chairman brought suit to challenge the legality of his removal, the Supreme Court agreed that the statutory removal-for-cause provision was a constitutionally proper limit on the President's removal power. Humphrey's Executor (Rathbun) v. United States, 295 U.S. 602 (1935). The Court suggested that these statutory limitations were necessary in order to maintain the constitutional, tripartite division of power. But the Court's reasoning seems questionable. Insofar as the agency exercises quasi-judicial power to adjudicate particular disputes, it seems apparent that Congress may legitimately decide to provide safeguards against executive domination. Indeed, due process requires some measure of independence for adjudicators in many agency settings. The situation is quite different, however, when the agency exercises executive or quasi-legislative powers. For these areas of policymaking, a substantial measure of political responsiveness and accountability to elected officials seems both desirable and permissible. When an agency like the Federal Trade Commission possesses combined powers to bring cases, adjudicate, and issue rules, there is no simple answer to the problem of striking an acceptable balance between independence and accountability.

Later decisions have not materially clarified the limits on the executive removal power. Several agencies, including the FCC and the SEC, are in an ambiguous position because they were created after the *Myers* decision suggested that the President's removal power could not be limited by Congress, but before the *Humphrey's* opinion made it clear that some limits were possible.

Thus, the commissioners of the SEC serve for fixed terms of years, but they have no explicit statutory protection against summary removal from office. It is not clear whether the President would be able to remove them without cause. A similar ambiguity may arise when an independent agency commissioner reaches the mandatory retirement age specified by statute before his term of office expires. Since the President has discretionary authority to exempt the commissioner from the mandatory retirement provision on a year-by-year basis, there may be a question as to whether he can effectively remove the commissioner by refusing to grant an exemption, or whether on the other hand the commissioner has effectively lost his independence if he is dependent on annual renewals by the President. ITT Continental Baking Co., 82 F.T.C. 1188 (1973).

As a practical matter, however, even fixed terms of office and removal-for-cause statutes do not pose serious obstacles to the President's ability to influence regulatory policy through the appointments process. Since regulators' terms of office are typically staggered in the multimember agencies and many commissioners do not serve out their terms, a newly elected President almost always has the opportunity to make key appointments early in his administration. Presidents Eisenhower, Kennedy, and Nixon each altered the direction of the NLRB (where political balance is not required) by the appointments that they made within a year of assuming office. Moreover, if the President formally requests an administrator's resignation, even an "independent" commissioner is not very likely to resist or to face the prospect of a removal-for-cause controversy.

The President also has the statutory power to designate one of the commissioners of an independent agency to serve as chairman, and to "demote" the chairman back to the rank of commissioner without cause. Since the chairman of a regulatory agency has the primary responsibility for managing its operations, including the hiring of new personnel, a change in agency leadership often results in policy changes. This was evident in the "revitalization" of the FTC during the early 1970's when the President responded to public criticism of the agency by appointing activist chairmen who initiated sweeping changes in staffing and regulatory policy. More recently, President Carter reacted to the Nuclear Regulatory Commission's handling of the Three Mile Island accident by replacing the chairman of the NRC and proposing a reorganization of authority in that agency. See p. 47, infra.

While the President's power to change an agency's policy by replacing its leadership is considerable, there are some practical limits. Dismissal of a high-ranking official may be politically costly to the President, particularly if the administrator has the support of a powerful constituency. Another kind of limitation on the Executive's removal power may arise when administrative rules are issued specifying that the official in question will not be removed without cause. This point was at issue in the litigation resulting from President Nixon's order to dismiss Archibald Cox as Watergate Special Prosecutor. Under pressure from Congress, the Justice Department had issued formal regulations providing that the Special Prosecutor "will not be removed from his duties except for extraordinary improprieties on his part." When the Acting Attorney General followed the President's directive to dismiss Cox without cause, the court ruled that this violation of a valid administrative regulation made the firing illegal. Nader v. Bork, 366 F.Supp. 104 (D.D.C. 1973). However, since a successor (Leon Jaworski) had been appointed in the meantime, Cox was not reinstated.

In the day-to-day functioning of the administrative process, the President's power of persuasion and the other less drastic tools of executive oversight are usually more significant factors than the threat of removal. One technique which has been more frequently used than the removal power is the President's authority to modify the organizational structure of the bureaucracy. Under the Reorganization Act, 5 U.S.C.A. §§ 901–13, the President may submit a "reorganization plan" to the Congress, transferring functions from one department to another. If the legislature does not vote to reject the plan within a fixed period of time, the transfer becomes effective. Thus, for example, the Environmental Protection Agency was created by Reorganization Plan No. 3 of 1970, 5 U.S.C.A. App. 1, which consolidated in one new agency a variety of programs that had been scattered among several executive departments.

Much of the work of executive oversight takes place within the organizations which comprise the Executive Office of the President, commonly referred to as "The White House." The Executive Office of the President includes not only the President's personal advisors, who comprise the White House Office, but also permanent organizations like the National Security Council and the Council of Economic Advisers. See 3 U.S.C.A. § 101. The most important of these units to the regulatory agencies is the Office of Management and Budget (OMB), which uses two principal methods to oversee the agencies. As its name suggests, OMB has primary responsibility for formulating the annual executive budget which the President transmits to the Congress. In performing this task, OMB receives budget requests from the individual agencies and modifies them in accordance with the administration's priorities. 31 U.S.C.A. § 16. Similarly, OMB reviews the agencies' requests for substantive legislation, including agency officials' proposed testimony before congressional committees, for consistency with the Administration's position. Both of these "clearance" procedures typically give rise to extensive negotiations between OMB staff and agency officials, and usually a compromise solution is reached. However, major disagreements are sometimes resolved by the President.

In recent years, the White House has attempted to exert more direct supervision and control over particular agency decisions in major rulemaking proceedings through the Regulatory Analysis Review Group (RARG). Under a series of Executive Orders issued during the Ford and Carter Administrations,[2] executive branch agencies are required to prepare a "regulatory analysis" or assessment of anticipated costs and benefits for any proposed rule which is likely to have a significant economic impact. These analyses are selectively reviewed by the RARG, which is made up of representatives of the cabinet departments, the EPA, and various units within the

2. E. g., Exec. Order No. 12044, 3 C.F.R. 152 (1978 compil.). The Reagan Administration has superseded this order and the RARG with its own Presidential Task Force on Regulatory Relief. E.O. No. 12291, 46 Fed.Reg. 13193 (Feb. 19, 1981). While distinctive in several respects, it continues and extends the basic analytical concepts discussed in the text.

Executive Office of the President. While the RARG review is ostensibly focused on the technical quality of the agency's cost-benefit analysis, it can also be a significant check on the political acceptability of proposed rules, particularly those which are likely to impose substantial costs on the regulated industry.

The regulatory analysis provides an essentially negative check on agency decisions, in the sense that the reviewers are looking for errors and deficiencies in the agency's proposals. For some years, commentators have suggested that the the President ought to have a more affirmative role in initiating and directing agency policy. One proposal recommends enactment of a statute generally authorizing the President to issue executive orders modifying or reversing agency policy, or directing an agency to consider and decide a particular matter within a fixed period of time. See Cutler & Johnson, *Regulation and the Political Process,* 84 Yale L.J. 1395 (1975). The President's order would have a delayed effective date, and during this waiting period either house of Congress could pass a resolution setting it aside. This approach is intended to provide greater political legitimacy for agency policymaking, by bringing the elected branches of government more directly into the process. However, the Congress generally has not been receptive to proposals which would increase executive power over the agencies, particularly the independent regulatory commissions which are partially insulated from executive oversight.

A final tool of executive oversight, which is often overlooked, is the President's power to control litigation affecting the agencies through the Department of Justice. See 5 U.S.C.A. § 3106. Although there are significant exceptions, most agencies lack the statutory authority to litigate on their own behalf. Rather, they must obtain representation from the Department of Justice, and the Department's refusal to advocate or defend a particular agency policy may mean that the agency's decision has no practical effect. One notable instance in which the Justice Department used this power occurred in 1977. Then Attorney General Griffin Bell sent an open letter to the heads of all departments and agencies, advising them that the government would not defend an agency against suits to compel disclosure of documents under the Freedom of Information Act, 5 U.S.C.A. § 552, even if the documents were exempt, unless the agency could show that disclosure was "demonstrably harmful." This directive was designed to implement the Carter Administration's belief that greater openness in govenment was desirable, and it appears to have been an effective means of compelling the agencies to abide by that policy.

Despite the wide array of formal oversight techniques and the considerable informal "powers of persuasion" that a President can bring to bear, direct Presidential involvement in many areas of regulatory policy is still rare or nonexistent. Part of the reason may be the sheer pressure of time and workload; the President and his personal advisors may often find that more pressing matters prevent them from getting too deeply involved in the intricacies of administrative regulation. On the other hand, when a regulatory policy issue is truly controversial and any decision is likely to offend some powerful interest group, the White House may think it prudent to avoid direct involvement which could make the President personally responsible for the final decision.

C. INDIRECT POLITICAL CONTROLS

The formal powers of legislative and executive oversight are supplemented by a network of informal relationships and activities which greatly influence agency policy. Most of these indirect political controls involve the acquisition and use of information, and in recent years a series of statutes have made it considerably easier for an outside party to gather detailed data about the inner workings of the agencies.

The first—and probably the most important—of these contemporary disclosure statutes was the 1966 Freedom of Information Act, 5 U.S.C.A. § 552, which set the pattern for many later enactments. The most notable feature of the 1966 FOIA was its presumption in favor of disclosure: "any person" had the right to see and copy any government records unless the documents requested fell within one of the statutory exemptions to the Act. These exemptions were designed to permit the withholding of records only when disclosure would harm some important governmental function or private interest. Thus, classified information which must be kept secret in the interest of national security is exempt (exemption 1), and so are internal deliberative documents which contain advice or recommendations, because disclosure might inhibit candid discussion within the agencies (exemption 5). When information relating to private parties is contained in government files, disclosure that could invade personal privacy (exemption 6), or destroy valuable trade secrets (exemption 4), or threaten the integrity of investigative files of law enforcement agencies (exemption 7) is not required. These exemptions have generally been given a narrow interpretation by reviewing courts, and in 1974 Congress enacted several amendments to FOIA which effectively increased the burden that agencies must meet in order to justify a refusal to release documents. Some of these amendments reinforced "the principle of harm," the notion that an agency should not be able to withhold records unless it can show some specific threat to a valid governmental or private interest if the particular documents were disclosed. Other amendments made it easier for private parties to enforce the rights conferred in FOIA, by authorizing the agencies to waive search and copying fees in the public interest, and by providing that parties who sue successfully under the Act may recover their costs and attorneys' fees.

Later statutes have extended the disclosure requirements of the Freedom of Information Act. The "Government in the Sunshine Act," 5 U.S.C.A. § 552b, requires that most meetings of the multimember regulatory agencies be open to public scrutiny. Another significant disclosure statute is the Privacy Act of 1974, 5 U.S.C.A. § 552a, which not only permits the individual citizen to inspect the files that government agencies have relating to him, but also enables the record subject to seek correction of erroneous or incomplete records. Like the FOIA, the Privacy and Sunshine Acts are judicially enforceable.

Some of the primary users of these disclosure statutes are the organized constituency groups which are sufficiently concerned about regulatory policy to conduct continuous monitoring of agency activities. The most familiar—and often the most numerous and influential—of these constituency groups are the regulated industries and their trade associations, but environmental, consumer, and other "public interest" groups have also become a significant factor in the administrative arena. By following agency activities and learning the basis of proposed actions, these constituency groups can often use persuasion or pressure to mold regulatory policy at the early stages of a proceeding, when participation is most effective. In many regulatory areas, the Freedom of Information Act, supplemented by personal contacts within the agencies, functions as a kind of informal "discovery" system which constituency groups use in preparing to make their "case" to the agency.

In some instances, this process of informal consultation between regulators and regulated is institutionalized through the establishment of an advisory committee. Typically, these committees are groups of private citizens who are asked to provide an agency with advice and recommendations regarding a particular issue or program. Some advisory committees are comprised of technical experts, like the scientific committees which advise the EPA on proposals to cancel the registrations of pesticides as safety or environmental hazards. Others may be designed to represent diverse political constituencies, as in the presidential committee which was appointed to investigate the nuclear reactor accident at Three Mile Island: it was composed not only of scientists and technicians, but also environmentalists, industry members, and citizens from the community where the accident occurred. Under the Federal Advisory Committee Act, 5 U.S.C.A. App. I, the meetings of the committees must generally be open to public scrutiny and participation.

Good information is not only vital for effective participation in the regulatory process, but also can be used to generate publicity and to mobilize pressure on the agency. Information finds its way from the regulatory bureaucracies to the press and the broadcast media through a great variety of channels. Investigative reporters, following in the tradition of the muckrakers, are always looking for an expose or a scandal; private or "public interest" groups may issue study reports attacking an agency for incompetence or malfeasance; and agency personnel may "leak" information as a means of "blowing the whistle" on improprieties or of serving some personal motive. The agencies, in turn, may try to generate favorable coverage through press releases, news conferences, or active public information offices.

From the regulators' perspective, adverse publicity may be both unpleasant and threatening: it can bring the unwanted attention of executive or legislative oversight bodies, undercut agency staff morale, and disrupt harmonious relationships with constituency groups. Thus, publicity can be an effective weapon, but it is also a fairly crude one. A nonexpert public is likely to condemn an entire agency for one official's misconduct or for the agency's failure in a single, highly visible program. Since a variety of actors may be trying to manipulate press coverage for their own ends, there is always risk of distortion or error. Moreover, press coverage often tends to concentrate on sensational events and simple explanations, when the real problems in agency performance are likely to be complex and undramatic. Despite these shortcomings, publicity is still an important link in the process of democratic controls on administration.

In several countries and a few jurisdictions in the United States, extralegal controls on agency performance are institutionalized in an "ombudsman"—a public official, usually responsible to the legislature, with broad authority to investigate individual complaints of administrative misconduct, to report on them, and to make recommendations. As the federal government has grown in size and complexity, there have been repeated proposals to create a national ombudsman, or to appoint similar officials within particular agencies. A few agencies, like the CAB, have responded by setting up separate offices to receive and respond to citizen complaints. However, it seems unlikely that a general federal ombudsman will be established. Given the size of the country and the scope and diversity of federal regulation, an ombudsman's office would have to be a fairly substantial bureaucracy in its own right. Thus, there is a legitimate concern that the ombudsman would simply become another bureaucratic layer insulating government officials from the citizenry. A more serious objection, in practical terms, is the reluctance of Congress to give up its own ombudsman or "casework" responsibilities, which many legislators regard as an important and popular service to constituents.

CHAPTER III
AN OVERVIEW OF JUDICIAL REVIEW

An important set of controls on administrative behavior—and the ones that are most directly of concern in Administrative Law—are those which arise from court review of agency action (or inaction). Unlike the political oversight controls, which generally influence entire programs or basic policies, judicial review operates to provide relief for the individual person who is harmed by a particular agency decision. Judicial review also differs from the political controls because it is a process of reasoned decisionmaking, requiring the agencies to produce supporting facts and reasoned explanations. Thus, judicial oversight may conflict with the oversight activities of the political branches, which depend heavily on pressure, bargaining and compromise rather than on reasoned analysis. In one important respect, however, judicial review is an essential supplement to political controls on administration. A major function of judicial review in contemporary Administrative Law is to assure that the agency is acting in accord with the will of the political branches, as expressed in the enabling legislation. Thus, a reviewing court can nullify agency action which exceeds the jurisdictional limits contained in the relevant statutes, or which is based on factors that the Congress did not authorize the agency to consider. Finally, judicial review may enhance the acceptability of administrative decisions by providing an independent check on their validity. In this respect, it may contribute to the political legitimacy of bureaucratic regulation.

Like the regulatory process, judicial review evolved over a period of years into a complex and not completely coherent system. A series of statutory, constitutional and judicial doctrines have been developed to define the proper boundaries on judicial oversight of administration. In some areas, the courts may lack institutional competence to review an administrative action because the decision in question is political, or the plaintiff is asking the court to render an advisory opinion; in other instances, the court may decline to intervene until the administrative process has had a chance to run its course. On the whole, however, the trend in the recent judicial decisions and in modern statutes like the APA is to make judicial review more widely and easily available.

This text postpones an extended analysis of the various avenues for obtaining judicial relief and the reasons for preventing review until the administrative decisionmaking process has been explored. There is no magic in this sequence. It proceeds on the assumption that it is easier to understand many of the reasons for granting or denying judicial review if one has a fairly clear idea of what, and how, the agency has decided. Frequently the availability of judicial review turns on the issue of whether judicial relief will disrupt agency operations or harm the regulatory program, and it is difficult to address those issues without some fairly detailed explanation of the ways in which agencies function.

Administrative action may take many forms. An order may grant a TV station license, deny a workmen's compensation claim, prohibit an unfair trade practice, make possible the collection of wage reparations by an illegally discharged employee, levy a tax, or award a second class mailing privilege. Also the administrative order may be interim or final. Again, the directly affected person may have been named as a party and may have participated in a hearing almost indistinguishable from the trial of a civil suit; or he may have participated only on his own initiative (and even then have been given merely an opportunity to submit his views in writing). However, regardless of the form of the order or the procedure relied upon, a significant administrative sanction generally cannot be imposed without an opportunity for judicial review.

Once judicial review is available, the question then becomes: how far can the court go in examining the agency decision? Technically, this issue is known as "scope of review" and, as Professor Davis has observed, the scope of review for a particular administrative decision may range from zero to a hundred percent. That is, the reviewing court may be completely precluded from testing the merits of an agency action, or it may be free to decide the issues *de novo,* with no deference to the agency's determination. Usually, however, the function of the reviewing court falls somewhere between these extremes.

The general rule of thumb is that the scope of review varies depending upon whether a particular issue is a question of law or a question of fact. Law questions are theoretically subject to full review under a "rightness" test. The court will determine the correctness of the agency's interpretation and may freely substitute its judgment for the administrator's on legal issues. (While reviewing courts have the power to substitute their judgment on questions of law, in practice they often grant some deference or presumption of correctness to the

[*58*]

agency's interpretation of relevant statutes.) Fact questions and inferences, by contrast, are reviewed under a "reasonableness" test: the court defers to the agency's determination if it has a rational basis—or unless it is so lacking in support as to be unreasonable.

This fact-law dichotomy can be traced through section 706 of the Administrative Procedure Act, the APA's basic scope of review provision. Three subsections of section 706(2) deal with review of facts, and each prescribes a different level of judicial deference to agency fact-finding. Subsection (A)'s "arbitrary and capricious" test, which applies generally to informal rulemaking and informal adjudication, is in theory the most deferential standard; it is often interpreted to mean only that the administrator's decision have some rational basis. The "substantial evidence" test prescribed by subsection (E) invites somewhat closer judicial scrutiny: there must be enough evidence in the record as a whole that a reasonable person could have reached the conclusion that the agency did. The substantial evidence test is most often applied to proceedings where there has been a formal trial-type hearing. Finally, subsection (F) indicates that in some instances, the court can find the facts *de novo*. The remaining subsections of this provision deal generally with questions of law, such as whether the Constitution has been violated (subsection B), or the agency has exceeded its statutory jurisdiction (subsection C), or has failed to use required procedures (subsection D), or has abused its discretion or otherwise acted "not in accordance with law" (subsection A). In these provisions, there is no express or implied requirement of judicial deference to the agency decision.

The reasoning behind the different scope of review for questions of law and questions of fact is primarily twofold. One factor is the relative competence of the courts and the agencies: as a general matter, the courts ought to be at least as expert as the agencies in interpreting constitutional and statutory requirements, and they are comparatively disinterested. An agency may tend to misinterpret a jurisdictional limitation in order to expand its power and authority, for example, and full judicial review of legal issues can counteract this tendency toward bureaucratic empire building. On the other hand, when the agencies are dealing with highly technical factual issues—whether the airborne pollutants generated by leaded gasoline are absorbed by human beings in sufficient quantities to pose a health hazard, or whether emergency core cooling systems on nuclear reactors are adequate to prevent releases of radiation in certain hypothesized accidents—then the courts, staffed by generalist lawyers, may be less well equipped to make the basic decision. Even if the issue is as simple as whether a welfare recipient has outside sources of income, however, the agency fact-finder who has heard the testimony and observed the demeanor of the witnesses may be in a better position to assess their credibility and decide where the truth lies. Considerations of economy and efficiency also argue in favor of limited judicial review of the facts. Fact finding, particularly if it is conducted through the trial-type procedures of the judicial system, is a very slow, costly, and labor intensive operation. If the courts essentially duplicated the agency fact finding process on a broad scale, the burden on the courts would be enormous and the delays intolerable. The costs to the participants and the government would also be formidable. In short, practical reasons of institutional competence and economy support the general practice of allowing only limited judicial review of the facts found in administrative proceedings.

While the different scope of review for fact and law questions generally makes sense, it is important not to treat the distinction too literally. Like most general principles of Administrative Law (or, for that matter, of law generally), it is subject to numerous qualifications and exceptions. An agency which has followed a particular statute through the Congress since its enactment and has implemented it for many years may well be more expert in its interpretation than a federal district judge who is seeing the act for the first time. Some reviewing courts have acknowledged this fact in the maxim that a longstanding interpretation of a statute by an agency charged with its implementation will be given great deference by the courts. See, e. g., FTC v. Mandel Bros., 359 U.S. 385, 391 (1959). A more fundamental difficulty is that issues cannot always be neatly divided into "questions of law" or "questions of fact"; there is a large gray area in between, sometimes referred to as "mixed questions of law and fact" or "application of law to fact." Because of this broad zone of ambiguity, and the impreciseness of the review standards, the courts have considerable latitude either to intervene deeply in agency determinations or to exercise restraint. These ambiguities in language and practice have bedeviled not only the courts themselves, but congressmen, scholars, and generations of students as well. But at least the doctrinal uncertainties give judges (and advocates) some room to maneuver, and to adjust the intensity of judicial scrutiny in particular cases to reflect factors such as the perceived competence of court and agency decisionmakers and the impact of the decision on affected interests.

As this brief discussion suggests, the law of judicial review does not lend itself to easy generalization. There are also many functional limitations inherent in judicial review. It is designed only to establish minimum standards, not to assure an optimal or perfect decision. Thus, above the threshold of minimum fairness and rationality, the agencies may still make unsatisfactory decisions or use poor procedures. Even a judicial reversal may have little impact on administrative policy, if there are strong bureaucratic or political reasons for the agency to persist in its view. The agency may simply produce a better rationalization for its action on remand, or reach the same result using different procedures, or misinterpret the court's directives (perhaps intentionally). And, of course, there are many decisions in which judicial review is not even sought. Judicial review is expensive and slow, and the outcome is never certain. These factors often combine to prevent parties from bringing even a meritorious claim, particularly when the person aggrieved is not wealthy or does not have a large financial stake in the outcome. Yet, despite the "limited office" of judicial review, it is generally regarded as the most significant safeguard available to curb the excesses in administrative action.

CHAPTER IV

DISCRETIONARY DECISIONS

A. THE NATURE OF ADMINISTRATIVE DISCRETION

Most agency enabling statutes authorize agency action; few compel it.[1] That is, the legislature usually delegates to the administrator not only jurisdiction over the subject matter but also broad discretion in determining whether he will in fact regulate the activity and, if so, how he should proceed. In deciding how to proceed, administrative choices range from informal pressures to formal prosecutions and include several intermediate choices such as policy announcements and binding rules. The administrator's negative discretion is almost unlimited. That is, he can decline to exercise jurisdiction even though the matter is within the scope of the agency's legislative mission. All regulatory authority overshoots the mark to some extent; not every violation can or should be punished.

In general, an administrator exercises discretion whenever he has the freedom and ability to choose among possible courses of action. A prosecutor may decide to file formal charges against a regulated company, or to investigate further, or to drop the matter entirely; a funding agency may grant or withhold money to build a highway, or require various modifications of the plans; a

1. For an illustration of a regulatory charter that often compels regulation and therefore confines administrative discretion—and thus does not fit much of the discussion here, see Clean Air Act, 42 U.S.C.A. §§ 7401 et seq. But see Ethyl Corp. v. EPA, 541 F.2d 1 (D.C.Cir.) (en banc), cert. denied, 426 U.S. 941 (1976).

licensing authority considering competing applications under a broad "public interest" delegation may have considerable latitude to decide which, if any, of the applicants will receive a license. In each instance, if the enabling legislation does not effectively dictate the result, the agency is exercising discretion.

It should be emphasized that in the conventional usage of Administrative Law, the scope of the agency's discretion is determined by reference to formal legal standards. However, in each of the examples given, there may be significant practical limits on the agency's freedom of action, despite the absence of legal checks. The administrator deciding whether to grant highway construction funds may be constrained by outside pressures from the media, constituency groups, and political oversight bodies; he may also have to accommodate bureaucratic pressures such as the need to "back up" his subordinates who are recommending a particular course of action, or to maintain the approval of his superiors, or to protect the agency from criticism; and his decision will likely be influenced by personal interests in reputation and in values like environmental protection or economic development. While these nonlegal constraints on administrative behavior are important both practically and conceptually, we are concerned here with the narrower question of legal techniques for controlling bureaucratic discretion.

In considering the legal system's approach to the problem of administrative discretion, it is useful to distinguish among several types of discretionary decisions. Each has a somewhat different functional justification, and each has been treated differently in the development of the applicable legal doctrines.

1. *Prosecutorial Discretion.* From the time that a potential violation comes to his attention until a decision is made to bring formal proceedings or close the case, the prosecuting official typically has very broad discretion to decide whether and how to proceed. Traditionally, several justifications have been given for this kind of discretion. Prosecuting agencies usually do not have sufficient resources to pursue all possible violations of the laws they administer; allocation of investigative and litigating manpower must be based on judgments about factors like the seriousness of the offense, the nature and quality of proof available, the likelihood of obtaining a consent settlement or a favorable decision, the deterrent value of a prosecution, the "opportunity cost" of other cases which will not be brought if resources are invested in this one, and the like. These are not matters which can easily be codified in legal standards and reviewed by the courts. But see K. Davis, *Discretionary Justice: A Preliminary Inquiry* (1969).

2. *Policymaking Discretion.* When an agency is delegated broad quasi-legislative power to make rules governing an area of regulatory activity, it may have discretion to set basic policy in that field. The FCC, for example, is authorized to issue licenses and make rules for radio and television broadcasting as "the public convenience, interest or necessity" may dictate. 47 U.S.C.A. §§ 303, 307. The language of this statute is broad enough to encompass a variety of strategies for regulating broadcasting. The FCC could define the economic structure of the industry

(for example, by limiting the number of stations in a particular area which can be owned by the same company, or by creating a preference for stations which are locally owned); it could prescribe quantitative standards for different types of programs (a maximum number of minutes per hour of commercials, or a minimum number of hours per week of news and public affairs programming); it could issue qualitative or content requirements for licensed stations (no obscene programs, equal time for competing political candidates); or it could follow a "deregulatory," free market approach (by granting as many licenses as technically feasible, and allowing them to be sold and transferred freely without regard to program content). Over the past 40 years, the FCC has experimented with elements of each of these strategies, and for the most part the courts have agreed that the governing statutes give the agency considerable latitude to choose among them.[2]

Policymaking discretion may be granted to an agency because a problem is novel (as the regulation of broadcasting was when radio first became technically and commercially feasible), or because the issues are highly technical (as in many fields of health and safety regulation), or because the legislature is not able to reconcile conflicts among competing values. The latter reason may help explain why the FCC's discretion in the broadcast licensing field has not been confined by later legislation.

---

2. The FCC's current posture (circa 1981) is not to regulate broadcast programming, at least insofar as radio is concerned. See Wall St. J., p. 28 (Jan. 15, 1981). Its initial effort at format deregulation was upheld only after considerable struggle, however. See FCC v. WNCN Listeners Guild, 101 S.Ct. 1266 (1981), reversing 610 F.2d 838 (D.C.Cir. 1979) (en banc).

Finding the appropriate tradeoffs between interests such as safeguarding freedom of expression and assuring quality programming, or between protecting the security of investment and encouraging the spur of competition, are controversial matters on which there is little political consensus. Legislatures have frequently been content to turn these intractable problems over to the agencies under a broad grant of policymaking discretion.

3. *Choice of Mode of Action.* Another type of agency discretion comes into play when the administrators have identified a problem area which needs corrective action, and a choice must be made as to what kind of proceedings should be initiated. If the Federal Trade Commission has reason to believe that hearing aid dealers are using deceptive sales practices in violation of the FTC Act, 15 U.S.C.A. § 45, it may use several different procedural techniques in attacking this problem. It could issue complaints to initiate cease-and-desist adjudications against the worst offenders; or it could begin rulemaking proceedings designed to impose general rules which would have the force and effect of law; or it could issue "policy statements" threatening to bring individual enforcement actions if the industry persists in its violations; or it might even go directly to court and try to enjoin the offenders pending further litigation. When the authorizing statutes give the agencies a range of procedural techniques to use, they generally confer discretion to choose among the different modes of action. Statutes often provide that relatively drastic summary remedies, such as seizures or injunctions, cannot be used unless there is an emergency, and due process may impose some procedural limits on summary action. Beyond these minimal restraints, how-

[*67*]

ever, many agencies remain free to select among various kinds of proceedings. Most of the disputes that have arisen in this area concern the agency's choice between adjudication and rulemaking. This topic is discussed separately in Chapter 10.

One reason for agency discretion to choose among different kinds of proceedings is the agencies' need for some freedom to manage and allocate their resources. A major rulemaking proceeding, for example, may consume much more time and effort than a series of adjudications, and it may inspire more resistance as well. In addition, the state of knowledge in a particular area may not be sufficient to warrant the issuance of a general rule; an experimental, case-by-case approach may be preferable. Finally, in recent years rulemaking proceedings have become more "judicialized" while opportunities for affected persons to intervene in adjudications have become more freely available. This means that an agency's choice of one form of proceeding rather than the other may have little practical effect on the rights of interested persons to contest the agency's proposal.

B. LEGAL CONTROLS ON DISCRETION

The Administrative Procedure Act contains two seemingly contradictory directions to courts reviewing discretionary administrative decisions. Section 706(2)(A) empowers the court to set aside administrative action which is "arbitrary, capricious, an abuse of discretion, or otherwise not in accordance with law." However, the introductory phrase of section 701(a)(1) states that the judicial review provisions of the APA are inapplicable "to the extent that . . . agency action is committed to agency discretion by law." In practice, this latter exception covers agency decisions that are so discretionary or unbounded by legal standards that there is "no law to apply"; one example would be the President's decision to award transatlantic airline routes to particular carriers after negotiations with foreign governments. This exception for actions "committed to discretion" is discussed separately in Chapter 11. The present discussion is concerned with the techniques courts use to control agency discretion under the "arbitrary, capricious, [or] abuse of discretion" language of section 706(2)(A). Analytically, these review techniques can be grouped into several categories.

1. *Consistency With Statutory Mandate.* Since the scope of an agency's discretion is determined by the statutory delegation giving it powers to make certain kinds of decisions, a reviewing court can control discretion by enforcing the limits set by the legislature. These limits can take a wide variety of forms. For example, the legislature can define unlawful conduct with great specificity, as it does when it sets the maximum speed limit at 55 miles per hour and prescribes penalties for those who are found guilty of violating it. This kind of statute gives the implementing agencies no discretion to make policy by setting the speed limit at 60 or 70 miles per hour; at most, the police and prosecutors would have discretion in deciding how to enforce the policy set by the legislature with respect to matters such as issuing warnings rather than citations, or accepting pleas to lesser offenses. While the commitment of enforcement resources—e. g., the number of police patrols, the use of radar—is a discretionary decision of equal import in

enforcing this policy, the legislature may attempt to thwart the use of even this discretionary power by specifying the level of enforcement required.

At the other extreme, the enabling legislation may impose minimal constraints on the agency's ability to make policy. If the statute merely said that "The State Liquor Commission may grant licenses to sell alcoholic beverages as the public interest may dictate," it would be difficult at best for the reviewing court to determine whether a particular grant or denial of a license application violated the legislative intent. Unless there was some evidence outside the statute indicating what the legislature intended— for example, legislative history, or a record of prior administrative practice—any policy short of a complete ban on the sale of alcoholic beverages might be within the proper scope of the agency's discretion.

More commonly, regulatory legislation falls somewhere between these extremes. Most delegations direct the agency to take account of particular factors or interests in making certain decisions, and these limits can be enforced by reviewing courts. Sometimes factors are explicitly listed in the statute; for example, the Federal Water Pollution Control Act Amendments of 1972 require EPA to "take into account" factors such as "the age of equipment and facilities involved," "the process employed," and "the non-water quality environmental impact" when the agency issues rules requiring manufacturers to use pollution control technologies. 33 U.S.C.A. § 1314(b)(1)(B). While the agency has considerable latitude in determining how much weight to give each of these factors, it could not completely refuse to take account of a factor made relevant by the statute. The EPA could not, for example, simply ignore evidence that a particular water pollution control technology would reduce air quality. See, e. g., Weyerhaeuser Co. v. Costle, 590 F.2d 1011, 1044–53 (D.C.Cir. 1978).

Even when the statute does not explicitly prescribe the factors which the agency must consider, judicial construction of broad statutory terms, guided by legislative history and other aids to interpretation, can establish boundaries on agency discretion. In Citizens to Preserve Overton Park, Inc. v. Volpe, 401 U.S. 402 (1971), the relevant statute provided that the Secretary of Transportation could not grant federal funds to finance construction of highways through public parks if a "feasible and prudent" alternative route existed. The Court interpreted this broad language as limiting the Secretary's decision: before taking park land, he must find that "as a matter of sound engineering judgment it would not be possible to build the highway along any other route" or that an alternative route would not be "prudent." In construing the latter requirement, the Court held that the legislature had given primary importance to the preservation of park land; thus, the Secretary could not approve a route through a park unless he found that alternatives presented "unique problems" or would impose cost and community disruption of "extraordinary magnitude." In other words, a court reviewing for abuse of discretion will construe the statute not only to determine what factors the legislature directed the agency to consider, but also to discover whether the statute required the agency to give special weight to one or more of these factors. Since the legislation in *Overton Park* required the agency to give great weight to the preservation of park land, and the record did not establish that the Secretary had done so, his decision was not shown to be within the scope of his authority. Thus, the case was remanded for a determination of whether the Secretary's decision was properly supported or supportable.

When the statute directs the agency to consider certain factors in making a particular type of decision, it may implicitly prohibit the administrator from taking other factors into account. This situation is illustrated by the "Three Sisters Bridge" case, D.C. Federation of Civic Ass'ns v. Volpe, 459 F.2d 1231 (D.C.Cir.), cert. denied, 405 U.S. 1030 (1972). There, the Secretary of Transportation had made a highway funding decision similar to the one challenged in *Overton Park.* This time, however, the appellants asserted that he had abused his discretion because he had yielded to pressure from an influential chairman of a congressional committee in granting his approval for the construction project. The reviewing court agreed: since the legislation directed the Secretary to consider the costs and benefits of the project "on the merits," the pressures brought to bear by one congressman were technically irrelevant to the decision. The matter was remanded with a directive to the Secretary to consider the merits of the project without regard to the irrelevant factor of political pressure. While the *Three Sisters Bridge* decision has been criticized for imposing unrealistic limits on the congressional oversight process, it nevertheless demonstrates the power of reviewing courts to require that discretionary decisions be based only upon those factors that the legislature as a whole has authorized or directed the agency to consider.

2. *Factual Support.* The Court in *Overton Park* noted that the APA directive to set aside administrative action which is "arbitrary, capricious [or] an abuse of discretion" required reviewing courts not only to assure that the decision in question was "based on consideration of the relevant factors," but also to determine whether the agency had made "a clear error of judgment." In other words, the reviewing court should determine whether the agency had an adequate factual basis for its decision.[3] Some review of the facts may be essential if the judicial controls on discretion are to be meaningful. Otherwise, an agency might be able to protect itself from reversal merely by saying that it had taken account of the relevant factors, without really considering the evidence for and against its position. However, the scope of review of facts in discretionary decisions has been a continuing source of difficulty in Administrative Law.

Section 706(2) of the APA contains three different standards of fact review. The "arbitrary and capricious" standard of subsection (A) is in theory the most lenient of these standards, and it is the one which is most broadly applicable: it will govern unless the agency's organic statute directs the court to use some other test, or unless one of the other two APA fact review standards comes into play. These other two APA standards are the "unsupported by substantial evidence" test found in

---

3. For a discussion of the Supreme Court's use of the "clear error of judgment" test in *Overton Park*, and an explanation that it was not meant to revamp the usual review standard ("that a reviewing court must defer if the agency has a rational basis for its decisions"), see Ethyl Corp. v. EPA, 541 F.2d 1, 34–35 n. 74 (D.C.Cir.) (en banc), cert. denied, 426 U.S. 941 (1976).

subsection (E), and the "unwarranted by the facts" test set forth in subsection (F). There has often been confusion and debate about when these two more stringent fact review standards should apply, and much regulatory legislation is ambiguous on this point. However, there are some helpful general principles to follow in deciding when to apply these two standards.

The language of the APA indicates that the applicability of the substantial evidence test is triggered by a particular kind of agency proceeding: substantial evidence is required in "a case subject to sections 556 and 557 of this title or otherwise reviewed on the record of an agency hearing provided by statute." In other words, if the agency decision was made after a trial-type, on-the-record hearing (a "formal adjudication" or "rule-making on a record"), then the substantial evidence test should apply. The APA is less helpful in indicating when the reviewing court is able (or required) to find the facts *de novo,* without any deference to the agency's factual determinations. Subsection (F) simply says that a reviewing court may reverse an agency decision which is unwarranted by the facts "to the extent that the facts are subject to trial de novo by the reviewing court." The Court in *Overton Park,* relying on the legislative history of the APA, determined that this plenary fact review is available primarily in two situations: either "the action is adjudicatory in nature and the agency factfinding procedures are inadequate," or "issues that were not before the agency are raised in a proceeding to enforce nonadjudicatory agency action." 401 U.S. at 415. Plenary fact review may also be specifically provided for by statutes other than the APA.

The second condition noted by the court in *Overton Park* refers primarily to a method for reviewing administrative rules which was common when the APA was enacted in 1946, but is fairly rare today. Before the 1960's, it was difficult to get "pre-enforcement" judicial review of an administrative rule at the time it was issued; instead, the person covered by the rule had to wait until the agency brought an enforcement action against him to challenge its validity. Since these actions were brought in the trial courts, it was possible to have an evidentiary hearing on the factual support for the rule. Gradually, however, the restrictions on pre-enforcement review were removed either by statute or by judicial interpretation. See Abbott Laboratories v. Gardner, 387 U.S. 136 (1967), discussed at p. 319 infra. Today, most significant or controversial substantive rules are challenged in court shortly after they are issued, and the review takes place in the courts of appeals, based upon the administrative record that was before the agency when it issued the rule. Thus, the *de novo* review of facts in an enforcement proceeding has little practical significance in contemporary Administrative Law.

The other situation when *de novo* fact review may be available under the APA and *Overton Park* is less clearly defined. The first branch of the inquiry is whether the agency action was an "adjudication." However, the APA defines the term quite broadly. Under section 551(7), an adjudication is any administrative process for the formulation of an order—and an order is defined by section 551(6) as the final disposition of any "matter other than rule making but including licensing." Since orders comprise such a broad residual category, a very large proportion of all agency decisions would technically be considered adjudications. Thus, the key often is whether "the agency factfinding procedures are inadequate." The *Overton Park* decision suggests that this test will rarely be met. The procedures used by the Secretary of Transportation in that case were extremely informal. There was no public hearing, no opportunity for interested persons to submit comments or otherwise participate, and no formal administrative record supporting the decision; the Secretary simply reviewed documents in the privacy of his office, consulted with subordinates and other officials as he thought appropriate, and then made the decision. He was not even required to issue written findings or an explanation of his action. Yet the Supreme Court found that the *de novo* fact review test did not apply. Instead, review was to be based upon "the full administrative record that was before the Secretary at the time he made his decision," supplemented if necessary by testimony from agency officials explaining the administrative action taken. Following *Overton Park*, reviewing courts have tended to treat whatever collection of papers was before the decisionmakers as the administrative record, and to subject that record to review under the "arbitrary and capricious" test.

Courts conducting this kind of review have varied in the degree of deference they have been willing to give to agency factual determinations under the APA's arbitrary and capricious test. The *Overton Park* decision itself has some seemingly contradictory directives on this point. While the Court noted that the administrative decision was entitled to a presumption of regularity and that a reviewing court is "not empowered to substitute its judgment for that of the agency," it also stated that the agency decision should be subjected to "a thorough, probing, in-depth review" and a "searching and careful" inquiry into the facts. Subsequent decisions have not fully reconciled these conflicting pressures. Some courts have followed the traditional assumption that the arbitrary and capricious test is less stringent (that is, more deferential to the agency) than the substantial evidence test, though the difference in intensity of review is not possible to capture in a simple phrase. Other courts have suggested that there really is no difference between the two fact review standards, at least when the issue under consideration is one which lends itself to relatively straightforward factfinding. See, e. g., Associated Indus. of New York State, Inc. v. United States Dept. of Labor, 487 F.2d 342 (2d Cir. 1973); cf. Industrial Union Dept., AFL–CIO v. Hodgson, 499 F.2d 467, 474–76 (D.C.Cir. 1974). Perhaps the most that can be said is that courts reviewing discretionary decisions under the arbitrary and capricious test will determine whether the agency's factfinding is within the zone of reasonableness. The size of that zone will often depend upon a variety of subtle factors such as the nature and complexity of the issues involved, the consequences of an erroneous determination, the agency's reputation for competence and fairness, and the judge's philosophy of judicial review.

3. *Consistency With Administrative Policy.* Even though an administrator's discretionary decision is in accord with governing statutes, it may be suspect because it is inconsistent with the agency's own policy. If an agency has issued valid interpretive rules stating that it

will grant a license or confer some benefit upon all who meet certain criteria, for example, a decision rejecting an applicant who met the conditions stated in the rules would be reversible as an abuse of discretion. See generally Note, *Violations by Agencies of Their Own Regulations,* 87 Harv.L.Rev. 629 (1974). Departure from agency precedents embodied in prior adjudicative decisions can also constitute an abuse of discretion, if the reasons for the failure to follow precedent are not adequately explained. See, e. g., Sunbeam Television Corp. v. FCC, 243 F.2d 26 (D.C.Cir. 1957) (FCC's failure to give a "demerit" or negative weight to a contract between a network and one competing applicant for a television station license constitutes reversible error when similar arrangements had been treated as negative factors in prior licensing proceedings). As in the case where the agency has violated its own regulations, this sort of inconsistency may deny regulated parties fair notice of agency policy and an opportunity to comply. In addition, differential treatment of parties who are similarly situated raises questions as to whether the agency is administering its program in a fair, impartial and competent manner. However, reviewing courts have generally refrained from requiring agencies to follow precedent as closely as trial courts must. Since conditions in a regulated industry may change rapidly and the agency often needs some latitude to adjust and develop its policies, rigorous adherence to precedent could frustrate the objectives of the regulatory program. Thus, when a reviewing court finds that a particular administrative decision is inconsistent with the agency's own precedents, it may remand the matter to the agency for a fuller statement of reasons rather than reversing the decision.

4. *Compelling Agency Rulemaking.* Since the legislative limitations on administrative discretion are often minimal and many agencies are slow to clarify their own policies in rules or precedents, some commentators have argued that reviewing courts should modify the delegation doctrine to compel agency articulation of policy. Thus, an agency operating under a broad delegation of authority could be ordered to issue administrative rules confining its discretion. K. Davis, *Discretionary Justice: A Preliminary Inquiry* 55–59 (1969).

Traditionally, reviewing courts have not restricted the agencies' discretion to deal with a particular problem through adjudication or rulemaking, or to refrain from clarifying policy. See generally Chapter 10. On a few occasions, however, courts have effectively required the agencies to issue administrative rules before taking particular actions. In Hornsby v. Allen, 326 F.2d 605 (5th Cir. 1964), the court ruled that a disappointed applicant could enjoin the distribution of retail liquor licenses by the mayor and board of aldermen to political favorites; ascertainable standards and fair procedures were possible and constitutionally required in this instance.[4] Holmes v. New York Housing Auth., 398 F.2d 262 (2d Cir. 1968), applied a similar rationale to public housing applications where the demand for public housing far exceeded supply. Finding that public housing was an important interest often not otherwise satisfied, and that rational criteria could readily be developed (e. g., by filling vacancies from a chronological waiting list or by giving

---

4. But see Atlanta Bowling Center, Inc. v. Allen, 389 F.2d 713, 716 (5th Cir. 1968) ("traditional local interest in regulating the liquor business calls for the use of broad discretion and flexible procedures").

preference according to need), the court held that "due process requires that selections among applicants be made in accordance with 'ascertainable standards.'" Id. at 265 (quoting Hornsby v. Allen, supra).

A similar case that has puzzled commentators is Morton v. Ruiz, 415 U.S. 199 (1974). There the Court reversed a decision of the Bureau of Indian Affairs denying benefits to Native Americans under a federal assistance program. The Bureau had developed an internal policy of denying assistance to claimants who lived outside of the reservations, but it had never communicated this policy to the public through rules or precedents. The Court held that even though this policy might be consistent with congressional intent and have a rational basis due to the limited funds available, it could not be implemented through *ad hoc* decisions; the Bureau had to issue valid administrative rules before it could cut off the claimants' eligibility in this fashion. Although the result in *Ruiz* can be justified by the claimant's need to know what the agency's policy is before he unwittingly forfeits his eligibility, the Court's rationale is obscure. The Court expressly declined to decide the case on constitutional grounds—the apparent foundation of *Hornsby* and *Holmes*—and neither statute nor agency rule appeared to support the requirement. Thus, the *Ruiz* decision has not generally been used as authority for reviewing courts to compel agency rulemaking, and the constitutionally based rule of *Hornsby* and *Holmes* appears to be limited to the allocation of scarce government benefits. However, Congress has imposed mandatory rulemaking requirements, sometimes under strict time deadlines, in several recent regulatory programs.

5. *Procedural Rights.* Another technique that reviewing courts can use to control agency discretion is to require that agencies making discretionary decisions use fair and open procedures. Section 706(2)(D) of the APA empowers the reviewing court to set aside actions which are taken "without observance of procedure required by law," and courts may enforce this requirement strictly when they have doubts about the substantive wisdom or propriety of a discretionary decision. The right to a hearing or other opportunity to participate in the decisionmaking process may be based upon agency regulations, statutory provisions, or the constitutional requirements of procedural due process. Regardless of their nature or source, however, procedural protections have a limited effect on the agency's exercise of discretion. Without some substantive leverage to confine or affect the agency's choices, procedural safeguards can become a mere formality which the agency must complete before it announces a predetermined outcome.

CHAPTER V

ACQUIRING INFORMATION: INVESTIGATIONS

Without information, administrative agencies could not regulate industry, protect the environment, prosecute fraud, collect taxes, or issue grants. Good decisions require good data, and if an agency does not fully understand the nature of the problems confronting it or the consequences of possible actions, its programs are likely to be either unduly burdensome or ineffective. Indeed, one of the strongest arguments for "deregulating" major sectors of the economy is the claim that agencies often cannot learn enough about the regulated industry to make sound policy. Access to complete and accurate information is also an important determinant of the fairness of the administrative process, and many of the procedural protections found in judicial and administrative proceedings are designed to give interested persons an opportunity to discover, present, and challenge relevant information. In addition, collection and disclosure of information serves the interest of public and political accountability, by revealing areas where administration is ineffective and reform is necessary.

Much of the information needed to make the administrative process work is freely available from published sources, voluntary submissions by regulated persons and organizations, citizen complaints, and studies conducted by agency staff or outside parties. Frequently, however, the necessary information can be obtained only from members of the regulated industry or other private parties who are not willing to give it to the government. Personal privacy and freedom from governmental intrusion have long been considered fundamental elements of liberty, and these interests are constitutionally protected by the Fourth Amendment's prohibition of unreasonable searches as well as the Fifth Amendment's ban on compulsory self-incrimination. The growth of regulatory and benefit programs in recent years has greatly increased the government's demand for sensitive private information, and the computerization of files has heightened popular fears that agencies may misuse personal data.

Beyond these legitimate concerns about abuse of official power, however, there are some strong practical incentives for regulated persons and firms to resist disclosure. Withholding requested information is often an effective way of avoiding unwanted regulation or delaying it; even if the agency ultimately succeeds in forcing disclosure, conditions may have changed sufficiently to make the data useless or irrelevant. Moreover, some of the data sought by the regulatory agencies may be commercially valuable material such as trade secrets, and companies may fear that information will "leak" from the agencies' files to their competitors. Cost is also an important factor in many situations where private parties refuse to provide information voluntarily. When the FTC ordered large manufacturing firms to provide detailed financial information broken down by product category or "line of business," some companies fought the demand through the courts for years because they did not keep records according to the categories requested by the agency. As a result, it would have been extremely costly for them to reconstruct the data from existing business records. See, e. g., In re FTC Line of Business Report Litigation, 595 F.2d 685 (D.C.Cir.), cert. denied, 99 S.Ct. 362 (1978).

Because the stakes to the agency and to the regulated industry are often high, conflicts over access to information frequently result in litigation. Over the years, a complex body of law has developed to govern the agencies' power to demand data from private persons, and the data source's ability to prevent the agency from disclosing sensitive information.

A. JUDICIAL CONTROLS ON INVESTIGATORY POWERS

The power to compel private parties to submit information, like other administrative powers, must be based upon a valid legislative delegation of authority, and the agency must observe the standards and procedures specified in the relevant statutes. Traditionally, however, Congress has granted the agencies great discretion to investigate and compel disclosure of information; many statutes impose only minimal constraints on the agency's use of compulsory process. Another source of legal limitations on agency data gathering is the Constitution. Because the government's attempts to gather information can threaten constitutionally protected privacy interests, the agency's activities must be measured against the requirements of the Fourth and Fifth Amendments. Applying these established general principles has often proven difficult, however, because the agencies are engaged in widely diverse activities and the constitutional protections, which were designed primarily to deal with criminal law enforcement proceedings, cannot be mechanically applied to all agency activities. Administrative inquiries may be directed toward an eventual criminal prosecution, as in the case of an IRS tax fraud investigation, but they may also be designed to support a civil penalty, or a cease and desist order, or the setting of rates for the future, or the formulation of general policy. Moreover, much of the work of the regulatory agencies takes place outside of formal proceedings. The Equal Employment Opportunity Commission mediates discrimination complaints; the Food and Drug Administration negotiates "voluntary" recalls of potentially hazardous food products; the Federal Reserve Board exercises continuing supervision over banks. The agency's (and the public's) need to compel disclosure of information may vary in each of these settings, and so also may the potential harm to the regulated if that power is unchecked. See generally Freedman, *Summary Action by Administrative Agencies,* 40 U.Chi.L.Rev. 1 (1972).

Another source of difficulty is the fact that agencies use a variety of techniques for gathering data, and these techniques vary in their burdensomeness and intrusion on protected interests. In some Federal Trade Commission investigations, for example, the Commission can issue subpoenas for documents or testimony, or it can demand to inspect records in the office where they are kept, or it can require companies to fill out special "report orders"; in other instances, the FTC can issue "civil investigative demands" which are subject to different standards and procedures; and presiding officers in adjudicative proceedings can issue discovery orders much like those used in the federal courts. Other agencies, particularly those enforcing health and safety regulations, have the power to inspect facilities and seize suspicious goods. As might be expected, the courts' attempts to adapt the constitutional protections to the administrative process have produced a large and not entirely consistent body of law.

A threshold question which arises in disputes over agency access to information is how the party who is presented with an agency demand for records or other data may contest the legality of the request. In many agencies, rules or statutes explicitly provide a procedure similar to the motion to quash a subpoena that is used in the courts. When such a process is available, the party served with a subpoena must present his objections before the agency or he may be barred from raising them in the courts under the doctrine of exhaustion of administrative remedies. McClendon v. Jackson Television, 603 F.2d 1174 (5th Cir. 1979); see also pp. 316–18 infra. If the agency does not accept the party's objection, the matter may then move into the courts. While courts can enforce their own subpoenas directly by use of the contempt power, agencies generally cannot; they must bring an enforcement action and obtain a court order directing compliance with the subpoena. In this enforcement action, the party who is resisting disclosure may present his objections to the subpoena, and the court will review the legality of the agency's use of compulsory process. If the court upholds the supoena, it will issue an order enforcing it, and a violation of this order is punishable as contempt of court. Thus, a party resisting an agency subpoena typically does not incur any risk of penalties or legal liability until after court review. Some statutes do provide that a party who refuses to comply without just cause is subject to fines or criminal penalties from the time the agency subpoena is issued. See, e. g., Securities Exchange Act, 15 U.S.C.A. § 78u(c) (failure to comply with SEC subpoena is a misdemeanor punishable by fine or imprisonment). These immediate sanctions are rarely enforced, however, and a party can usually obtain judicial review of administrative subpoenas with no real risk that substantial penalties will accrue.

B.   GENERAL PRINCIPLES

When a private party contests an agency's demand for records, testimony, or other information, the reviewing courts will test the legality of the agency's demand by applying general principles that have evolved to control the use of compulsory process. These basic standards can be divided into four categories.

1.   *The Investigation must be Authorized by Law and Undertaken for a Legitimate Purpose.* Because administrative agencies can exercise only those powers which the legislature has delegated to them, the first inquiry is whether the relevant statutes have conferred the power to conduct the investigation in question. Section 555(c) of the APA restates this principle by providing that compulsory process may not be issued or enforced "except as authorized by law." In practice, however, this jurisdictional limit on administrative investigations is generally easy to satisfy. Both the substantive delegation of regulatory power to the agency and the grant of investigative authority may be drafted in such broad terms that the reviewing court will find it difficult to conclude that the investigation is *ultra vires.* When the issue of agency jurisdiction is arguable or unclear, the court may

well decide that it should let the investigation go forward because an injured party will usually have an opportunity to challenge the scope of the agency's power on review of a final decision. Moreover, a judicial attempt to fix the boundaries of agency jurisdiction at the preliminary stage of subpoena enforcement may be premature. This question can usually be litigated in subsequent agency proceedings, and as a result the issues may be more clearly defined if review is postponed until there is a final administrative decision. Alternatively, the question may become moot if the agency ultimately decides not to exercise regulatory power over the complaining party. Thus, the courts generally conclude that the question of statutory coverage is to be determined by the agency in the first instance. See, e. g., Oklahoma Press Pub. Co. v. Walling, 327 U.S. 186 (1946).

A jurisdictional argument may succeed when the complaining party is able to show a clear congressional intent not only to exempt it from regulation, but also to protect it from particular agency investigations. A common carrier which was subject to regulation by the ICC and explicitly exempted from investigative or regulatory activities of the Federal Trade Commission was able to resist compliance on this ground in FTC v. Miller, 549 F.2d 452 (7th Cir. 1977). Another situation in which reviewing courts are likely to take a close look at agency demands for information is when the complaining party can make a convincing showing that the investigation was undertaken in bad faith for some improper purpose such as harassing or persecuting the respondent. United States v. Powell, 379 U.S. 48 (1964). However, if the administrator has a colorable basis for requesting the information in question, the complaining party will have to satisfy a substantial burden of pleading and proof in establishing an improper motive. Id.

2. *The Information Sought must be Relevant to a Lawful Subject of Investigation.* The Fourth Amendment prohibits the issuance of search warrants unless there is probable cause to believe that a specific violation of law has occurred, and during the early years of administrative regulation a similar standard applied to administrative subpoenas. The leading case was Federal Trade Commission v. American Tobacco Co., 264 U.S. 298 (1924), where the Court strictly construed the FTC's investigative authority in order to avoid the constitutional question: if the statute did not require "[s]ome evidence of the materiality of the papers demanded," it might well violate the Fourth Amendment.

A few years later, however, the Court relaxed this seemingly stringent requirement. In Endicott Johnson Corp. v. Perkins, 317 U.S. 501 (1943), the Secretary of Labor had requested payroll data from a government contractor for the purpose of determining whether certain factories were covered by the minimum wage law. The Court concluded that the issue of whether the factories were covered should not be litigated in the subpoena enforcement proceeding; so long as "[t]he evidence sought by the subpoena was not plainly incompetent or irrelevant to any lawful purpose of the Secretary in the discharge of her duties under the Act," the district court should grant enforcement. The constitutional basis for this result was further explained in Oklahoma Press Pub. Co. v. Walling, 327 U.S. 186 (1946). There, the Court distinguished between actual searches and seizures like those that are commonly used in criminal law enforcement and the "figurative" or "constructive" search which takes place when a regulatory agency demands to see the records of a regulated company.

The *Oklahoma Press* opinion emphasized that there was a long history of legislative provisions requiring corporations to maintain records which were open to public and government scrutiny, while individuals had been protected against "officious intermeddling" in their affairs. In essence, the threat to legitimate expectations of privacy was less in the regulatory setting, while the public interest in access to corporate records was strong. In many fields of regulation, the only evidence of possible violations of law may be the records of regulated companies. In this situation, a strict probable cause requirement could make enforcement impossible. The Supreme Court recognized this necessity in United States v. Morton Salt Co., 338 U.S. 632 (1950), when it analogized the agency's investigative power to a grand jury's: an agency with a proper legislative authorization "can investigate merely on suspicion that the law is being violated, or even just because it wants assurance that it is not." There may also be strong policy reasons to minimize the probable cause requirement when an agency investigation is not directed at the disclosure of particular violations of law. Many agencies have responsibilities which extend beyond the enforcement of existing laws and rules. When administrators are delegated the power to make policy through rulemaking or are authorized to report to the Congress on matters that may require legislation, they will often need to obtain information from unwilling private parties.

Rigid application of the probable cause standard could undermine the quality of agency policymaking.

While the constitutional standard of relevance has become easy to satisfy, particular statutes may impose more rigorous requirements on agency investigations. When the Federal Trade Commission is investigating to determine whether a particular person or company has committed unfair or deceptive practices, for example, its sole form of compulsory process is a "civil investigative demand" which must state "the nature of the conduct constituting the alleged violation . . . and the provision of law applicable to such violation." FTC Improvements Act of 1980, § 13, 94 Stat. 375 (1980). It is also important to remember that physical inspections and other administrative searches are subject to more intensive judicial scrutiny than agency demands to produce records or witnesses. See pp. 98–102 infra.

3. *The Investigative Demand must be Sufficiently Specific and not Unreasonably Burdensome.* The Fourth Amendment's prohibition of unreasonable searches and seizures has also been modified in its application to administrative investigations. As the Court noted in the *Oklahoma Press* case, this requirement implies that the subpoena must adequately describe the materials sought; however, the sufficiency of the specifications is "variable in relation to the nature, purposes, and scope of the inquiry." Other factors bearing on the reasonableness of the subpoena are the cost of assembling and copying the requested materials; the disruption of the data source's business or activities that will result from compliance with the agency's request; the repeated or excessive nature of

the agency's demands for data; and the risk of competitive harm if trade secrets or other commercially valuable information is released by the agency. While claims of unreasonable burden are frequently made, they are rarely successful. At most, the reviewing court may inquire whether there is adequate assurance, through protective orders or other procedural devices, that the respondent will be protected against the loss of proprietary information.

4. *The Information Sought must not be Privileged.* The extent to which constitutional, common law, or statutory privileges limit the agencies' powers of compulsory process has been the subject of continuing debate. Much of the controversy has concerned the Fifth Amendment's privilege against self-incrimination. The extent of this protection is discussed in the next section. Other testimonial privileges, such as the common law protection for husband-wife and lawyer-client communications, as well as the more recent state statutes like those protecting newsmen and their sources or accountants and their clients, have rarely been litigated in the administrative context. Agency statutes and regulations are usually silent on this point, and there is no general federal law governing the applicability of nonconstitutional privileges to administrative proceedings. However, a few reviewing courts have assumed that at least the traditional common law privileges should apply. See, e. g., CAB v. Air Transport Ass'n, 201 F.Supp. 318 (D.D.C. 1961). In some instances, the common law privileges and the constitutional protection against self-incrimination may both be relevant to a subpoena enforcement action. In Fisher v. United States, 425 U.S. 391, 402–05 (1976), the Internal Revenue Service sought to subpoena documents which taxpayers

had given to their lawyers while seeking legal advice. The Court held that the documents were covered by the lawyer-client privilege, but only to the extent that they would have been protected from disclosure if they had remained in the custody of the taxpayers. Since the taxpayers' Fifth Amendment rights would not be violated by the subpoena, and no other privilege was applicable, the subpoena could be enforced. See also pp. 94–97 infra.

C. COMPELLED TESTIMONY, REQUIRED REPORTS, AND SELF– INCRIMINATION

When an agency seeks to compel a witness to testify, its attempts may conflict with the Fifth Amendment's assurance that no person "shall be compelled in any criminal case to be a witness against himself." Although the agency which is seeking the testimony will not normally have the power to impose criminal sanctions itself, the witness may fear that the information he provides will later be used against him in a criminal prosecution. When there is a risk that criminal sanctions will be imposed, the witness may refuse to answer questions which will incriminate him or provide a link in a chain of evidence against him. However, there are some significant limitations on the use of the privilege in administrative investigations or hearings.

1. *The Threatened Penalty must be Criminal Rather than Civil in Nature.* In many regulatory areas, the sanction which the witness fears may be labeled a "civil penalty," a "forfeiture," or some similar term rather than a crime. When this occurs, the court must determine whether the statutory penalty is sufficiently punitive in

purpose or effect to be considered criminal. See Flemming v. Nestor, 363 U.S. 603, 613–21 (1960). In making this determination, the court will consider a variety of factors, such as whether the penalty is designed to promote retribution and deterrence rather than to compensate damages, or whether the sanction in question is excessive in relation to its claimed purpose. United States v. L. O. Ward, 100 S.Ct. 2636 (1980) (requirement that persons responsible for oil spills in navigable waters must report the spills to appropriate government agencies not a violation of Fifth Amendment despite civil penalties of $5,000 for each spill); see also Kennedy v. Mendoza-Martinez, 372 U.S. 144, 168–69 (1963).

2. *The Privilege is Available Only to Natural Persons and cannot be Asserted on Behalf of Corporations, Associations, or other Persons.* Since the purpose of the self-incrimination privilege is to protect individuals from the government's use of the "third degree" and similar coercive tactics to extract confessions of personal wrongdoing, it does not exempt the officers of corporations and other business associations from testifying about the affairs of their firms. Bellis v. United States, 417 U.S. 85 (1974). Moreover, because the privilege is personal to the witness, an individual cannot refuse to testify on the ground that his testimony might incriminate some other person. See, e. g., Couch v. United States, 409 U.S. 322 (1973) (taxpayer's Fifth Amendment rights not violated by summons directed against his accountant because the taxpayer was not subjected to personal compulsion); California Bankers Ass'n v. Shultz, 416 U.S. 21, 71–72 (1974) (banks lack standing to assert Fifth Amendment

rights of their customers when customers' assertions of privilege would be premature); cf. United States v. Miller, 425 U.S. 435 (1976) (defendant's Fourth Amendment privacy rights not violated by government subpoena of his records from a bank where he maintained an account, even though subpoena was defective).

3. *The Privilege Attaches Only to Compelled Testimonial Utterances and Not to Other Communications.* The Fifth Amendment's protection is limited to compelled testimony, and a number of cases have dealt with the question of whether a particular statement has been coerced, or whether it is testimonial in nature. Generally, the recent cases take a restrictive view of both requirements. Thus, in Couch v. United States, 409 U.S. 322 (1973), subpoenaed documents that were in the hands of the taxpayer's accountant were not privileged because no such privilege is recognized under federal law and, in any case, there could be "little expectation of privacy" because the documents were needed to prepare the individual's tax return. Moreover, the subpoena did not compel the taxpayer to give testimony because it was directed to his accountant. On the other hand, workpapers which had been prepared by an accountant but were in the hands of the taxpayer's attorney and were otherwise protected by the attorney-client privilege were held not to be immune from production in Fisher v. United States, 425 U.S. 391 (1976). The taxpayer could have been required to produce them himself, and his tacit acknowledgement that the papers existed—which is all the subpoena required of him—was not sufficiently "communicative" to constitute a testimonial utterance. Finally, even if the documents sought are personal records which

are in the possession of the individual and contain handwritten notations, the agency may still be able to obtain them by using a search warrant rather than a subpoena. Here, also, the individual is not compelled to testify against himself, and so the Fifth Amendment does not apply. Andresen v. Maryland, 427 U.S. 463 (1976).

The Fifth Amendment analysis may be different if the agency seeks to compel an individual to report information rather than trying to get access to existing records or documents. One early case, Shapiro v. United States, 335 U.S. 1 (1948), suggested that the government had broad power to require that individuals keep business records and make them available to the government on demand, so long as the underlying regulatory program was a proper exercise of governmental power. The recordkeeping requirement was viewed as a less drastic form of regulation than a complete prohibition of the activity in question. However, this broad power to compel disclosure was later narrowed by a series of cases involving requirements that criminal conduct be reported to the government. In Marchetti v. United States, 390 U.S. 39 (1968), the Court relied on the Fifth Amendment in striking down a requirement that persons whose income resulted from accepting wagers must provide information about their activities to the Internal Revenue Service. Since bookmaking was a criminal offense under state and federal laws, Marchetti was forced either to violate the law by not registering or to incriminate himself. The Court found several bases for distinguishing Marchetti's situation from the *Shapiro* decision. *Shapiro* had involved a price control program in which the individual was only required to preserve and make available business records which he normally kept; Marchetti, by contrast, was required to report information which was unrelated to his customary business records. In addition, the records at issue in the *Shapiro* case had "public" rather than private aspects, and they involved "an essentially non-criminal and regulatory area of activity." Neither factor was present in Marchetti's situation; instead, he was part of a group which had been singled out as "inherently suspect of criminal activities." See also Grosso v. United States, 390 U.S. 62 (1968); Haynes v. United States, 390 U.S. 85 (1968). The scope of the *Marchetti* exception to the required records rule is somewhat unclear, but it seems likely that most administrative reporting requirements would be more closely analogous to the *Shapiro* provisions than to the unusual facts of the *Marchetti* case.

4. *The Privilege can be Defeated by a Grant of Immunity from Prosecution.* Even if the Fifth Amendment has been validly invoked by the subject of an administrative investigation, the agency can still compel the individual to testify by granting him immunity from prosecution. Under 18 U.S.C.A. § 6004, the agency must find that the testimony is "necessary to the public interest," and it must obtain the approval of the Attorney General before immunizing the witness. A grant of immunity will not prevent the government from bringing a criminal prosecution based on independent evidence, see Kastigar v. United States, 406 U.S. 441 (1972), and it will not protect the witness against use of the information in a noncriminal administrative proceeding, see Burley v. U. S. Drug Enforcement Administration, 443 F.Supp. 619 (M.D.Tenn. 1977).

D. ADMINISTRATIVE SEARCHES AND INSPECTIONS

Many agencies gather information through direct observation. Administrative inspections cover a wide range of activity, including safety tests of commercial equipment and personal cars, sanitary inspections of restaurants and hotels, environmental monitoring of factory emissions, and fire and health checks of apartments and homes. Although they are occasionally used for law enforcement purposes, the primary function of administrative inspections is to prevent and correct undesirable conditions. Physical inspections or tests may also take the place of formal hearings. The Administrative Procedure Act provides an exception to the Act's trial-type hearing procedures when an adjudicative decision "rest[s] solely on inspections [or] tests." 5 U.S.C.A. § 554(a)(3). Regardless of the reason for which it is undertaken, however, an administrative inspection must not violate the Fourth Amendment's prohibition against unreasonable searches and seizures, and its requirement that search warrants can only be issued upon a showing of probable cause. Much of the litigation on administrative searches has involved the application of the warrant clause to agency inspections.

At one time administrative inspections were considered exempt from the constitutional warrant requirement. Thus, a health inspector did not need a search warrant to enter a house in search of a source of rats that had been infesting the neighborhood if the authorizing statute imposed reasonable safeguards such as a requirement that the inspector adequately identify himself and conduct his inspections only during normal business hours. Frank v. Maryland, 359 U.S. 360 (1959). It was not necessary to obtain prior judicial authorization for this kind of limited investigation because the strong public interest in sanitation and the historic acceptance of such inspections outweighed the individual's interest in privacy. However, this view was rejected in two later inspection cases, Camara v. Municipal Court, 387 U.S. 523 (1967) (apartment building), and See v. Seattle, 387 U.S. 541 (1967) (commercial warehouse). Although routine fire and health inspections may be less hostile and less intrusive than the typical police search for evidence of a crime, the Court reasoned that "[i]t is surely anomalous to say that the individual and his private property are fully protected by the Fourth Amendment only when the individual is suspected of criminal behavior." Moreover, health and fire codes are frequently enforced by criminal processes, and refusal to permit entry may be a separate crime. Thus, the individual's privacy interests are entitled to the protection of the warrant requirement.

At the same time, the Court in *Camara* and *See* recognized that inspections are essential to effective enforcement of health and sanitary standards, and that the concepts of probable cause developed in criminal law enforcement could not be mechanically applied to these administrative searches. In place of the criminal law standard requiring a showing of probable cause to believe that a violation had occurred and that fruits, instrumentalities, or evidence of a crime would be recovered at the place specified, the Court established the rule that an administrative search warrant could issue when "reasonable legislative or administrative standards for conducting an area inspection are satisfied." The standards would vary according to the nature of the regulatory program, and they might be based upon factors such as "the passage of time, the nature of the building . . . , or the condition of the entire area, but they will not necessarily depend upon specific knowledge of the condition of the particular dwelling."

The *See* decision left open the possibility that warrants would not be required for administrative searches in situations where a license was required to conduct the business in question and the grant of a license was effectively conditioned on the applicant's consent to warrantless searches. Two later cases, Colonnade Catering Corp. v. United States, 397 U.S. 72 (1970) (licensed retail liquor establishment), and United States v. Biswell, 406 U.S. 311 (1972) (firearms dealer), confirmed that warrantless searches were permissible in industries subject to a licensing system which involved intensive regulation. Lower courts began to expand this exception, upholding warrantless searches in regulatory areas where there was no licensing requirement and the regulatory power extended to only a part of the business' operations. See generally McManis & McManis, *Structuring Administrative Inspections: Is There Any Warrant for a Search Warrant?*, 26 Am.U.L.Rev. 942, 953–60 (1977).

This trend toward judicial approval for warrantless administrative inspections was halted by the Supreme Court's decision in Marshall v. Barlow's, Inc., 436 U.S. 307 (1978). The Occupational Safety and Health Administration, acting under a statute which explicitly authorized it to conduct warrantless searches, argued that surprise inspections of workplaces were both necessary for effective protection of workers, and reasonable within the meaning of the Fourth Amendment. However, the agency's assertion that unannounced searches were necessary to uncover hazards that could be hidden if the employer had notice was undercut by OSHA's own practice: the agency's rules provided that inspectors should seek compulsory process when they were denied entry. Moreover, the Court interpreted the *ColonnadeBiswell* exception to the warrant requirement as a narrow one, applicable only when the target of the search was part of a "pervasively regulated" industry which has been subject to a "long tradition of close supervision." For all other inspections, a warrant was still necessary. As in *Camara* and *See*, the warrant would not require "specific evidence of an existing violation"; it could be based on reasonable legislative or administrative standards, including "a general administrative plan for the enforcement of the Act derived from neutral sources such as . . . dispersion of employees in various types of industries across a given area." In the Court's view, the warrant requirement would protect employers against arbitrary or harassing invasions of their privacy, and give them notice of the proper scope of the inspection. At the same time, it would not prevent the agency from implementing a rational enforcement plan or impose an intolerable administrative burden. In practice, the scope of the protection afforded by the warrant requirement may well depend on the diligence of reviewing courts in scrutinizing agency requests for warrants to conduct

[*101*]

inspections. Experience in the field of criminal law enforcement suggests that some courts may be willing to grant approvals routinely, with only a perfunctory review of the agency's justification.

Administrative inspections also may fall within exceptions to the warrant requirement which have evolved in the context of criminal law enforcement. If the individual consents to the search of the premises, no warrant is required. Marshall v. Barlow's, Inc., supra. The consent may be valid even if permission to search is a condition to receiving important benefits. Wyman v. James, 400 U.S. 309 (1971) (requirement that recipients of welfare benefits consent to home visits by caseworkers not a violation of the Fourth Amendment). Nor is a warrant necessary if the evidence gathered by the inspector is in "plain view" from roadways or other public areas. Air Pollution Variance Bd. of Colorado v. Western Alfalfa Corp., 416 U.S. 861 (1974) (emissions from smokestack visible from public areas of factory grounds).

E. PUBLICITY AND CONFIDENTIALITY

When an agency gathers sensitive information in the course of an investigation, it may encounter conflicting pressures to release the information to the public, or to protect the confidentiality of data supplied by private parties. The public interest in a liberal disclosure policy is generally stong. Effective public and political oversight requires detailed knowledge of agency activities, and without disclosure of investigative data it may be impossible to determine whether the agency is either ignoring violations of law, or harassing innocent persons and organizations. The exposure during the 1970's of the FBI's extensive efforts to suppress political dissent graphically demonstrates that when investigative powers are exercised in secrecy, they can readily be abused to subvert fundamental rights. In addition to the concern for agency accountability and the need to protect civil liberties, disclosure of investigative data may serve other important policy goals. When the purpose of a regulatory program is to protect consumers from worthless or unsafe products, disclosure may help the public make more informed purchase decisions. Information about pending investigations can also be useful to regulated firms who may want to change their practices voluntarily in compliance with current agency policies. But disclosure of investigative file data also carries with it some very substantial risks. Premature release of information about pending investigations can impede the enforcement of regulatory laws by alerting wrongdoers to hide or destroy evidence, or by discouraging potential witnesses from cooperating with investigators. Public disclosure can invade personal privacy and damage the reputations of persons or firms before they have had a chance to establish their innocence. It may also destroy commercially valuable trade secrets, or give competitors an unjustifiable advantage.

In contemporary administrative practice, the effort to reconcile these conflicting objectives is governed by a series of information disclosure statutes. See pp. 51–54 supra. The most important of these is the Freedom of Information Act, 5 U.S.C.A. § 552, which requires that investigative file data and other agency records must be disclosed to any person upon request unless the material in question falls within one of the exemptions to the Act.[1] The FOIA contains several exemptions which are designed to protect the investigative functions of the agencies and the rights of those who are the targets of investigations. The government's interest in effective law enforcement is acknowledged in exemption 7, 5 U.S.C.A. § 552(b)(7), which permits the agency to withhold "investigatory files compiled for law enforcement purposes" when disclosure would cause some particular harm such as revealing the identity of a confidential source or endangering the physical safety of an officer. This provision also authorizes the withholding of investigatory records when the release would "interfere with enforcement proceedings," and under this exemption the agency can make a generic determination that disclosure of certain types of material will interfere with pending cases. Thus, in NLRB v. Robbins Tire & Rubber Co., 437 U.S. 214 (1978), the Labor Board's policy of refusing to give access to witness statements gathered during unfair labor practice investigations was upheld. The Court noted that disclosure would permit employers or unions to coerce potential witnesses into changing their testimony, or not testifying

---

1. However, before a court can order that agency records be released, it must find that the agency has "(1) 'improperly' (2) 'withheld' (3) 'agency records'." Kissinger v. Reporters Committee for Freedom of Press, 100 S.Ct. 960, 968 (1980) (summaries and transcripts of conversations involving former Secretary of State removed from Department and given to the Library of Congress under a grant of confidentiality were not "withheld" or "agency records" within custody and control of State Department); Forsham v. Harris, 100 S.Ct. 978, 983 (1980) (55 million records generated by physicians and scientists studying diabetic patients under NIH grants not "agency records").

at all. In addition, some persons might refuse to provide information to investigators if they knew that their statements would become public documents. In light of this "possibility that a FOIA-induced change in the Board's prehearing discovery rules will have a chilling effect on the Board's sources," it was not necessary for the Board or the courts to conduct a burdensome case-by-case inquiry into the harm that was likely to result from a particular disclosure of witness statements.

Several statutory provisions protect the privacy rights of individuals whose personal data is incorporated into investigative files or other agency records. The law enforcement exemption to FOIA explicitly authorizes agencies to withhold investigatory files if release would "constitute an unwarranted invasion of privacy." 5 U.S.C.A. § 552(b)(7)(C). Exemption 6 extends the same protection to agency personnel and medical records, in slightly different language. 5 U.S.C.A. § 552(b)(6). Both of these provisions enable the reviewing court to balance the threat to the data subject's privacy interests against the requester's need for access to the data in question. A third source of protection for individuals is the Privacy Act, 5 U.S.C.A. § 552a. It applies to all agency systems of records in which files can be retrieved by the individual's name or identifying number. The Act requires agencies to publish notice of all "routine uses" of personal information, and it provides damages and injunctive relief for the record subject if the agency makes any other disclosures of his file without his consent. This is one of the few situations in which the Congress has provided injured persons with a damage remedy for the government's misuse of information.

Another private interest which is frequently threatened by government use of investigatory files is the commercial value of trade secrets and other proprietary information. Exemption 4 to the Freedom of Information Act, 5 U.S.C.A. § 552(b)(4), allows the agencies to withhold "trade secrets and commercial or financial information obtained from a person and privileged or confidential." Further protection is provided by the Trade Secrets Act, 18 U.S.C.A. § 1905, which makes it a crime for government officials to disclose trade secrets. However, from the viewpoint of the company submitting proprietary information, these provisions leave a great deal to be desired.

The legal definition of trade secrets is not clearly established, and the applicability of exemption 4 to commercially valuable material which is not a trade secret is even more problematic. See National Parks & Conservation Ass'n v. Morton, 498 F.2d 765 (D.C.Cir. 1974). Even if the material is exempt from disclosure, the agency may still decide to release it as a matter of discretion. The Trade Secrets Act may not be a very powerful deterrent in this situation, because the Justice Department is not likely to prosecute a bureaucrat for releasing documents to the public. On the other hand, in GTE Sylvania, Inc. v. Consumers Union, 100 S.Ct. 1194, 1200 (1980), the Court held that an agency has not "improperly" withheld records under FOIA if the agency is subject to a court order enjoining the agency from disclosing the requested records. It thus seems likely that protective orders will now be sought before sensitive data is turned over to an agency. In this situation, the protective order would have to be vacated before FOIA access is permissible. See also FTC Improvements Act of 1980, §§ 4 & 14, 94 Stat. 375 (1980) (FTC denied discretionary authority to make public any information exempt from disclosure under exemption 4 of FOIA as well as any material received in FTC investigation of law violations).

As a result of these doubts about the public's access to agency files, companies supplying valuable or sensitive information to the government have developed a variety of legal theories in an effort to prevent the agencies from disclosing their proprietary data. One of these "reverse FOIA" plaintiffs scored a limited success in Chrysler Corp. v. Brown, 441 U.S. 281 (1979). There, several Chrysler employees had sought copies of affirmative action compliance reports submitted by the company to the Department of Defense Logistics Agency; Chrysler in turn sought to enjoin the release of these reports by asserting that they were exempt from disclosure under FOIA. The Court rejected two of the company's legal theories. The Trade Secrets Act does not create an implied right of private action to enjoin disclosures which might be illegal, so the company could not base a claim for relief on that statute. Nor are the exemptions to the Freedom of Information Act mandatory; FOIA is a disclosure statute, and it merely gives the agency discretion to withhold material which falls within the statutory exceptions. But this discretion is not unbounded. A decision to release exempt documents is a final agency action subject to judicial review under the APA, and the reviewing court must decide whether the administrative determination was "arbitrary, capricious, an abuse of discretion, or otherwise not in accordance with law." Since a disclosure which violated the Trade Secrets Act would not be "in accordance with law," the reviewing court could prohibit disclosure.

The Court did not have to interpret the Trade Secrets Act in *Chrysler*, or to address the question of how much discretion the agencies have to release exempt material other than trade secrets. Presumably an agency would abuse its discretion if it disclosed proprietary information in violation of its own regulations or in disregard of its validly given promises of confidentiality. Beyond these relatively straightforward situations, the scope of the protection afforded by the *Chrysler* decision is not clear. When discretionary releases are challenged, agencies which have carefully structured their discretion are more likely to be successful in convincing the court that their decisions should be upheld than those which do not have a clearly articulated policy. The Food and Drug Administration, which handles a large volume of proprietary data in the process of evaluating the safety and efficacy of drugs, is an example of an agency that has taken the initiative in developing standards for the release of exempt material and in providing data suppliers with an opportunity to challenge proposed disclosures. See 21 CFR Part 20 (1980).

Occasionally agencies will seek to use investigative file data in an affirmative fashion, rather than simply responding to public requests for records. When "disclosure" becomes "publicity," some different considerations come into play. Administrators may seek publicity for a variety of reasons. One of the strongest justifications for an agency to seek press coverage of investigative activities is the need to protect the public from hazardous products which have already been distributed. Consumers need to know if cans of a particular brand of soup may cause botulism, or a new toy which is on store shelves has a defect that can harm their children. Reports by the press and the broadcast media may be the only effective way to warn people of these risks, but the effect on the regulated industry can be devastating. Products and companies have been driven out of business by this kind of unfavorable publicity, and often it turns out that the warning was a false alarm. Yet, those who are damaged have no redress unless the Congress passes a private bill. The agency can also use the threat of adverse publicity to enhance, if not exceed, its delegated powers. The FDA, for example, was able to conduct a series of "voluntary" recalls of suspect food products, despite the absence of any explicit statutory authority, because the companies knew that they would be subject to adverse publicity if they refused to cooperate. Finally, agencies may be tempted to use publicity as a sanction or weapon, by exposing the regulated to embarrassment or retaliation.

There are few statutory restraints on the agencies' use of publicity. As long as the publicity-seeking activity is not clearly in violation of the agency's enabling act, the injured party will have no grounds to seek judicial relief unless the statements reflect a prejudgment of the facts constituting a denial of due process. Compare FTC v. Cinderella Career & Finishing Schools, Inc., 404 F.2d 1308 (D.C.Cir. 1968) (factual press release describing the issuance of a deceptive practices complaint against the company not a denial of due process), with Cinderella Career & Finishing Schools, Inc. v. FTC, 425 F.2d 583

(D.C.Cir. 1970) (speech by Commissioner suggesting belief that the practices in question were in fact deceptive constituted prejudgment violative of respondent's due process rights).   See also pp. 162–65 infra.

CHAPTER VI

THE INFORMAL ADMINISTRATIVE PROCESS

Although Administrative Law cases and materials are primarily concerned with decisions which are subject to the procedural requirements of the Administrative Procedure Act, the great bulk of administrative decisions are made informally. The APA imposes procedural requirements only when the agency is formulating policy for the future through substantive rulemaking[1] (5 U.S.C.A. § 553), or when it is adjudicating the application of established rules to a particular fact situation using formal trial-type hearings (5 U.S.C.A. § 554). See pp. 180–236 infra. All other administrative decisions, including the many important decisions that are typically made during the preliminary stages of a formal proceeding, fall within the broad category of "informal action." While informal decisions are not directly covered by the APA, that statute does provide for judicial review if the agency action is not "committed to agency discretion" or otherwise precluded from review. Citizens to Preserve Overton Park v. Volpe, 401 U.S. 402 (1971), discussed p. 71 supra; see also pp. 300–07 infra. Nonetheless, informal action is generally not subject to the procedural constraints familiar to administrative law. This may

---

1. Under the APA, there are two kinds of substantive rulemaking proceedings: "notice-and-comment" rulemaking under section 553, and the rarely used "rulemaking-on-a-record" procedure which is similar to a formal adjudication. See generally pp. 244–55 infra.

seem anomalous for, as one study concluded, informal administrative procedures "are truly the lifeblood of the .administrative process."

While they are an essential component of effective administration, informal decisions raise questions about the accountability of the decisionmakers and the fairness of the process. The basic requirements of procedural fairness, implicit in the concept of due process, are adequate notice and a meaningful opportunity to be heard before the government takes action which can seriously harm the individual. When the agency acts informally, procedural safeguards are often minimal or nonexistent. Moreover, informal decisions are often highly discretionary; there may be only vague standards, or none at all, limiting the administrator's freedom of action, and judicial review is often curtailed as a consequence. In this situation, there is a risk that the administrator will act arbitrarily or fail to give equal treatment to parties who are similarly situated. Unless the disparities are so great that they violate the constitutional requirements of equal protection of the laws, the only real safeguard may be the agency's willingness to issue rules or other substantive standards confining its own discretion, or to provide for internal "quality control" reviews that can assure some minimal consistency in decisionmaking.

The Freedom of Information Act, 5 U.S.C.A. § 552, and the Privacy Act, 5 U.S.C.A. § 552a, do provide some opportunities for the affected individual to discover information which may be used against him in informal decisions. The FOIA provides that administrative orders, policy statements, rules, staff manuals, or instructions that affect an individual's rights cannot be relied on or cited as precedent unless the person has actual notice or the materials have been made available to the public. 5 U.S.C.A. § 552(a)(2). Both the FOIA and the Privacy Act permit the individual to obtain documents relating to his claim or defense, unless the material requested falls within one of the statutory exemptions. However, neither of these statutes allows the frustrated claimant to contest the factual basis of agency action; at best, the Privacy Act gives the individual a limited right to insert a short statement in his file giving his version of the relevant facts. 5 U.S.C.A. § 552a(d) (2)–(3). In addition, the statute creating the particular program may require that some limited procedural rights be given, or the agency may voluntarily provide procedural opportunities for individuals to participate in informal decisions affecting their interests, without going to the extreme of requiring a full trial-type hearing. Finally, when neither the relevant statutes nor the agency's own rules of practice provide adequate procedural rights, the constitutional requirements of procedural due process may create some safeguards for the individual. The application of procedural due process standards to informal administrative action is covered in Chapter 7; the following discussion is designed to provide context and background for that analysis, by reviewing the most common types of informal administrative decisions.

A. NEGOTIATION AND SETTLEMENT

The caseload of administrative tribunals is enormous, far exceeding that of the judicial system. Agencies which are responsible for enforcing economic, environmental, or health and safety regulations generally have the power to bring enforcement actions against those who may be in violation of statutes or agency rules, and agencies which have the power to grant or revoke licenses are usually authorized to adjudicate the licensee's rights. To cope with the adjudicative workload that they face, agencies have developed informal settlement and negotiation procedures.

Several factors contribute to the prevalence of settlements in administrative practice. Regulated industries have to live with the agencies which oversee their operations, and the company accused of a violation may be reluctant to earn the reputation of being uncooperative by resisting when it is in the wrong. At the same time, an agency which has become familiar with the respondent through continuing supervision or prior dealings may have access to ample information establishing the violation. When the agency has issued rules clearly stating its policy and its interpretation of statutory authority, this may discourage parties from seeking a formal adjudication. Finally, the costs of litigation, including the harm to the company's reputation with consumers and the uncertainty resulting from prolonged litigation, often create a powerful incentive to settle a pending charge.

Settlement of pending claims is also a common method of resolving disputes in the courts, but there are some significant differences in the administrative setting. In contrast to a negotiated compromise between two private litigants, the agency adjudication usually has a strong public interest dimension: the rights and interests of consumers, competitors, or other parties who are not directly represented can be greatly affected by the agency's decision. Negotiated settlements increase the efficiency of the administrative process, but they may do so at the expense of other interests. Decisions made without full testing of the facts and adversary debate on matters of law and policy may have a higher risk of error than those made in formal proceedings, and affected persons may feel that they are less fair than actions taken after trial-type hearings. In recognition of these risks, many agencies have codified the process of settlement in their rules of practice, and have provided an opportunity for interested members of the public to comment on proposed settlements. This approach has been extended by statute to the settlement of civil antitrust cases brought by the Department of Justice. 15 U.S.C.A. § 16.

Section 554(c) of the APA requires agencies to give respondents in complaint cases an opportunity for settlement "when time, the nature of the proceeding, and the public interest permit." Similarly, license applicants must be given an "opportunity to demonstrate or achieve compliance with all lawful requirements." 5 U.S.C.A. § 558(c). While the APA thus imposes a duty on the agencies to consider settlement offers, it does not limit their discretion in accepting or rejecting proposed compromises. The decision to settle a pending case is generally considered a part of the administrator's unreviewable prosecutorial discretion—that is, an action committed to agency discretion—in part because these decisions often are based upon bargaining between the agency staff and the respondent rather than a process of applying general principles to particular facts. In addition, the courts would have little "law to apply" in reviewing such a decision, because the agency typically considers a wide variety of factors that cannot be reduced to simple principles, such as the precedential effect of a favorable decision, the need to devote resources to other cases or investigations, and the likelihood that the agency will prevail in litigation.

Usually, consent negotiations can take place either before or after the issuance of a formal complaint. The respondent signing a consent order agrees to comply with the order's remedial requirements, but it does not formally admit that it has committed a violation of the applicable laws. As a result, the party signing the consent settlement would not be estopped from denying legal liability if a private party, such as a competitor or a customer, later brought a civil damage action against the respondent based on the same set of facts. This opportunity to avoid a formal adjudication of wrongdoing is often a major incentive for the respondent to settle. Once a consent settlement has been signed, it has the same legal effect as a final agency order. See, e. g., NLRB v. Ochoa Fertilizer Corp., 368 U.S. 318, 322 (1961).

B.   APPLICATIONS AND CLAIMS

One of the most common reasons for creating administrative agencies is to provide for the fast processing of large numbers of claims and applications. The agencies which are responsible for dispensing welfare benefits or regulating individual conduct, such as the Veterans Administration, the Immigration and Naturalization Service, or the Internal Revenue Service, process thousands or even millions of cases every year. The scope of the modern administrative state is illustrated by the Social Security Administration's disability benefits system, which is only one of the programs administered by that agency. In a recent fiscal year, nearly two million disabled workers were receiving SSI benefits, and the state agencies administering the program made more than a million initial determinations of disability. More than 200,000 disappointed claimants requested reconsideration of initial denials, and another 75,000 persons sought formal hearings after their claims were denied on reconsideration. Even though formal hearings were requested in only a small proportion of the claims processed, the agency was unable to keep up with its adjudicative workload; by the end of the year, more than a hundred thousand cases were awaiting hearings, and the average processing time was about seven months—a delay which could cause serious hardships to a disabled worker. See generally J. Mashaw et al., *Social Security Hearings and Appeals* (1978).

Faced with the need to make an enormous number of decisions quickly, many of the agencies which process individual claims have developed sophisticated informal procedures in an effort to minimize the use of formal hearings. One of the most familiar examples is the Internal Revenue Service. Despite the formidable complexity of the tax laws, the IRS has developed forms which are relatively simple to complete, and has produced a variety of informational pamphlets and simplified instructions for taxpayers. It also provides direct assistance and advice through regional offices located throughout the country. Computerized audit routines and cross-checks with state tax records "flag" suspicious returns for further analysis. When a question arises, a system of administrative reviews and a simplified "small claims" procedure serve to resolve most disputes. Thus, out of more than a hundred million tax returns filed annually, about two and a half million may be examined; approximately a thousand cases are referred for prosecution, and normally fewer than a hundred of these will actually go to trial.

An effective system for resolving disputes administratively, and for establishing some quality control over routine decisions, is essential if the claims processing agencies are to avoid administrative paralysis. As discussed in Chapter 7, the courts and the agencies have been concerned in recent years with the hearing rights that are available to individual claimants when a dispute arises. However, it may well be that greater improvements in the quality of administrative justice could be realized if more attention were devoted to improving the procedures used to handle routine cases and to avoiding disputes. See Mashaw, *The Management Side of Due Process,* 59 Corn.L.Rev. 772 (1974).

C. TESTS AND INSPECTIONS

A person seeking a driver's license must usually pass a written exam, an eyesight check, and a driving test. All of these are administered by trained inspectors who do not use formal judicialized procedures in making the decision to grant or deny the license. Routine use of trial-type procedures for these kinds of decisions would be not only slow and cumbersome, but also pointless:

courtroom procedures such as sworn testimony and cross-examination may be useful for testing the credibility and veracity of witnesses and the accuracy of eyewitness testimony, but they would contribute relatively little to the straightforward processes of measurement and observation that are the basis of many administrative decisions. See also 5 U.S.C.A. § 554(a)(3) (excepting inspections and tests from trial-type hearing requirements). Tests and inspections are used in a variety of regulatory programs where technical criteria or other objective standards are applied. Informal inspections determine whether cars, planes and trains are in compliance with safety rules, agricultural products can meet quality standards, or periodicals can obtain second class mailing privileges. They may also form the basis of agency decisions as to whether foods and drugs are contaminated, pilots are physically fit to operate aircraft, or factories are in compliance with environmental standards. Agencies may also conduct tests and publish the results for the purpose of assisting consumer choice, as when the FTC releases statistics on the tar and nicotine content of cigarettes or the EPA measures the gas mileage of automobiles.

Although the savings in time and resources are great and the threat of inaccurate decision is generally small, the widespread use of administrative tests and inspections does give rise to some procedural concerns. Even when the test is simple and the results unambiguous, there is still a risk that the official conducting it will be careless or corrupt, or use defective measuring equipment. Moreover, many decisions based on tests or inspections require a considerable amount of judgment or interpretation. The decision whether to certify a newly designed airplane as "airworthy" to carry passengers requires a series of decisions involving engineering judgments about the problems that the plane is likely to encounter in operation, and its ability to withstand a variety of predictable stresses and failures. Tests can provide the basis on which these judgments are made, but they will not necessarily furnish a clear answer. Decisions like the airworthiness certification may also involve an implicit value choice on matters such as whether the public interest is best served by allowing relatively easy certification so that manufacturers and airlines can bring new airplanes into service quickly and cheaply, or whether the paramount interest in safety requires a high level of prior assurance even though this may raise prices and stifle innovation. Basic policy choices of this nature should be made in visible, public proceedings with ample opportunities for interested persons to participate; yet, if the established criteria are vague or incomplete, the policy decisions may in effect be made by the technicians who conduct tests and inspections. Fairness to the regulated may also be lacking if a decision is based on a test or inspection which they have no real opportunity to contest. When the environmental inspector takes an incriminating reading of the opacity of smoke rising from the company's stack, or draws a sample of the river water near its drain pipe, there may be no practical or effective way to contest the alleged violation unless there has been prior notice and an opportunity to conduct independent tests, or at least to observe the sampling procedure.

Several steps and strategies have been developed to minimize these risks. The skills and integrity of inspectors can be checked by setting minimum qualifications for these personnel, and by providing expert supervision (especially through unannounced spot checks). Apart from emergency situations, such as the discovery of contaminated perishable foods or livestock with contagious diseases which must be destroyed immediately, it is usually possible to provide a check on the inspector's discretion by having a second official reinspect the goods, or even by providing the right to a trial-type hearing. The Fourth Amendment warrant requirement, discussed in Chapter 5, also assures that the target of an administrative inspection will usually receive some notice, and thus be able to prepare a defense—or that an independent review of the need for the inspection has occurred (and that appropriate checks on administrative arbitrariness exist).

D. SUSPENSIONS, SEIZURES, AND RECALLS

Many agencies have the authority to remove a product from the market, to seize property, or to suspend a license or a rate pending full adjudication of alleged violations. Federal agencies can summarily seize adulterated or misbranded foods and drugs, stop public trading in securities, and take control of banks which have become fiscally unsound. The licenses of doctors, lawyers, horse trainers, and innumerable others whose occupations are regulated at the state or federal level can usually be suspended when the responsible authorities have reason to believe that a licensee has failed to observe minimum professional standards. The power to issue orders summarily terminating risks to the public health, safety, or economic welfare has historical antecedents in the common law power to abate public nuisances, but in the modern regulatory state the delegation of powers to take summary action has become widespread.

The justification for summary administrative powers is generally straightforward. When private conduct is arguably in violation of regulatory statutes and poses an immediate threat to the health, safety, or economic interests of the public, the responsible agency should not have to wait months or years until it can complete a formal trial-type proceeding before protecting the public from harm. But summary action can also have a devastating impact on those who are regulated, both in lost income and in damage to reputation. Recalls of defective or dangerous products or suspensions of occupational licenses for corruption or incompetence are often newsworthy events that carry a lasting stigma. Moreover, since summary action often must be taken on the basis of incomplete or untested information, there may be a high risk that the agency is wrong. In recognition of these risks, some agencies are required to obtain court approval for summary actions, such as the Consumer Product Safety Commission's decision to remove appliances or other products from the market as imminent hazards. 15 U.S.C.A. § 2061. Another procedural protection against hasty or unauthorized summary action is the requirement that the agency hold a full hearing promptly after it has suspended a license or

[*122*]

removed a product from the market. If the agency's rules or the relevant statutes do not provide a prompt post-termination hearing, procedural due process may require it. See Barry v. Barchi, 443 U.S. 55 (1979) (horse trainer's license could be suspended without prior hearing when horse trained by him had been drugged, but trainer had a constitutional right to a prompt postsuspension hearing), discussed pp. 156–57 infra.

E. SUPERVISION

In many regulated industries, the agency's constant surveillance of business activities is similar to the physical inspection of regulated products. National bank regulation is one field where pervasive regulation takes place through informal supervision rather than through formal proceedings. Administrators determine who can open a bank, whether a branch bank can be established and where it can be located, what cash reserves must be maintained, what auditing procedures must be followed, whether the bank can enter other businesses, and the like. The administrator is even empowered to take over a bank at his discretion and without a prior hearing in order to protect its creditors. Fahey v. Mallonee, 332 U.S. 245 (1947). Compliance with this extensive regulatory framework is enforced by daily supervision and periodic (often unannounced) visits by bank examiners. When problems or potential violations are uncovered, they are usually resolved quietly by mutual consent. This system of intensive but informal regulation has worked in the banking field because banks are extremely concerned with maintaining public confidence in their fiscal soundness. A bank will surely lose business, and perhaps have

to close its doors, if its financial stability is publicly
questioned by a regulatory agency. Thus, the agency's
decision simply to institute a formal proceeding may be a
severe sanction.

Continuing supervision is also used in regulatory
programs where the industry is not so dependent upon
public confidence. The FCC's control over interstate
telephone rates has traditionally been exercised through
extensive reporting requirements and informal negotiations with the industry. Formal ratemaking proceedings
have rarely been used; routine reporting and disclosure
have had the effect of constant surveillance. Supervision
has narrowed the range of factual disagreements between
the FCC and the industry, and encouraged settlements.
Finally, informal supervision and attempts to secure
voluntary compliance are sometimes used in industries
that are not extensively regulated. This technique has
often been used in place of formal wage and price
controls. In recent years, for example, the Council on
Wage and Price Stability has been responsible for
monitoring inflationary trends in the economy, establishing voluntary wage and price guidelines, and "jawboning"
or exhorting firms and unions which violate the guidelines
to come into compliance.

The principal risk of continuing supervision is that the
agency will have too much or too little "leverage" to
enforce compliance with its policies. When the regulated
industry is effectively precluded from challenging agency
decisions in formal proceedings or on judicial review, as is
often the case in bank regulation, the agency may be
under little pressure to explain and rationalize its policies,
or to apply them consistently. See Scott, *In Quest of*

Reason: The Licensing Decisions of the Federal Banking Agencies, 42 U.Chi.L.Rev. 235 (1975). Here, as elsewhere, the development of "secret law" may result in inadequately considered policy choices and unfair or arbitrary treatment of the regulated. On the other hand, if the agency is unable to back up its supervisory efforts with a credible threat of formal proceedings or other sanctions, the regulatory program may be ineffective. Voluntary wage and price guidelines have not been notably successful in stopping inflation,[2] and economic analysts have concluded that the FCC's supervision of the interstate phone companies has not kept long distance telephone rates below what they would be in an unregulated market. The FCC's experience also suggests that when an agency becomes too heavily dependent upon informal supervision, it will not develop the resources and staff expertise required to conduct formal proceedings effectively when the need arises.

F. ADVICE AND DECLARATORY ORDERS

The most frequent contacts between private parties and administrators involve requests for advice about agency policies, procedures, or legal interpretations. The practice of providing advice or information in response to public inquiries has substantial advantages for both the agency and the private party. Many regulatory statutes confer

---

2. However, the problem here appears to transcend the issue of formal controls. Most sophisticated observers, for example, are now persuaded that wage and price controls only postpone rather than cure or control inflation—for the causes of inflation are numerous and lie elsewhere. See generally Jones, *Government Price Controls and Inflation—A Prognosis Based on the Impact of Controls in the Regulated Industries,* 65 Corn.L.Rev. 303 (1980).

broad discretion, and the agency's rules and precedents may not provide a clear statement of how the agency will deal with a particular act or practice. Thus, even when the private party has access to good legal advice, he may be unsure about his duties and liabilities. By learning the agency's current interpretation of the law and perhaps also its enforcement intentions, he can make better decisions and avoid unexpected liabilities. In addition, when the agency staff has technical expertise in a particular field, they may be able to suggest efficient ways of complying with agency standards or regulations. A staff member of an environmental agency, for example, may have more detailed knowledge of available pollution control technologies than many businessmen working in the affected industries. The opportunity to obtain legal or technical advice from administrators can be particularly important to small businesses, both because they often lack the resources to master the requirements of all of the regulatory programs they encounter, and because they may be more severely damaged if an unwitting violation leads to an enforcement action. From the agency's perspective, advice to the public can be a useful way of producing voluntary compliance at minimal cost. Typically, advice is sought when a private party is contemplating a major business decision, and it is easier for the requesting party to come into compliance before resources and effort have been invested in a new project. Preventing violations is usually simpler and more effective than trying to remedy them after the fact. Giving advice is also cheaper and faster than conducting a formal proceeding, or even a major investigation. Thus, advisory services can be beneficial to both the regulators and the regulated.

Agency advisory activities take many forms. At the simplest and most common level, an agency staff person may provide information over the telephone or reply to a written inquiry. In some instances, however, the transaction or the point of law involved may be sufficiently important that either the agency or the private party will want a more formal statement of policy from a higher level of the bureaucracy. As a result, some agencies have developed elaborate informal processes for rendering advisory opinions. The Internal Revenue Service's revenue ruling procedure is a sophisticated system which issues tens of thousands of rulings annually. The Service distinguishes between two categories of written advice: unpublished "private letter rulings" issued by branch offices without extensive internal review, and published rulings which are approved in the Commissioner's office. Published revenue rulings are official statements of agency policy, and they can be relied on by the public. However, the Service takes the position that private letter rulings should not be relied upon by other taxpayers, even if their situations are identical, because these opinions have not been given thorough consideration at the highest levels of the agency.

The IRS revenue ruling system illustrates some of the dilemmas an agency faces in trying to develop a sound advisory opinion practice. At one extreme, a process which involves careful exploration of relevant policy, factual, and legal issues, and review by high level officials, can become so formal as to lose most of the advantages of speed and low cost previously mentioned. Private parties may become reluctant to ask the agency for advice, and the agency may become reluctant to give it, as costs and delays increase. Moreover, the agency might prefer to use notice-and-comment rulemaking procedures for significant policy decisions because rulemaking provides for better public notice and more opportunities for interested persons to participate. However, a policy of freely authorizing staff members to give advice to the public creates a risk that important policy issues will be decided by low level employees without adequate analysis, investigation, or review by supervisors. The IRS solution of decentralizing private letter rulings and refusing to be bound by them in future cases has also been criticized for allowing inconsistent treatment of similarly situated taxpayers and for discouraging reliance on administrative precedent. Each agency which is frequently called upon to give advice must try to strike a balance between the conflicting goals of careful, reasoned consideration and prompt, informal response to public inquiries. Ideally, routine inquiries in areas of settled policy could be handled at the staff level while unresolved issues of law or policy are referred to higher levels of the agency for more formal consideration. In practice, however, it is often difficult to apply this distinction to a particular request—or even to decide who should make this initial determination.

A related question which arises when agencies give advice to the public is whether the requesting party can confidently rely upon the advice it receives. Viewing the issue from the administrator's side, is the agency estopped from changing its position if the regulated party relies on advice which is later found to be erroneous? The unfairness to the private party who sought the advice can be substantial, particularly if he has changed his position significantly in reliance on the agency's opinion. On the other hand, when the advice in question was not formally endorsed by the head of the agency, the administrator can argue that any reliance was not reasonable and that the agency should not be bound by the opinions of low level personnel. Since the purpose of most regulatory programs is to protect the public, it is also possible that the interest in realizing the statutory goals will override the private party's reliance interest. A clear illustration of this principle is Wilmington Chem. Corp. v. Celebrezze, 229 F.Supp. 168 (N.D.Ill. 1964), where the manufacturer of a basement waterproofing compound argued that the FDA could not require a more stringent label on cans of its paint which had already been marketed, because the cans had been labeled in reliance on an earlier advisory opinion. The court rejected this contention when the FDA pointed out that it had later learned that a "mere spark"—such as a house furnace starting up—had touched off explosions killing users of the improperly labeled product. Typically, however, the public interest in allowing the agency to revoke an advisory opinion is not so clear and substantial. The application of estoppel to informal advice seems to depend upon the nature and extent of the reliance, and the harm to the public and the regulatory program that may result if the agency is bound by its earlier opinion. Compare Federal Crop Ins. Corp. v. Merrill, 332 U.S. 380 (1947), with Moser v. United States, 341 U.S. 41 (1951).

Another difficult question which arises when agencies give advice to the public is whether their opinions are subject to judicial review. The answer may depend in part upon the formality of the agency procedure for rendering advice. Perhaps the most formal type of advice is the "declaratory order" provided by the APA. Section 554(e) states that the agency "may issue a declaratory order to terminate a controversy or remove uncertainty," and it stipulates that these orders are to have "like effect as in the case of other orders." In other words, a declaratory order is binding on both the agency and the private party, and it is reviewable in the same manner as a cease and desist order issued after a formal adjudication. See Weinberger v. Hynson, Westcott & Dunning, Inc., 412 U.S. 609, 627 (1973). However, the APA declaratory order practice has some significant limitations. One deficiency is that the declaratory order provision is applicable only when the agency decision must be based on a formal trial-type hearing, which eliminates the great majority of situations where advisory opinions are sought. In addition, section 554(e) provides that the issuance of declaratory orders is within the "sound discretion" of the agencies, and apparently none of them has exercised that discretion to make declaratory orders widely available. Thus, the question of reviewability seldom arises, and then only when the requester or some other private party is dissatisfied with the agency's informal advice.

Since agencies generally are not required by statute to give advice to the public, the courts have been sensitive to the risk that judicial review would make advisory opinions so cumbersome and costly that the agencies would stop giving them. Review might also force the agency to litigate questionable interpretations of law or policy before the administrator's position had fully crystallized, in a forum and a factual setting not of the agency's choosing. However, the complete denial of review usually means that the only way a private party can have his rights and liabilities finally determined is by ignoring the agency's advice and risking civil or criminal sanctions. Two cases involving SEC "no-action letters" demonstrate the difficulties that the courts have had in reconciling these conflicting pressures.

Companies subject to the securities laws can ask the SEC for advice as to whether certain actions, such as the refusal to include a shareholder's proposal in a proxy statement, would be considered a violation of the Act. If the agency concludes that the activity in question would not violate the law, or if it believes that there might be a technical violation not worthy of corrective action, it will issue a letter stating that the Commission will not take any action against the company. In Medical Committee for Human Rights v. SEC, 432 F.2d 659 (D.C.Cir. 1970), vacated as moot, 404 U.S. 403 (1972), the court granted limited review of an SEC no-action letter upholding the decision of a chemical company to exclude from its proxy statement a proposal by a group of antiwar stockholders that the company stop manufacturing napalm for use in Viet Nam. The court noted that the no-action letter had been approved by the full Commission, and that the decision was based upon an interpretation of the relevant statutes rather than upon an exercise of the SEC's prosecutorial discretion. Thus, the letter had sufficient formality and finality to permit review of the agency's legal analysis. However, when a similar issue arose in Kixmiller v. SEC, 492 F.2d 641 (D.C.Cir. 1974), the court reached the opposite result: the advice in that case had been given at the staff level rather than by the Commissioners, and the court concluded that there was no reviewable final order. Thus, the *Medical Committee* exception to the general nonreviewability of advisory opinions appears to be a narrow one, applicable only when the heads of the agency personally approve the advice. However, both decisions were made under special statutory review provisions in the Securities Act, and the result could be different under other regulatory provisions.

When courts do permit review of agency advice, they may encounter constitutional limits on their powers. Article III of the Constitution limits the federal judicial power to "cases or controversies," and this provision has long been interpreted as prohibiting the courts from rendering advisory opinions on abstract or hypothetical fact situations. Thus, if an agency advisory opinion is based upon a party's mere statement of future plans or intentions, the court may itself be rendering an advisory opinion if it grants review. Helco Products Co. v. McNutt, 137 F.2d 681 (D.C.Cir. 1943). However, if the party requesting advice is accruing potential civil or criminal penalties by continuing its present practices, then the constitutional requirement should be satisfied. National Automatic Laundry & Cleaning Council v. Shultz, 443 F.2d 689 (D.C.Cir. 1971) (industry association representing laundry operators entitled to judicial review of administrator's letter concluding that laundry workers were covered by amendments to minimum wage law when employees would be entitled to double back pay for violations, and employers would be subject to criminal penalties); see also pp. 318–19 infra.

G. PUBLICITY

An administrator's decision to issue a press release, hold a news conference, grant an interview, or "leak" a story to the press is usually made informally, yet these publicity-seeking activities can have more severe impact than a formal rule or order. Media coverage of agency activities serves several purposes. Agencies frequently use publicity to warn consumers about dangerous products or fraudulent sales practices. As in the case of seizures, recalls, or suspensions, this form of summary action can be a valuable method of protecting the public—provided that the threatened harm is serious and imminent, and the administrator has taken reasonable care to learn the true facts. Other uses of publicity may be dubious, however. When the regulated industry is very sensitive to adverse publicity, the agency can threaten disclosure to induce compliance, or use press coverage as a sanction to punish violators for past offenses. The Equal Employment Opportunity Commission has reportedly used adverse publicity to supplement weak statutory penalties for employment discrimination. Press coverage may also be helpful in establishing the agency's credibility with constituency groups, or in bringing pressure to bear on other government agencies. When it was first created, the Environmental Protection Agency vigorously publicized a series of pollution cases it had referred to the Justice Department for prosecution, with the apparent intent of establishing EPA's reputation as a tough enforcement agency (and perhaps also with the idea of making it difficult for the Justice Department to drop the cases).

News coverage of agency activities is essential to assure the public and political accountability of the regulatory bureaucracies, but the possibility that agencies will use publicity as a weapon raises concerns about the fairness of the administrative process. Normally, administrators cannot impose a sanction until the respondent has been afforded notice, an opportunity for a hearing, a reasoned agency decision, and judicial review of final agency action. The publicity sanction has none of these prior safeguards, and the target of adverse publicity will typically have no redress after the fact: the government is not liable for damages caused by adverse publicity, and public denials or even agency recantations cannot cancel out the lingering effects of a damaging public accusation. Moreover, the agencies' ability to resort to a publicity sanction may prevent the development of legal penalties and procedures, and leave dubious theories or policies untested.

A few agencies have issued internal rules or guidelines confining their own discretion to publicize pending matters. See, e.g., 28 CFR § 50.2 (Justice Department). Some statutory provisions also confine the agency's discretion to release damaging information. The Consumer Product Safety Commission, for example, cannot disclose information relating to manufacturers of consumer goods unless the agency has first provided the manufacturer with a summary of the information in question and an opportunity to comment on it. The CPSC also must take "reasonable steps" to assure the accuracy of the information it releases, and publish a retraction if that information turns out to be wrong. However, these protections do not apply when the agency believes that a product is an imminent hazard to consumers. 15 U.S.C.A. § 2055; cf. CPSC v. GTE Sylvania, Inc., 100 S.Ct. 2051 (1980) (release of file information under the Freedom of Information Act must also comply with Consumer Product Safety Act requirements of fairness and accuracy).

In the absence of such statutes or administrative rules, a reviewing court would be primarily concerned with whether the agency's informational activities were authorized by statute, and whether prehearing statements by decisionmakers in a formal proceeding constituted a prejudgment of the facts. See pp. 108–10 supra. When adverse publicity is equivalent to a formal accusation of criminal wrongdoing, due process may compel the agency to allow the accused some opportunity to present evidence and cross-examine adverse witnesses. Compare Hannah v. Larche, 363 U.S. 420 (1960) (Civil Rights Commission not required to identify adverse witnesses or permit cross-examination in investigative hearings on racial discrimination), with Jenkins v. McKeithen, 395 U.S. 411 (1969) (state commission holding hearings on labor racketeering required to permit accused individuals to present live testimony and confront and cross-examine witnesses because commission's investigative hearings were limited to alleged criminal violations); see also pp. 162–65 infra.

H. CONTRACTS AND GRANTS

The government can also seek to implement policy when it spends money to procure goods and services, or awards grants and benefits. For example, the spending power has been used extensively to promote racial equality. Under a series of executive orders, firms and universities contracting with the federal government have been required to agree that they will refrain from discriminating on the basis of race, religion, or sex, and to take affirmative action to increase minority employment. In addition, some grant programs include a requirement that a specified portion of the money awarded be used to hire minority businesses. See, e. g., Fullilove v. Klutznik, 100 S.Ct. 2758 (1980) (requirement that a percentage of grants for public works be set aside for minority businesses upheld against equal protection challenge).

Federal expenditures are largely made through informal action; rules relating to government "loans, grants, benefits, or contracts" are exempt from the notice-and-comment rulemaking procedures of the APA (5 U.S.C.A. § 553(a)(2)), and trial-type hearings are rarely available unless there is a major dispute over performance under a previously awarded grant or contract. If the agency administering the program does not have a well developed informal system for resolving complaints about the grantee's compliance with applicable standards, the frustrated beneficiary or grantee may be forced to resort to the courts. See Tomlinson & Mashaw, *The Enforcement of Federal Standards in Grant-In-Aid Programs: Suggestions for Beneficiary Involvement*, 58 U.Va.L.Rev. 600 (1972). Agency enforcement of conditions in grants involves a variety of informal techniques, such as compliance reviews prior to awards, reporting requirements and site inspections, and complaint resolution and negotiation.

I. MANAGEMENT

The government also makes or implements policy in its role as manager, especially through the management of the public lands. Approximately a third of the nation's land area is in government ownership, and agencies such as the Forest Service, the Bureau of Land Management, and the National Park Service often have considerable discretion in determining how the resources in these federal lands will be used. Issuance of grazing and timber harvesting permits and mineral leases, operation of recreational facilities, construction of public works ranging from backcountry hiking trails to massive dams and reservoirs, and provision of firefighting and rescue services are only a few of the activities which the land management agencies undertake. Like the grant and contract functions, management activities are exempt from the APA rulemaking procedures (5 U.S.C.A. § 553) and have traditionally been conducted informally. Many of the statutes governing the management of the federal lands state broad, conflicting objectives such as wilderness preservation and economic development, and therefore provide few checks on agency discretion. However, some of the recent environmental statutes, particularly the National Environmental Policy Act, 42 U.S.C.A. §§ 4321–61, have imposed some procedural requirements and provided opportunities for public participation. Under NEPA, major actions which will significantly affect the environment must be preceded by public release of an environmental impact statement assessing the costs and benefits of the proposal and reviewing alternatives. Interested groups and individuals may submit comments on the impact statement, so that major land use policy decisions are made in a process that resembles the APA's informal rulemaking procedures. However, NEPA does not confine the agencies' substantive discretion, and it does not

reach the many decisions which do not constitute a major
federal action.   Kleppe v. Sierra Club, 427 U.S. 390
(1976).

CHAPTER VII

PROCEDURAL DUE PROCESS AND THE RIGHT TO AN ADMINISTRATIVE HEARING

When the applicable statutes and regulations permit administrators to act informally, a claim is often made that the agency's summary decisionmaking procedures violate the constitutional rights of those who will be adversely affected. The Fifth Amendment, applicable to the federal agencies, provides that no person shall "be deprived of life, liberty, or property, without due process of law," and the Fourteenth Amendment contains a similar limitation on state action. The concept of procedural due process implies that official action must meet minimum standards of fairness to the individual, which generally encompass the right of adequate notice and a meaningful opportunity to be heard before the decision is made. However, it is often difficult to determine what process is due in the administrative setting. Informal regulatory decisions affect a wide range of interests, many of which do not fit easily into the traditional categories of life, liberty, and property; moreover, the government's justification for summary action varies from one setting to the next. In many instances, there is also little consensus as to whether a particular procedural right, such as the opportunity to confront and cross-examine adverse witnesses or the right to be heard by an impartial decisionmaker, will contribute materially to the accuracy and fairness of the process. While the judicial decisions applying the due process clauses to administrative action may not be entirely consistent, the analytical framework used by the courts can be divided into three parts.

A. IS THERE A THREAT TO LIFE, LIBERTY OR PROPERTY INTERESTS?

Since the due process clauses are applicable only when the official action constitutes a denial of life, liberty, or property, the threshold question is whether an adverse decision will deprive a person of one of these protected interests.[1] Very few administrative decisions pose threats to life;[2] thus, the major difficulties have arisen in determining when a protected property or liberty interest exists.

1. *Property.* Traditionally, the property interests protected by the due process clauses were defined quite narrowly. Many government benefits and grants were considered mere gratuities or "privileges" rather than rights; like a private donor, the government could impose whatever conditions it wished on its gift, or even remove

1. Prior to *Roth* and *Sindermann,* considered pp. 145–46 infra, the question of whether a protected interest was being threatened was not considered separately. Thus in Goldberg v. Kelly, 397 U.S. 254 (1970), the scope of the property interest was evaluated only in deciding "what process was due" under the circumstances.

2. A possible exception is suggested by the Court's statement in Goldberg v. Kelly, supra, that an erroneous decision to terminate welfare benefits under the Aid to Families with Dependent Children (AFDC) program could deprive eligible recipients of "the very means by which to live," because that program is designed to enable needy persons who have no other means of support to procure the necessities of life.

the benefit at will. This approach is exemplified by Justice Holmes' famous dictum, in upholding the firing of a police officer for political activities, that "[t]he petitioner may have a constitutional right to talk politics, but he has no constitutional right to be a policeman." McAuliffe v. Mayor of New Bedford, 155 Mass. 216, 29 N.E. 517 (1892). However, later decisions reflected a gradual recognition that Holmes' epigram was too broad and absolute: if taken literally, it would permit the government to do indirectly what it would be constitutionally prohibited from doing through direct regulation or prohibition. The resulting principle, known as the doctrine of "unconstitutional conditions," held that the government could not require citizens to give up their constitutional rights as a condition of receiving benefits. Thus, it has been held that the First Amendment's free speech guarantee prevents the government from requiring that low-level employees be members of a particular political party. Elrod v. Burns, 427 U.S. 347 (1976); Branti v. Finkel, 445 U.S. 507 (1980). Similarly, the government cannot condition the grant of a license to practice law or the opportunity to work as a policeman on the applicant's willingness to waive his Fifth Amendment right against self-incrimination. Garrity v. New Jersey, 385 U.S. 493 (1967); Spevack v. Klein, 385 U.S. 511 (1967).

The doctrine of unconstitutional conditions protected the individual only when the government's action abridged a specific constitutional right; in the absence of such an encroachment, the right-privilege distinction still permitted agencies to condition or revoke benefits at will. During the 1960's however, as welfare rolls grew and public concern for the victims of poverty increased, the

[*141*]

soundness of the right-privilege distinction was questioned. Commentators pointed out that not only welfare payments but also a wide variety of other forms of wealth, ranging from TV station licenses to truck routes to jobs and occupational licenses, could be stripped of due process protections by the right-privilege distinction. As government expanded, these new forms of wealth, which were directly or indirectly attributable to government largess, had become increasingly vital to the individual; often, the loss of a government job, or an occupational license, or a welfare payment, could deprive a person of his livelihood. Thus, to maintain the balance between government and individual, and to assure some protection against denial or invasion of these new interests, it was necessary to reject the right-privilege distinction and extend the protections of due process to this "new property." See generally Van Alstyne, *The Demise of the Right-Privilege Distinction in Constitutional Law,* 81 Harv.L.Rev. 1439 (1968); Reich, *The New Property,* 73 Yale L.J. 733 (1964).

The Supreme Court finally abandoned the right-privilege distinction in Goldberg v. Kelly, 397 U.S. 254, 261–63 (1970). It held that welfare beneficiaries' claims that their payments had been terminated without due process of law could not be defeated simply by asserting that the benefits were gratuities or privileges; instead, the relevant inquiry was whether the recipient would be "condemned to suffer grievous loss" if his support were cut off. Since many welfare recipients are destitute, a person who had been the victim of an erroneous decision to terminate his benefits could be deprived "of the very means by which to live." It was also significant that the welfare program in question was based on a system of statutory entitlement in which all applicants who met the conditions defined by the legislature were entitled to receive public assistance. Given the nature and magnitude of their interest in continued payments, the welfare recipients were deemed to have an interest which was protected by the due process clause and which could not be terminated without, in this instance, an oral hearing.

With the demise of the right-privilege distinction, it became necessary to determine in each instance whether the claimant had a sufficient "entitlement" to an important benefit to invoke the constitutional protection. In the welfare field, the line seems to have been drawn between programs like the Aid to Families with Dependent Children (AFDC) benefits in *Goldberg* which provide assistance directly to all persons who meet the statutory criteria, and those which seek to aid the poor indirectly by providing subsidies or market incentives for private parties to furnish low-cost goods or services like housing or nursing care. Compare Mathews v. Eldridge, 424 U.S. 319 (1976) (provision of Social Security Act making disability benefit payments available to all covered workers who were medically "unable 'to engage in any substantial gainful activity'" created protected property interest), with Hahn v. Gottlieb, 430 F.2d 1243 (1st Cir. 1970) (program which gave loan guarantees and subsidies to landlords who provided low income housing did not require an oral evidentiary hearing in advance of a rent increase in subsidized housing). Thus, in O'Bannon v. Town Court Nursing Center, 100 S.Ct. 2467 (1980), the Court held that patients of a subsidized nursing home did not have a property interest which would give them the right to participate in proceedings to revoke the home's certification and terminate its subsidy. Even though the revocation would force the elderly patients to relocate and thus expose them to some risk of physical harm, the statute did not give the patients the right to remain in a particular nursing home; their entitlement was limited to choosing among the private providers who had met the Medicaid criteria for certification.

The Court's reluctance to provide constitutional protection for indirect benefits may reflect its concern that a different result would greatly increase the number of persons entitled to participate in decisions, and thereby disrupt the functioning of welfare or regulatory programs. Moreover, when the program uses market incentives rather than direct payments, any increase in cost or delay resulting from greater procedural safeguards is likely to decrease the effectiveness of the economic incentive.[3] Whatever the underlying rationale, however,

---

3. This risk is more apparent in a case like *Hahn*, where the interests of the beneficiaries and the provider are adverse (because the landlord seeks higher rents, while the tenants want to block the increase), than it is in a case like *O'Bannon*, where the nursing home operator and the patients both want to block decertification. Even in *O'Bannon*, however, the incentive structure created by the program might be distorted if the beneficiaries could assert procedural rights to stop or delay the decision. For the nursing home, the risk that the government subsidy will be revoked is the substitute for the market discipline that exists when a seller knows that the buyer will go elsewhere if the quality of his service declines. Because the elderly patients in *O'Bannon* lacked the resources to purchase nursing care on the private market, and could be physically or emotionally harmed by relocation, the normal market discipline was weakened. If the risk of losing the subsidy became even more remote because the patients could intervene to delay a decertification decision, the provider might be more tempted to cut corners on services.

the *O'Bannon* opinion illustrates the Supreme Court's tendency in its recent decisions to examine very carefully the precise nature and extent of the entitlement created by the relevant statutes and regulations.

Public employment is another area in which the line between protected property interests and other interests which are not subject to the due process clause has been difficult to discern. (As discussed at pp. 150–53 infra, dismissal from a government job may also affect the employee's liberty interests.) The Supreme Court's decisions concerning the due process rights of government employees seem to have gone through several cycles in recent decades. When the right-privilege distinction was in effect, an employee of a concessionaire at a defense plant could have her security clearance summarily revoked and thus lose her job without any specification of charges or opportunity to know and refute adverse evidence. Cafeteria & Restaurant Workers Union v. McElroy, 367 U.S. 886 (1961); see also Bailey v. Richardson, 182 F.2d 46 (D.C.Cir. 1950), aff'd by an equally divided court, 341 U.S. 918 (1951). In the wake of *Goldberg*, however, the Court was called upon to reexamine the status of public employees, and it concluded that some employment relationships could confer property rights.

In Board of Regents of State Colleges v. Roth, 408 U.S. 564 (1972), an untenured college instructor at a state institution was held not to have a due process right to be heard when the college refused to renew his contract; to invoke the constitutional guaranty, the individual had to have a "legitimate claim of entitlement" rather than a mere "unilateral expectation" of continued employment.

The companion case of Perry v. Sindermann, 408 U.S. 593 (1972), indicated that the claim of entitlement did not have to be based upon a written contract or a statutory grant of job tenure. There, the dismissed teacher claimed that the college had a de facto tenure system: policy guidelines issued by the state education system indicated that teachers who had successfully completed a probationary period, as the respondent had, could expect continued employment. The Court analogized this informal tenure system to an implied contract term, and concluded that it was sufficient to give the dismissed teacher a constitutionally protected property interest.

The *Roth* and *Sindermann* decisions addressed only a few of the many relationships that commonly exist between public institutions and their employees. The next major case to reach the Court, Arnett v. Kennedy, 416 U.S. 134 (1974), saw the justices sharply divided over the question of whether a protected property interest had been created. The discharged worker in *Arnett* had been employed by a federal agency. He was fired after accusing his superior of illegal activities. Relevant statutes provided that employees in the respondent's job category could be dismissed "only for such cause as will promote the efficiency of the service," but the statute and implementing regulations also provided limited hearing rights before dismissal. The discharged employee was entitled to written notice, a reasonable time to file a written response, and a written statement of reasons. A plurality of three justices concluded that this set of standards did not create a protected property interest, because the employee's reasonable expectation of entitlement had been limited by the procedures specified in the statute. The other justices disagreed that the procedures provided by the statute could so condition the individual's statutory interests as to make the due process clause inapplicable, but they divided over the question of whether the Constitution required a pretermination evidentiary hearing in this situation.

The notion that statutory grants of limited procedural rights could limit or defeat a constitutional property interest was not raised when the Court again considered the issue of due process employment rights in Bishop v. Wood, 426 U.S. 341 (1976). The city ordinances at issue in *Bishop* conferred no procedural rights on the petitioner, who had been fired from his job as a city policeman; but they did provide that a permanent employee like the petitioner could be dismissed only for cause such as negligence or inefficiency on the job. Notwithstanding this seemingly clear language, the Court considered prior judicial interpretations of state law and concluded that the petitioner "held his position at the will and pleasure of the city." Since there was no substantive limitation on the government's ability to dismiss the petitioner, he did not have a sufficient property interest to trigger the due process protections.

The Court's insistence on the presence of a clear statutory or contractual right to continued employment before it will find a constitutionally protected property interest may have several policy bases. One seems to be the concern expressed in *Bishop* that a less restrictive approach could involve the federal courts in reviewing "the multitude of personnel decisions that are made daily by public agencies." When those decisions are made by state or local agencies, considerations of federalism may also make the federal judiciary reluctant to overturn the procedural systems created by state and local governments. In addition, many public employees have alternative protections against arbitrary dismissal. At most levels of government, there are at least limited procedural and substantive safeguards for civil service employees created by statutes, regulations, and judicial decisions. With the spread of collective bargaining in government, unions and contractual grievance procedures often provide an additional source of protection against improper dismissal or suspension. Finally, the doctrine of unconstitutional conditions, particularly in the recent applications of First Amendment principles, provides an additional constraint on the power of agencies to remove or discipline employees. Recent decisions have made clear that government employees cannot be dismissed for their political beliefs or affiliations unless "the hiring authority can demonstrate that party affiliation is an appropriate requirement for the effective performance of the public office involved." Branti v. Finkel, 100 S.Ct. 1287, 1295 (1980) (attorneys in public defender's office cannot be dismissed for political party affiliations); Elrod v. Burns, 427 U.S. 347 (1976) (requirement that process servers and other employees of sheriff's department be members of a particular political party violates First and Fourteenth Amendments).

In other areas of procedural due process, the Court has been more willing to conclude that the individual has a constitutionally protected property interest. Licenses to engage in an occupation have been considered protected property, see Barry v. Barchi, 443 U.S. 55 (1979) (state license to work as a horse trainer), as have drivers' licenses. Mackey v. Montrym, 443 U.S. 1 (1979); Dixon v. Love, 431 U.S. 105 (1977); Bell v. Burson, 402 U.S. 535 (1971). Once a driver's license has been issued, its "continued possession may become essential in the pursuit of a livelihood." Bell v. Burson, supra. Thus, even a temporary suspension of the license will trigger the due process protections. Similarly, when the state grants all children the right to attend public schools, it cannot suspend or revoke that right for alleged misconduct without giving the student at least a limited prior hearing. Goss v. Lopez, 419 U.S. 565 (1975). Even utility service may be a constitutionally protected property right; when the government undertakes to provide gas or electric service to the populace, it cannot cut off service for alleged nonpayment of bills without giving the customer a right to contest the amounts charged. Memphis Light, Gas & Water Division v. Craft, 436 U.S. 1 (1978). In all of these situations, however, the nature and extent of the entitlement created by statutes or regulations is still an important factor. In the *Memphis Light* case, for example, the majority placed considerable emphasis on the fact that state law did not allow a utility to stop serving a customer for nonpayment of a disputed bill but instead required that any termination be "for cause." Since the existence of a property right was not contested in most of the recent license cases, it is impossible to predict whether the strict construction of statutory or contractual entitlements evident in employment cases like *Bishop*, where the Court deferred to a narrow state interpretation of its law, will be carried forward into other areas as well.

2. *Liberty.* A few administrative agencies such as prison bureaucracies and parole boards have the power to restrict individual freedom directly. When the decisions of such bodies determine whether a convicted criminal who has been conditionally released will be jailed because of some alleged misconduct, the courts have had little difficulty in concluding that the threat to personal liberty triggers due process protections. See, e. g., Gagnon v. Scarpelli, 411 U.S. 778 (1973) (probation revocation); Morrissey v. Brewer, 408 U.S. 471 (1972) (parole revocation). If the threat to personal freedom is less substantial and direct, however, the question of whether there is a sufficient liberty interest to require procedural safeguards is often difficult to answer. In the prison area, for example, a disciplinary proceeding to revoke an inmate's "good time" credits—which would effectively increase the time he must actually serve on his sentence— was held subject to the requirements of procedural due process. Wolff v. McDonnell, 418 U.S. 539 (1974). The accrual of good time credits was a statutory right, which could be forfeited only for serious misconduct. By contrast, a decision to transfer prisoners to less favorable conditions does not necessarily implicate any constitutionally protected liberty interest; a criminal conviction extinguishes the inmate's general interest in personal freedom, and he has no due process rights if the state law does not impose conditions on the prison authorities' power to order transfers. Meachum v. Fano, 427 U.S. 215 (1976).

Outside of the prison context, protected liberty interests may be found when the state imposes bodily restraint or corporal punishment, or when it stigmatizes the individual by publicly accusing him of wrongdoing or otherwise damages his reputation. The Supreme Court has been sharply divided, however, on the questions of when these actions are sufficiently harmful to constitute a denial of liberty, and what kinds of procedural rights must be provided before the harmful action is taken. Thus, in Ingraham v. Wright, 430 U.S. 651 (1977), the Court held that a state statute and local school board regulations which authorized teachers to paddle students for misconduct were a sufficient threat to liberty to invoke the constitutional guaranty; yet the majority concluded that due process did not require that the students be given any right to notice or a hearing before the punishment was inflicted. Under state law an injured student could bring a damage action if the teacher used excessive force, and this was considered adequate protection to satisfy the requirements of due process.

The existence of a tort remedy is also relevant when a person claims that an agency has unfairly stigmatized him; see, e. g., Paul v. Davis, 424 U.S. 693 (1976). Before reaching that question, however, the plaintiff will have to satisfy a high standard of pleading and proof to establish the existence of a constitutionally protected interest. The plaintiff in *Paul* had his name and picture included in a police flyer listing "active shoplifters" which had been distributed to hundreds of merchants in the plaintiff's home town. Despite Davis' claim that distribution of the leaflet impaired his future job opportunities and made him reluctant to enter stores for fear of being apprehended, the majority concluded that he had not suffered any injury to a constitutionally protected liberty interest. Since the leaflet did not alter Davis' legal status, prior cases recognizing a liberty interest in

avoiding stigma were distinguishable.[4] A similar result
was reached in *Bishop,* where the discharged policeman
claimed that the department's allegations of incompetence
unfairly stigmatized him and deprived him of future job
opportunities. Since the agency had not yet communicated the damaging information to potential employers or
disclosed it publicly, his claim of stigmatization was
premature. See also Codd v. Velger, 429 U.S. 624 (1977)
(similar claim by discharged policeman rejected, even
though he had shown harmful disclosure, because he had
not alleged the existence of a factual dispute which
required a hearing to resolve).

Taken together, these decisions indicate that an
individual claiming a denial of due process from government stigmatization must plead not only that a damaging
disclosure was made, but also that the information
disclosed was wrong and that his legal status or
entitlement was altered as a result. Even when these
conditions are met, the plaintiff may still find his due
process claim rejected if a tort action for defamation or
some other damage remedy is available. As in the recent

4. In Wisconsin v. Constantineau, 400 U.S. 433 (1971), the Court
    had ruled that the state practice of "posting" or giving written
    notice to liquor stores that certain persons were considered
    hazards to themselves, their families, or the community as a
    result of their excessive drinking, constituted stigmatization
    within the meaning of the Fourteenth Amendment. In *Paul* the
    majority distinguished *Constantineau* as a case which also
    involved a change in legal status, because stores were prohibited
    from selling liquor to a person who had been "posted."
    Similarly, the students in *Goss* had based their due process
    claim in part upon the allegation that suspension from school
    would stigmatize them among their classmates and with future
    employers or educational institutions. *Goss* was also distin-
    guishable from the situation in *Paul* because the suspension
    altered the students' legal right to attend school.

cases defining constitutionally protected property interests, a majority of the Supreme Court seems concerned that a host of small claims will be presented to the federal courts if the due process threshold is lowered. Several of the justices also assume that existing systems of legal remedies are adequate and should not be superseded by constitutional protections unless the individual can show that he has no practicable means of redress.

B. WHAT ARE THE INTERESTS OF GOVERNMENT AND THE INDIVIDUAL?

Once it has been determined that a constitutionally protected liberty or property interest exists, the next stage of the due process analysis is a balancing of the agency's interest in summary adjudication against the individual's interest in obtaining a hearing or other procedural protections before adverse action can be taken. This interest balancing influences the ultimate determination of what procedures are required in the particular case, because as the Court ruled in *Mathews,* the need for additional procedural rights is determined by "the risk of an erroneous deprivation of [the private] interest through the procedures used, and the probable value, if any, of additional or substitute procedural safeguards." Conceptually, however, the balancing of governmental and private interests is distinguishable from the final cost-benefit analysis that must be performed in determining whether the procedures should be required.

As is often the case in constitutional adjudication, interest balancing is not a precise or objective process. The indeterminate nature of interest analysis is perhaps most evident in the courts' assessment of private interests. When individuals have asserted a right to continued receipt of welfare benefits, the Supreme Court has considered the general likelihood that the person will have sufficient resources to survive pending a post-termination hearing. Thus, in *Goldberg* the AFDC recipients by definition had no alternative sources of income because the statutory entitlement was based on a showing of need; when an eligible recipient is denied assistance, his situation "becomes immediately desperate." By contrast, the interest of the disability claimant in *Mathews* was not considered so pressing: despite evidence in the record that claimants generally had few personal assets to rely upon, and that the particular claimants had lost their home and even had their furniture repossessed, the majority concluded that other welfare programs such as food stamps and AFDC were available to provide temporary support. The year before *Mathews,* however, the Court had concluded in *Goss* that a ten-day suspension from high school was a sufficiently severe loss to warrant a brief presuspension hearing. In the *Goss* opinion, the Court quoted with approval its prior decision in *Roth,* for the proposition that " 'we must look not to the "weight" but to the *nature* of the interest at stake.' . . . [A]s long as a property deprivation is not *de minimis,* its gravity is irrelevant to the question of whether account must be taken of the Due Process Clause." Even after *Mathews,* the Court has accorded due process protections to private interests that seem less compelling than the claim for disability benefits. Thus, in *Memphis Light,* the Court reasoned that a possible cutoff of utility service in a billing dispute was sufficient to trigger procedural rights because "[u]tility service is a necessity of modern life" and "discontinuance of water or heating for even short periods of time may threaten health and safety." Yet, as the dissent pointed out, there was no indication that health-threatening cutoffs had actually occurred, or that the customers were unable to continue service by paying the bill and then bringing a court action for the overcharge.

A possible means of harmonizing these cases is by focusing on the varying interests on the government side of the balance, and the low or minimal costs associated with the procedures imposed. In *Mathews*, the claimant sought a full trial-type hearing and the continuation of benefit payments pending adjudication. The Court reasoned that the prospect of continued payments would create a strong incentive for rejected claimants to request a hearing, and it observed that "experience with the constitutionalizing of government procedures suggests that the ultimate additional cost in terms of money and administrative burden would not be insubstantial." By comparison, the procedures required in cases like *Goss* and *Memphis Light* were quite simple. The suspended students were entitled only to oral or written notice of the charges against them, and an opportunity to tell their side of the story; they were not necessarily allowed any delays to prepare their case, or any opportunities to confront adverse witnesses. Similarly, the procedural rights of the utility customers in *Memphis Light* were confined to notice that a dispute settlement process was available, and the opportunity to meet with a responsible employee before service was terminated for nonpayment. In both cases, the mandated procedures were considered more helpful than harmful to the government. The majority in *Memphis Light* observed that a "utility—in its own business interests—may be expected to make all reasonable efforts to minimize billing errors and the resulting customer dissatisfaction and possible injury." The opportunity for the student to tell his side of the story in *Goss* was described as possibly "less than a fair-minded school principal would impose upon himself in order to avoid unfair suspensions." A different result was reached in *Ingraham*, when students sought similar procedural protections before school authorities imposed corporal punishment for misconduct. In that situation, the Court was concerned that a prior hearing requirement would deter teachers from paddling students and thereby undermine their disciplinary authority.

The government's interest in summary decisions is generally considered greatest when there is a need for immediate action to prevent a risk of serious harm to the public. See generally Freedman, *Summary Action by Administrative Agencies,* 40 U.Chi.L.Rev. 1 (1972). Thus, a prehearing seizure of potentially dangerous or mislabeled consumer products has been upheld. Ewing v. Mytinger & Casselberry, Inc., 339 U.S. 594 (1950); North American Cold Storage Co. v. Chicago, 211 U.S. 306 (1908). Drivers' licenses may also be summarily suspended if the state has developed a policy of automatic suspension for certain categories of drivers thought to pose a risk to the public, such as those who have been convicted of a fixed number of offenses, Dixon v. Love, supra, or those who have refused to take a test for drunkenness, Mackey v. Montrym, supra. However, if the suspension is designed to serve some other purpose, such as assuring that the driver will be financially responsible for compensating the victims of a past accident, a prior hearing may be required. Bell v. Burson, supra. Serious financial risks to the public or to the government's revenues may also justify summary action. See, e. g., Fahey v. Mallonee, 332 U.S. 245 (1947) (removal of bank officers without prior notice and hearing upheld when regulatory agency had reason to believe that management was undermining the fiscal soundness of the bank); Phillips v. Commissioner, 283 U.S. 589 (1931) (summary seizure of taxpayer's property to assure payment of taxes upheld against due process challenge). Even a threat to the integrity of state-sanctioned wagering on horse races has been held sufficient to justify summary suspension of the license of a trainer suspected of drugging horses. Barry v. Barchi, supra. In the latter situation, however, the Court has added an important qualification: due process requires a prompt postsuspension hearing so that the individual will have a reasonable opportunity to clear his name and the deprivation will not be unnecessarily prolonged. See also Mackey v. Montrym, supra (prior hearing on driver's license suspension not required when the state provided an immediate postsuspension hearing).

C. WHAT PROCEDURES ARE COST–JUSTIFIED?

Closely related to the balancing of governmental and private interests in contemporary due process analysis is an assessment of the utility of the procedural rights that are being requested. The reviewing court will perform a "procedural cost-benefit analysis." That is, it will

[*157*]

determine whether the projected gains in accuracy of the decision and fairness of the process which will result from additional procedures will exceed the costs in time, effort, and program disruption that can be expected if the agency is required to use more formalized procedures. The analysis is not limited to a choice between the informal procedures the agency is now using, or a full trial-type hearing. Rather, each procedural right must be analyzed separately, and alternatives or intermediate procedural models must be considered. In practice, the procedural rights which have most frequently been considered in due process litigation can be grouped into several broad categories.

1. *Adequate Notice.* "An elementary and fundamental requirement of due process in any proceeding which is to be accorded finality is notice reasonably calculated, under all the circumstances, to apprise interested parties of the pendency of the action and afford them an opportunity to present their objections." Mullane v. Central Hanover Tr. Co., 339 U.S. 306, 314 (1950). Without proper prior notice to those who may be affected by a government decision, all other procedural rights may be nullified. Due process may require that notice be given both of the charges or facts that would support an adverse decision, see Goss v. Lopez, supra, and of the procedural opportunities that are available to influence the decisionmaker, see Memphis Light, Gas & Water Div. v. Craft, supra. However, if the agency has reason to believe that an emergency situation exists, it will not violate due process if it seizes property or takes other summary action without giving prior notice or opportunity to be heard. See, e. g., Fahey v. Mallonee,

supra (summary appointment of conservator to operate bank upheld when agency had reason to believe that bank's management had undermined its financial stability). In these situations, the affected parties may have a constitutional right to a prompt hearing after the summary decision has been made, and they would have the right to receive adequate notice of those proceedings.

2. *An Impartial Decisonmaker.* In judicial proceedings, it is generally assumed that the presiding judge must be an impartial official who decides between the parties solely on the basis of the evidence and argument presented at the trial. To assure this impartiality, judges are given long terms of office (life tenure in the federal judiciary), and are usually protected against arbitrary removal from office or other political reprisal. Some agency officials have similar protections. Administrative law judges (ALJs, formerly known as "hearing examiners") are formally independent from the agencies that employ them, and their duties are generally limited to presiding in trial type hearings and issuing initial decisions. See 5 U.S.C.A. §§ 556(b), 557(b), 3105, 5362, 7521. However, many due process issues arise in less formal proceedings where the decisions are made by other officials—including political appointees who serve "at the pleasure" of the chief executive. See pp. 42–46 supra. The question then is, when does the decisionmaker's organizational or personal stake in the outcome create a sufficient threat to the fairness of the decision to violate due process?

One well established ground for disqualification is the administrator's personal financial stake in the outcome. Thus, in Tumey v. Ohio, 273 U.S. 510 (1927), the Court held that a mayor who received a share of the fines levied on persons convicted in the town court could not constitutionally preside over their trials. The same conclusion has been reached when financial benefit accrues to the agency or unit of government making the decision and the person making the decision is closely identified with the operation of that agency. See, e. g., Ward v. Village of Monroeville, 409 U.S. 57 (1972) (violation of due process when fines levied in traffic court by the mayor increased village revenues). Another type of indirect financial stake which may require disqualification of the decisionmaker arises when the administrator is affiliated with a business, and he has the power to eliminate or restrict competition through his official acts. This situation frequently arises in state occupational licensing systems, where the licensing boards are customarily made up of individuals who practice in the regulated industry. See generally W. Gellhorn, *The Abuse of Occupational Licensing,* 44 U.Chi.L.Rev. 6 (1976). In Gibson v. Berryhill, 411 U.S. 564 (1973), a state board composed solely of optometrists who were in practice for themselves had brought a disciplinary action against optometrists who were in practice as employees of a corporation, charging that the corporate business connection was an unethical practice. The Court held that the board members' possible pecuniary interest in excluding competitors was sufficient to render the impartiality of the board constitutionally suspect. See also Friedman v. Rogers, 440 U.S. 1 (1979), rehearing denied, 441 U.S. 917 (similar claim held premature when no disciplinary proceeding had yet been brought against the complaining party). However, not every indirect financial interest is sufficient to disqualify an administrator. For example, school board members who were involved in wage negotiations with striking teachers could decide to terminate the employment of some of the teachers on the ground that the strike was illegal. The Board members did not have the kind of official stake in the outcome that rises to the level of a constitutional violation, and the record did not indicate that there was personal animosity between the board members and the striking teachers. Hortonville Joint Sch. Dist. v. Hortonville Educ. Ass'n, 426 U.S. 482 (1976).

As the *Hortonville* case suggests, personal conflict between the decisionmaker and one of the litigating parties is grounds for disqualification. See, e. g., Mayberry v. Pennsylvania, 400 U.S. 455 (1971) (due process required that contempt charges be tried before a different judge when criminal defendants attacked the judge with "highly personal aspersions" and "fighting words" during the course of the trial); Offutt v. United States, 348 U.S. 11 (1954) (attorney's summary contempt conviction for disrespectful conduct during trial reversed because transcripts showed "an infusion of personal animosity" between judge and attorney). However, this kind of psychological stake in the outcome is fairly rare in the administrative process; more commonly, the question is whether the administrator has prejudged the facts of a matter pending before him, or has some other form of bias that makes it impossible for him to render an impartial decision.

If the administrator has been personally involved in investigating the facts of a pending case, then his participation in the final decision may violate due process. American Cyanamid Co. v. FTC, 363 F.2d 757 (6th Cir. 1966) (FTC commissioner who had served as staff counsel during congressional investigation of antitrust violations could not participate in the decision when the FTC conducted an antitrust adjudication involving the same parties and facts). Strong external pressures which undermine the administrator's independent judgment may also violate due process. In Pillsbury Co. v. FTC, 354 F.2d 952 (5th Cir. 1966), a congressional oversight committee had subjected some of the commissioners of the FTC to prolonged and hostile questioning about an interlocutory ruling they had issued in a pending case. The court concluded that all commissioners who were involved should have disqualified themselves from participating in the case when it returned to the Commission for a final decision.

Due process is concerned with both the appearance and the reality of fairness. Thus, if an administrator delivers a speech or issues a public statement which creates the impression that he has prejudged the facts of a pending matter, he must disqualify himself, even if he actually has an open mind about the case. See, e. g., Cinderella Career & Finishing Schools, Inc. v. FTC, 425 F.2d 583 (D.C.Cir. 1970) (*Cinderella II*). However, there are some important limitations on the due process right to be heard by an official who has not prejudged the case. One major exception is the general rule that an administrator's actual or apparent prejudgment violates due process only if it concerns specific facts in a pending adjudication; expressions of opinion on matters of law or policy usually are not sufficient to disqualify. See, e. g., Laird v.

Tatum, 409 U.S. 824 (1972) (Supreme Court justice not required to disqualify himself even though he had testified in Congress and given speeches prior to his appointment to the Court arguing for the constitutionality of government practices that were at issue in a pending case). Even when specific facts are at issue, some prior statements or activities are not violations of due process. For example, the issuance of a factual press release which simply describes the filing of a complaint does not violate the respondent's right to an impartial decisionmaker. FTC v. Cinderella Career & Finishing Schools, Inc., 404 F.2d 1308 (D.C.Cir. 1968) (*Cinderella I*).

In many agencies which adjudicate violations of regulatory statutes and regulations, the agency heads who will make the final decision also make the preliminary determination to initiate the proceeding by voting to issue a complaint. In doing so, they may examine evidence gathered by the staff for the purpose of determining whether they have "reason to believe" a violation has occurred. This practice has long been considered constitutional. See, e. g., FTC v. Cement Inst., 333 U.S. 683 (1948). Due process does not require a strict "separation of functions" between prosecuting and decisionmaking officials, and "mere exposure to evidence presented in nonadversary investigative procedures is insufficient in itself" to demonstrate unconstitutional unfairness. Withrow v. Larkin, 421 U.S. 35 (1975) (not a violation of due process for members of state board of medical examiners who voted to initiate disciplinary proceedings to make the final decision on revocation of a license). Finally, a different standard may apply when the agency action being challenged is rulemaking rather than adjudication.

[*163*]

In Ass'n of Nat'l Advertisers, Inc. v. FTC, 627 F.2d 1151 (D.C.Cir. 1979), cert. denied, 100 S.Ct. 3011 (1980), the court concluded that the FTC chairman should not be disqualified from participating in a rulemaking proceeding to ban advertisements directed at young children, even though he had previously made statements and written letters indicating that he very strongly favored some regulatory action against the advertisers. The court reasoned that the standard for disqualification should be higher in policy rulemaking than in adjudication—notwithstanding the fact that Congress had required the agency to use oral hearings and cross-examination to resolve disputed issues of material fact in its rulemaking proceedings. In rulemaking, the court held, the test is whether "clear and convincing evidence" showed that the decisionmaker had an "unalterably closed mind" on the pending matters.

The cases dealing with agency bias and prejudgment demonstrate the difficulty of generalizing from one agency function to another. Administrative officials, particularly the heads of the major regulatory commissions, are given a wide variety of duties, some of them openly political. An agency head is expected to be actively involved in formulating policy through the initiation of rulemaking and adjudicatory proceedings, and in explaining and defending policy through speeches, congressional testimony, and other public statements. An overly stringent test for disqualification on the grounds of bias or prejudgment could undermine the administrator's ability to perform these essential functions and perhaps even decrease the political accountability of the agencies. Yet, the same individuals are expected to adjudicate particular disputes over alleged violations, and the potential unfairness seems obvious—especially in comparision to the treatment accorded similar disputes in the courts. So long as legislatures continue to delegate combined powers to regulatory agencies, and administrators make policy by bringing and deciding individual adjudications, the constitutional standards governing the impartiality of the decisionmaker are likely to remain an uneasy compromise among these conflicting objectives. See generally Gellhorn & Robinson, *Rulemaking "Due Process:" An Inconclusive Dialogue,* 41 U.Chi.L.Rev. 201 (1981).

3. *A Decision Based on the Record.* Traditionally, the only agency proceedings that were required to be based on a defined administrative record were formal adjudications and rulemaking proceedings governed by sections 556–57 of the APA. See pp. 218–21 infra. In such proceedings, the testimony and exhibits introduced at the hearing and other papers publicly filed constituted "the exclusive record for decision," 5 U.S.C.A. § 556(e); thus, a participant was assured that all materials affecting the decision could be found in a defined record. *Ex parte* contact between decisionmakers and interested parties, or other consideration of off-the-record factual materials, was grounds for reversal in such a proceeding. See generally Greater Boston Television Corp. v. FCC, 444 F.2d 841 (D.C.Cir.), cert. denied, 403 U.S. 923 (1971). When the proceeding was not governed by the APA formal hearing requirements, however, there was no assurance that all of the relevant material would be included in a single, defined record; agency file documents, or information supplied in informal conversations

between regulators and spokesmen for participants, might also influence the decision.

In *Goldberg*, the Supreme Court indicated that due process might require some informal adjudications to be based solely on a defined administrative record. After concluding that welfare recipients must be given an informal oral hearing before their benefit payments were terminated, the Court observed that an "elementary requirement" of due process was that the decision "must rest solely on the legal rules and evidence adduced at the hearing." Here, as in other areas, the courts began to realize during the 1970's that even a highly informal decision could generate an administrative "record" as it moved through the agency to final resolution, and that this record could be an important means of assuring fairness to those who would be affected by the decision. See, e. g., Citizens to Preserve Overton Park v. Volpe, 401 U.S. 402 (1971), discussed pp. 73–77 supra; Pedersen, *Formal Records and Informal Rulemaking*, 85 Yale L.J. 38 (1975). A defined administrative record serves this objective in several ways. To the extent that the record for decision is publicly available (and the Freedom of Information Act assures that all nonexempt documents will be released on request), a record complements the requirement of adequate notice: it informs the participants about the facts and policy considerations that will shape the decision, and it suggests where they should direct their efforts to influence the decisionmaker. In addition, it makes judicial review of the final decision more effective, by revealing to the reviewing court the data base that was before the administrator when the decision was made. In the absence of a record requirement, the reviewing court would be faced with after-the-fact rationalizations for agency action, and data which had been gathered to support the decision only after a court challenge was filed. A record compiled at the time the decision was made would be a much truer reflection of the actual bases for the agency's decision.

While several significant recent decisions acknowledge the importance of the administrative record, the Supreme Court has stopped short of requiring that the agency decision be based solely on a defined record in every situation where due process requires some procedural opportunity to be heard. It did not, for example, explicitly require that the presuspension disciplinary hearing mandated in *Goss* be limited to a defined record. Given the need to remove disruptive students from the school quickly and the fact that an ongoing relationship existed between the teacher and the student, the only procedure that was constitutionally necessary was an informal discussion at which the student would have an opportunity to tell his side of the story. An informal hearing of this nature does not generate a record, and the imposition of a record requirement could have formalized the suspension decision unduly.

4. *Oral Hearings.* Usually, a litigant claiming a denial of due process will ask the court to hold that the agency must afford him procedural rights similar to those used in judicial trials or formal administrative trial-type hearings—including the rights to present testimony orally and to confront and cross-examine adverse witnesses. However, trial procedures have traditionally been considered essential only for resolving certain kinds of issues; they

are not appropriate for every government decision that might affect an individual. The recent Supreme Court decisions have distinguished several kinds of issues in analyzing the need for oral hearings.

A basic assumption of the due process cases is that oral hearings and other trial procedures are useful primarily for resolving questions of fact. Thus, if the only dispute is over a question of law, due process does not require the agency to hold a hearing. Mackey v. Montrym, supra. An agency which has rulemaking authority can therefore issue rules confining its discretion, and refuse to grant hearings on possible mitigating factors. In this situation, the loss in individualized consideration is offset by other gains in the fairness of the system: a general rule "provides [those who are covered by it] with more precise notice of what conduct will be sanctioned and promotes equality of treatment among [persons] similarly situated." Dixon v. Love, supra; see also United States v. Storer Broadcasting Co., 351 U.S. 192 (1956). However, many of the issues decided by administrative agencies do not fit easily into the categories of "law" and "fact," and the decisions have not been entirely consistent in dealing with issues that might be described as "application of law to fact" or "policy questions." In *Goldberg,* the Court concluded that oral procedures were particularly important not only when recipients had challenged the factual premises of a particular decision, but also when they alleged "misapplication of rules or policies to the facts of particular cases." Similarly, when the decision involves a determination of whether a convicted criminal's parole or probation should be revoked, due process requires that a hearing be granted both on the specific facts of the alleged misconduct, and on "whether if he did commit the act his parole should, under all the circumstances, therefore be revoked." Codd v. Velger, supra (citing Morrissey v. Brewer, supra, and Gagnon v. Scarpelli, supra). But if the claim involves unfair stigmatization resulting in loss of employment, then it is necessary to allege some dispute over specific, past facts before a hearing will be granted. Id. See also Yee-Litt v. Richardson, 353 F.Supp. 996 (N.D.Cal.), aff'd, 412 U.S. 924 (1973) (welfare agency regulation permitting prehearing termination of benefits when recipient's appeal raised only policy issues held unconstitutional when experience indicated that the agency could not apply the distinction without making numerous errors).

Even if the claimant alleges the existence of a factual dispute, he may be met with the contention that trial procedures are not necessary to resolve it. Oral testimony and cross-examination are considered most useful for finding specific "adjudicatory" facts about the past conduct of the parties to the dispute; as the Court observed in *Goldberg*, "written submissions are a wholly unsatisfactory basis for decision" in proceedings where "credibility and veracity are at issue." However, if the dispute concerns general or "legislative" facts rather than specific facts about past conduct, due process does not require an oral hearing. Cf. United States v. Florida East Coast Ry. Co., 410 U.S. 224 (1973), discussed pp. 256–57 infra. The same result applies when the issues are highly discretionary and there are no standards for the court to apply, as in the academic decision on whether a medical school student had done passing work in her courses. Board of Curators v. Horowitz, 435 U.S. 78

(1978). Finally, a hearing may not be necessary when the questions to be resolved are sufficiently straightforward or objective that oral testimony will not materially contribute to their resolution. This distinction has been applied to technical or scientific decisions, such as a medical judgment about a claimant's disability, *Mathews*, or the interpretation of a chemical test which shows that a racehorse has been drugged, Barry v. Barchi, supra. It also has been used to support the decision that no oral hearing is necessary when the agency is making a purely clerical determination, such as the computation of "points" against a driver's license upon conviction of specified traffic offenses, Dixon v. Love, supra. See also 5 U.S.C.A. § 554(a)(3) (adjudications not required for "proceedings in which decisions rest solely on inspections, tests, or elections"). However, it apparently does not include computations made with the aid of a computer, *Memphis Light*.

An additional consideration affecting the need for an oral proceeding is the ability of the participants to represent their interests effectively in writing. Thus, in *Goldberg*, the court noted that the opportunity to file written submissions was an "unrealistic option" for most AFDC recipients, because they "lack the educational attainment to write effectively" and often "cannot obtain professional assistance." On the other hand, the wage earner who sought disability benefits in *Mathews* apparently did not suffer from any comparable disadvantage; he could obtain assistance in completing the necessary forms from the local Social Security office, and most of the important medical evidence was provided directly by treating physicians who were presumably competent to communicate clearly in written reports. Since due process requires that "[t]he opportunity to be heard must be tailored to the capacities and circumstances of those who are to be heard," an oral pretermination hearing was mandated in *Goldberg* but not in *Mathews*.

Finally, the decisions have emphasized that a due process oral hearing "need not take the form of a judicial or quasi-judicial trial." Goldberg v. Kelly, supra. In the *Goldberg* decision, the Court required that the welfare recipient have an opportunity to testify orally and ask questions of opposing witnesses, but it stopped short of mandating that the agency follow "a particular order of proof or mode of offering evidence," and it did not require that counsel be provided to recipients who were unable to retain a lawyer. Due process hearings in other contexts have been even more summary. The suspended students in *Goss*, for example, were entitled only to an oral statement of the charges against them, and a chance to tell their side of the story. Similarly, the municipal utility customer in *Memphis Light* could demand only that he receive proper notice of the reason for termination of service, and an opportunity to meet informally with a responsible representative of the utility. Between the extremes of a formal trial-type hearing and the informal conversation in *Goss* are many intermediate models which have not yet been fully considered by the courts. Since the nature of the oral hearing that will be required in a particular situation seems heavily dependent upon factors which are unique to the litigants and the agency program, it is difficult to project the application of these holdings to other administrative decisions.

5. *The Right to Counsel.* Section 555(b) of the APA provides that "[a] person compelled to appear in person before an agency or representative thereof is entitled to be accompanied, represented, and advised by counsel." Despite this broad statutory right to counsel in administrative proceedings, there are still many situations in which representation is not available and due process questions can arise. Since the APA applies only to the federal agencies, it does not reach the numerous state and local bureaucracies whose procedures must satisfy the due process clause of the Fourteenth Amendment. Even within the federal establishment, the APA may be overridden by more specific agency statutes; moreover, it says nothing about the person who is effectively denied representation because he cannot afford to retain a lawyer. Finally, since section 555(b) applies only to those compelled to appear, voluntary appearances effectively involve an automatic waiver of right to counsel, although the agency may thereafter be forced to advise the witness of this result. Thus, due process analysis sometimes encounters two related questions concerning the right to counsel: is the agency constitutionally prohibited from excluding retained counsel, and does it have to provide appointed counsel for those who are unable to procure representation on their own?

In most administative settings, the courts have stopped short of holding that due process requires the appointment of counsel for indigent participants in agency hearings.[5] Even when the administrator's decision can

5. One agency, the Federal Trade Commission, has concluded that due process requires the appointment of counsel for indigent respondents in deceptive practice adjudications before the agency.

result in a loss of personal freedom, appointed counsel may not be necessary. In *Gagnon*, the Court concluded that determinations of the need for counsel in probation revocation hearings "must be made on a case-by-case basis in the exercise of a sound discretion by the state authority." Similarly, the welfare recipients in *Goldberg* were not entitled to appointed counsel, even though they could be deprived "of the very means by which to live" if the agency wrongfully terminated their payments. However, they did have a due process right to be represented by retained counsel—if they hired a lawyer or obtained one through legal aid.

One reason for the Court's reluctance to conclude that counsel must be appointed for indigents may be the great expense that such a requirement could entail, particularly with respect to welfare or ciminal justice agencies which deal with large numbers of poor people. Since the agencies' authority to spend appropriated funds is circumscribed by statute, an agency may not be able to provide counsel for indigents unless the legislature is willing to amend its authorization. In any event, funds which are expended providing counsel to indigents may well be diverted from other agency programs, or subtracted from the amounts which are available to assist needy clients. Providing counsel can also increase administrative costs in other ways. The presence of counsel for a claimant may require similar representation for the agency, and lead to delays and increased

American Chinchilla Corp., 76 F.T.C. 1016 (1969). One factor undoubtedly was the risk that the entry of a cease and desist order against the respondent could materially interfere with his ability to earn a living.

formalism in the administrative process. When the decision in question is not a purely adversary fact-finding process, these costs of providing counsel may exceed the expected benefits.

Similar considerations may have influenced judicial decisions upholding statutes or administrative regulations which limit the participation of counsel or exclude legal representatives from agency hearings. In Wolff v. McDonnell, supra, the Supreme Court concluded that due process did not require the presence of either retained or appointed counsel at prison disciplinary proceedings. The reasons for this holding were essentially the same as those underlying the Court's earlier conclusion in *Gagnon* that due process did not require the appointment of counsel for indigents in probation revocation hearing. The function of the hearing was not purely factfinding, but rather "rehabilitative" as well; the decision was based on "predictive and discretionary" determinations as to what would be best for the offender. The presence of counsel and the resulting increase in procedural formality would not, in the Court's judgment, necessarily produce a better decision; indeed, it might make the agency "less tolerant of marginal deviant behavior." Thus, the presence of counsel might be harmful to both the offender and the agency. See also Madera v. Board of Educ., 386 F.2d 778 (2d Cir. 1967), cert. denied, 390 U.S. 1028 (1968) (no violation of due process to exclude attorney from "guidance conference" between parents of suspended student and school officials because presence of counsel might destroy the educational purpose of the conference).

Despite this recognition that lawyers are not essential or even useful in every conceivable administrative setting, it may well be true that the existing due process standards leave many persons who need legal assistance without access to counsel. Several studies have found that welfare or benefit claimants who are represented have a significantly better chance of prevailing on their claim than those who are not. These statistical studies are not conclusive, but they do confirm the common sense notion that many persons, particularly the poor, have considerable difficulty in dealing effectively with large bureaucracies and complex regulations. Since full legal representation seems certain to remain prohibitively expensive, it is likely that any further attempts to fill this gap in representation will rely upon paralegal personnel, "lay advocates," ombudsmen, or similar officials.

6. *Findings and Conclusions.* The final stage of the administrative process is the issuance of a decision, and due process may also impose some minimal requirements on this agency action. In a formal adjudication governed by the APA, the agency's decision must include a statement of "findings and conclusions, and the reasons or basis therefor, on all the material issues of fact, law, or discretion presented on the record." 5 U.S.C.A. § 557(c)(3)(A). Even when the agency is engaged in informal rulemaking under the APA, it is required to "incorporate in the rules adopted a concise general statement of their basis and purpose." 5 U.S.C.A. § 553(c); see also pp. 249–50 infra. A statement of reasons may be important not only to the perceived fairness of the process, but also to the quality of the decision. The need to prepare a written explanation of its decision may impose some discipline on the agency, by

pressuring decisionmakers to consider the evidence more carefully and to examine the legal and policy justification for the action more closely. When the grounds for the decision are committed to writing, it is easier for a higher level administrator to review it, and thereby provide a check on the discretion of the lower-level officials. Finally, a reasonably detailed statement of reasons makes it possible for a reviewing court to examine the actual basis of the agency's decision, rather than rationalizations it has produced after the fact. See pp. 73–77 supra; Rabin, *Job Security and Due Process: Monitoring Administrative Discretion Through a Reasons Requirement*, 44 U.Chi.L.Rev. 60 (1976).

The Supreme Court has acknowledged the importance of an agency statement of reasons in several decisions, by holding that due process required the agency to give some explanation of its action to affected individuals. However, the Court has not required that the statement be as detailed as the findings and conclusions that are typically issued in a formal adjudication. Thus, in *Goldberg*, the Court noted that "the decisionmaker should state the reasons for his determination, though his statement need not amount to a full opinion or even formal findings of fact and conclusions of law." Comparable requirements that the administrators inform the accused of the information and evidence relied upon have been imposed in prison disciplinary hearings, Wolff v. McDonnell, supra, and parole revocation proceedings, Morrissey v. Brewer, supra. When the required due process hearing is as informal as the presuspension discussion between the accused student and his teacher in *Goss*, however, no written statement of reasons is required.

D. THE FUTURE OF THE "DUE PROCESS REVOLUTION"

The Supreme Court's recent due process decisions may not have been entirely consistent, but the overall trend is clear: after the initial expansion of procedural rights ushered in by *Goldberg*, the Court has become markedly more reluctant to find that agency action has infringed a constitutionally protected interest, and also more skeptical about the value of trial-type procedures. Part of the reason may lie in the nature of constitutional adjudication, and in the kinds of issues that arise in due process analysis.

Because the Supreme Court speaks with finality on matters of constitutional interpretation, the codes of administrative procedure it promulgates when it finds that an agency has violated due process are highly resistant to change. This fact might not be cause for serious concern if there were reasonable assurance that the procedural solutions which the Court imposes were appropriate and workable in every circumstance; however, many of the questions that are posed by the contemporary due process calculus cannot be answered with confidence. To perform the procedural cost-benefit analysis which is required by *Goldberg* and its progeny, the Court should have reliable information about the likely impact of different procedural models on the program in question (and on similar programs which might be affected by the decision)—how much the procedures will cost in time, effort, and money, and what contributions they will make to the accuracy and perceived fairness of the process. Unfortunately, however, reliable information about either the inherent attributes of individual procedural devices or their operation in particular program areas is extremely limited. See, e. g., Mashaw, *The Management Side of Due Process*, 59 Corn.L.Rev. 772 (1974); cf. D. Horowitz, *The Courts and Social Policy* (1977). In the face of this uncertainty, the Court in recent years has frequently decided to let the other branches of government take the initiative in matters of procedural reform.

Some commentators have suggested that this approach gives insufficient weight to nonquantifiable values which should be protected by the due process clause. Professor Van Alstyne has criticized the Court's increasing reluctance to find protected property or liberty interests, and has argued that freedom from arbitrary adjudicative procedures should be regarded as a substantive element of personal liberty. Van Alstyne, *Cracks in "The New Property,"* 62 Corn.L.Rev. 445 (1977). Professor Mashaw has raised similar objections to the interest-balancing analysis used in the Supreme Court's recent due process decisions. In his view, the Court's utilitarian focus on procedural costs and benefits often ignores society's interest in preserving the dignity of the individual and preventing unequal treatment of persons similarly situated. This imbalance might be remedied, and the problem of inflexible constitutional requirements avoided, if the courts adopted a different strategy in due process litigation: instead of specifying the minimum procedures that are constitutionally required in a particular situation, courts could limit their reviewing function to the tasks of elaborating "a structure of values within which procedures would be reviewed," and then assuring "that the administrator had carefully considered the effects of his chosen procedures on the relevant constitutional values and had made reasonable judgments concerning these effects." Mashaw, *The Supreme Court's Due Process Calculus for Administrative Adjudication in Mathews v. Eldridge*, 44 U.Chi.L.Rev. 28, 58 (1976).

Unless the Supreme Court is willing to reexamine the underlying premises of its due process analysis, however, the primary responsibility for assuring the fairness of informal administrative action will lie with the legislature and the agencies themselves. The feasibility of drafting a general statutory code of procedure to govern informal adjudications—an "Informal Administrative Procedure Act"—has been debated for some years in the law journals.[6] The federal agencies' experience under the Privacy Act of 1974, 5 U.S.C.A. § 552a, discussed pp. 112–13 supra, suggests that it may be possible to draft workable legislation imposing minimum standards of fairness on agencies which process a high volume of individual claims. For the near future, at least, this seems a more promising route to general improvements in the fairness of informal adjudications than due process litigation.

6. E. g., Gardner, *The Procedures by Which Informal Action Is Taken*, 24 Ad.L.Rev. 155 (1972); Gardner, *The Informal Actions of the Federal Government*, 26 Am.U.L.Rev. 799 (1977); Davis, *Informal Administrative Action: Another View*, 26 Am.U.L.Rev. 826 (1977).

CHAPTER VIII

FORMAL ADJUDICATIONS

The procedures used by administrative agencies to adjudicate individual claims or cases are extremely diverse. Hearing procedures are shaped by the subject matter of the controversy, the agency's traditions and policies, the applicable statutes and regulations, and the requirements imposed by reviewing courts. Thus, any general description of administrative adjudications must be subject to numerous exceptions and qualifications.

Within the federal system, the APA establishes some minimum standards for administrative adjudications. However, it is important to remember that the APA's coverage is limited, and that its procedural requirements apply to only a relatively small proportion of agency adjudications. Under the APA, every final agency action which produces an "order" is technically an adjudication. 5 U.S.C.A. § 551(7). The term "order" is defined very broadly to include the final disposition "in a matter other than rule making but including licensing." 5 U.S.C.A. § 551(6). Thus, adjudication is a broad residual category that includes the great majority of agency decisions affecting private parties. But the fact that a particular agency decision is an adjudication does not imply that the agency must use trial-type procedures, or even that those who will be affected by the decision have any right to be heard. The APA establishes procedural requirements for only one class of adjudications: those which are "required by statute to be determined on the record after opportunity for an agency hearing." 5 U.S.C.A. § 554(a).[1] This means that the APA's adjudication procedures are mandatory only when some other statute directs the agency to conduct an evidentiary hearing in adjudicating particular kinds of cases.[2] However, they may also be applicable by reason of due process considerations. In Wong Yang Sung v. McGrath, 339 U.S. 33 (1951), the Court held that even though the relevant statute said nothing about a "hearing," due process required a trial-type hearing in deportation cases. As a consequence, the deportation statute was read as requiring on-the-record hearings in order to preserve its constitutionality, and the procedures of section 554 were applied.[3] Formal adjudications under the APA are sometimes called "evidentiary hearings," "full hearings," or "trial-type hearings." The latter term is probably the most accurate and descriptive, although as will be seen below, there are some

1. Section 554(a) of the APA contains a number of specific exceptions to the Act's formal hearing requirements. Trial-type hearings are not required, for example, in "proceedings in which decisions rest solely on inspections tests, or elections," or in "the conduct of military or foreign affairs functions." 5 U.S.C.A. § 554(a)(3), (4).

2. For example, section 5(b) of the FTC Act provides that if the Act's prohibition of unfair or deceptive practices is violated, the Commission shall issue a complaint "stating its charges," providing the named party a "hearing" at which the party "complained of shall have the right to appear . . . and show cause why an order should not be entered by the Commission." 15 U.S.C.A. § 45(b).

3. However, insofar as *Wong Yang Sung* applied to aliens not protected by constitutional due process requirements, Congress overruled the Court's separate requirement that the agency process provide for separate investigative and adjudicative functions. 8 U.S.C.A. § 1252(b); see Marcello v. Bonds, 349 U.S. 302 (1955) (upholding statute).

significant differences between agency trial-type hearings and court trials.

Even though formal adjudications comprise only a small proportion of the decisions made by the agencies, the total volume of administrative trial-type hearings is substantial. In fiscal year 1978, for example, more than 200,000 agency adjudications conducted by administrative law judges were closed, and about as many were opened—a figure which substantially exceeds the total number of cases filed in all of the federal district courts during the same calendar year. The great majority of these formal administrative proceedings were hearings on welfare and disability benefits conducted by the Social Security Administration, but approximately 20,000 formal adjudications were held in other agencies. Administrative Conference of the United States, *Federal Administrative Law Judge Hearings: Statistical Report for 1976–1978*, at 4, 33.

The discussion which follows is limited to agency adjudications which are "required by statute to be determined on the record after opportunity for an agency hearing," and therefore are governed by sections 554–57 of the APA. Other agency adjudications may be governed by special statutory procedures, and informal adjudications must always comply with the requirements of procedural due process. See pp. 139–76, supra. Beyond those limitations, the procedures used in agency adjudications which are exempt from the APA remain within the administrator's discretion.

A. PARTIES

1. NOTICE

An adversary decisionmaking process like formal adjudication depends upon the litigating parties to gather and present relevant evidence, and to challenge the evidence introduced by other parties. Thus, adequate notice is an essential prerequisite to fair and effective adjudication. As the Supreme Court noted in the second *Morgan* case, "Those who are brought into contest with the Government in a quasi-judicial proceeding aimed at the control of their activities are entitled to be fairly advised of what the Government proposes and to be heard upon its proposals before it issues its final command." Morgan v. United States, 304 U.S. 1, 18–19 (1938); see also pp. 158–59 supra. However, this does not mean that the complaint and other pleadings in an administrative adjudication are as formal as those used in civil litigation.

The APA provides that "persons entitled to notice of an agency hearing shall be timely informed" of the time and place of the hearing, the legal authority that the agency is relying on, and "the matters of fact and law asserted." 5 U.S.C.A. § 554(b). This language is generally interpreted as adopting the philosophy of "notice pleading": actual notice of the relevant facts and issues is sufficient, so long as the respondent has a fair opportunity to know and challenge the positions taken by adverse parties. Thus, proof may vary from the pleadings, and pleadings may be amended to conform to the proof. There are several reasons why technical defects in pleadings are less significant in administrative practice than in civil litigation. Many regulated industries have continuous dealings with the staffs of the agencies that oversee their operations, and in the process they often learn informally what facts and issues the agency considers crucial in a pending adjudication. In addition, administrative adjudications often are conducted under a vague "public interest" standard in which many factors are relevant to the ultimate decision. When the agency exercises broad discretion of this nature, there are no "elements of a cause of action" to plead and prove; rather, all of the litigating parties may present fact and argument supporting their view of the public interest. Finally, agencies do not necessarily follow the "continuous hearing" practice of the courts. Instead, they may adopt an "interval hearing" system in which, for example, the government presents its case and the hearing is then recessed for a period of weeks or months so that the respondent can prepare his defense. See, e. g., NLRB v. Remington Rand, Inc., 94 F.2d 862 (2d Cir.), cert. denied, 304 U.S. 576 (1938). However, if the agency changes or conceals its theory so that the respondent is deprived of a reasonable opportunity to challenge it, then a reviewing court may reverse because of inadequate notice. See, e. g., Sterling Drug, Inc. v. Weinberger, 503 F.2d 675 (2d Cir. 1974).

A common problem for agencies which conduct formal adjudications is determining when a proposed decision will have such a substantial collateral impact on parties other than the respondent that they must be given notice and an opportunity to be heard. Agency adjudications frequently affect competitors, customers, suppliers, or employees of a regulated company. An FCC decision to grant a television broadcasting license may affect not only the listening public and the employees and stockholders of the station, but also advertisers, newspaper publishers, competing broadcasters, performing artists, community groups, and political officials in the station's service area. Usually these indirectly affected persons or organizations are not "indispensable parties" to the adjudication, and they will not receive formal service of pleadings and other documents unless they take the initiative to intervene in the proceedings. However, in recent years many agencies have expanded their efforts to assure that potentially interested persons will receive notice of the pending adjudication. In broadcast licensing, for example, an incumbent licensee is required to announce to listeners that its license is due for renewal, and that interested persons may participate in the process. Agencies also use a variety of methods to reach potential participants directly, ranging from Federal Register publication to newspaper advertisements and public service announcements on television or radio.

2. INTERVENTION

When an agency adjudication affects individuals or organizations who are not named parties, they will often seek to participate in the hearing. The ways in which an interested person may participate in an agency adjudication are generally similar to those found in civil litigation: he may testify at the request of the agency staff or one of the named parties, or supply documentary evidence to them; he may request permission to file an amicus curiae brief and perhaps to present oral argument; or he may seek to intervene as a party. In recent years, as environmental, consumer, and other "public interest" groups have become more actively involved in the administrative process, there has been an increase in requests to intervene in agency adjudications as parties. Intervenor status generally has several advantages over more limited forms of participation, including the right to control the presentation of evidence supporting the intervenor's position, to cross-examine other parties' witnesses, and to appeal an adverse initial decision. However, intervention is also more costly to the agency in hearing time and other resources, and named parties in the case may fear that the intervenor's participation will be harmful to their interests. As a result, there is often a dispute over whether an interested person or group has a right to intervene in an agency adjudication.

The APA does not directly deal with the right to intervene in formal adjudications.[4] Consequently, an interested person's ability to participate may depend upon particular agency statutes or rules of practice. The standards contained in these sources are often vague, as in the provision of the Federal Trade Commission Act which simply states that intervention shall be allowed in formal

---

4. The APA's procedural requirements for the conduct of formal adjudications are generally phrased in terms of the rights of parties to the proceeding; see, e. g., 5 U.S.C.A. § 556(d) (party to formal adjudication entitled to present evidence and conduct cross-examination). The Act's notice provision simply states that "[p]ersons entitled to notice of an agency hearing shall be timely informed" of the time, place and nature of the hearing, without specifying what kinds of persons are entitled to notice. 5 U.S.C.A. § 554(b).

adjudications "upon good cause shown." 15 U.S.C.A. § 45(b); see Firestone Tire & Rubber Co., 81 F.T.C. 398 (1970). Because of this vagueness in the relevant statutes and rules, reviewing courts presented with intervention disputes have often been forced to resort to analogies and functional or policy analyses. One body of doctrine which has often been applied by analogy to intervention issues is the law governing standing to seek judicial review of administrative action, discussed at pp. 307–16 infra. See, e. g., Office of Communication of the United Church of Christ v. FCC, 359 F.2d 994 (D.C. Cir. 1966).

There are some obvious similarities between the standing and intervention questions, because both are basically concerned with whether the requesting party has a sufficient stake in the outcome of the controversy to make his direct participation desirable or necessary. However, there are also important differences. The standing doctrine is based on constitutional limits upon the powers of the federal judiciary as well as upon prudential considerations. For example, Article III of the Constitution confines the judicial function to resolution of "cases or controversies," and this provision has been interpreted as prohibiting the federal courts from acting in situations where the complaining party has not suffered a perceptible harm to a defined interest. In addition, judicial review is not an unlimited resource and standing has been used to control access to the courts. See pp. 314–16 infra. Administrative agencies are not subject to the same constitutional limitations, and they have greater flexibility than courts to adapt their procedures so that they can accommodate broad public participation without undermining fairness or efficiency. They are also charged with making decisions that have broad effects on persons and interests who are not named parties, but who may be able to contribute substantially to the agency's understanding of the relevant issues. Other prudential differences exist: for example, intervention usually just adds parties to an ongoing administrative proceeding, whereas the grant of standing to appeal often results in the initiation of a new proceeding. Thus, analogies to the standing doctrine must be applied with care.

Courts and commentators have sought to develop functional criteria that can be used to determine whether an intervenor should be allowed to participate in an administrative adjudication, and what the scope of his participation should be. See generally Gellhorn, *Public Participation in Administrative Proceedings*, 81 Yale L.J. 359 (1972). The Administrative Conference of the United States has recommended that administrators and reviewing courts should consider several factors in determining whether a person will be allowed to intervene in an agency adjudication. According to the Administrative Conference, the decisionmaker should take into account not only the intervenor's interest in the subject matter and the outcome of the proceeding, but also the extent to which other parties will adequately represent the intervenor's interest, the ability of the prospective intervenor to present relevant evidence and argument, and the effect of intervention on the agency's implementation of its statutory mandate. Recommendation 71–6, 1 CFR § 305.71–6.

In recent years, disputes over intervention in agency adjudications have declined. Agencies have become more aware of the positive contributions that intervenors can make to their decisions, and more sensitized to the practical costs (such as judicial reversals and congressional criticism) that may result from a refusal to permit public participation. The rapid expansion of administrative rulemaking may also be a factor. Important policy questions are increasingly being addressed through general rulemaking proceedings rather than through individual adjudications, and usually there is no question that all interested persons have the right to participate in a rulemaking proceeding. As the right to participate has become more widely accepted, attention has shifted to finding ways to assure that participation will be effective. For many public interest groups who themselves have no direct stake in the outcome but who represent consumers with a large (often financial) interest in the result, the principal barriers to effective participation are costs and attorneys' fees. The Comptroller General has ruled that many agencies have implied discretionary authority to reimburse public participants,[5] and a few

5. See generally Note, *Funding Public Participation in Agency Proceedings*, 27 Am.U.L.Rev. 981, 984–88 (1978). In Greene County Planning Bd. v. FPC, 559 F.2d 1237 (2d Cir. 1977) (en banc), cert. denied, 434 U.S. 1086 (1978), the court concluded that the Federal Power Commission (now the Federal Energy Regulatory Commission) did not have power to compensate intervenors in agency proceedings. See also Turner v. FCC, 514 F.2d 1354 (D.C.Cir. 1975) (FCC without inherent power to order a licensee to reimburse a "public interest" intervenor). However, the Department of Justice has taken the position that the *Greene County* decision does not preclude other agencies from adopting "implied authority" intervenor funding programs. Legal Times of Washington, June 26, 1978, at 4.

agencies have explicit statutory power to compensate groups and individuals who lack the resources to present their views in particular proceedings. For the most part, however, organizations that wish to participate in the administrative process are still dependent on the contributions of their members and occasional support from private foundations to finance their advocacy.

3. CONSOLIDATION AND THE COMPARATIVE HEARING

When an agency conducts adjudications in licensing proceedings, and there are multiple applicants for a single license, the agency's discretion to determine which parties will be heard may be limited by the "*Ashbacker* doctrine." The principle was first articulated in Ashbacker Radio Corp. v. FCC, 326 U.S. 327 (1945), where the FCC had received applications from two companies seeking licenses to provide radio broadcast services on the same frequency in adjoining communities. The applications were mutually exclusive because if both were granted each station's signal would cause electrical interference with the other's, making it impossible for most listeners to hear the programs. The statute provided that the agency could grant a license without a formal hearing, but it required an opportunity for trial-type hearing before a license application was denied. The FCC granted the first license application without hearing, then set the other down for evidentiary hearing. The Supreme Court concluded that this procedure violated the second broadcaster's statutory right to a "full hearing," because the prior grant to the first applicant made the subsequent hearing a sham. To preserve the hearing rights of both parties, the Commission was required to consolidate the mutually exclusive applications and hold a single "comparative hearing" in which each licensee would have an opportunity to show that he was best qualified to serve the public interest.

The *Ashbacker* principle has been applied not only in FCC broadcast licensing, but also in air route proceedings, gas pipeline certifications, motor carrier route cases, and other fields where multiple applicants compete for valuable operating rights. The doctrine is easy to apply in situations where it is physically impossible to grant both licenses and the second applicant has been summarily denied the right to a hearing. However, difficult questions have arisen when these conditions are not met. One problem has involved "economic mutual exclusivity"—the claim that one or both of the applicants will be driven out of business if both licenses are granted because there is not enough business in the relevant market area to support both of them. See, e. g., Carroll Broadcasting Co. v. FCC, 258 F.2d 440 (D.C.Cir. 1958) (comparative hearing required on broadcast license application when existing station made a substantial preliminary showing that grant of an additional license might damage or destroy service). Another problem can arise when the agency's procedural rulings or rules of practice do not explicitly prohibit the comparative hearing, but rather make it extremely difficult for the competing applicant to obtain one. This was the essence of the claim made in Citizens Communications Center v. FCC, 447 F.2d 1201 (D.C.Cir. 1971). The FCC had issued a policy statement providing that a broadcaster who wished to challenge the renewal application of an existing licensee could not obtain a comparative hearing unless the Commission had first concluded that the incumbent had not rendered "substantial service" to the listening public. The court held that this policy violated the statutory hearing right as interpreted in *Ashbacker*, because it unduly limited the challenger's right to a comparative hearing on all of the relevant issues.

If it is read broadly, the *Citizens Communications Center* decision may be inconsistent with a basic proposition of Administrative Law: an agency which has been delegated rulemaking authority may issue substantive standards refining the applicable statutory language, and then use summary judgment or similar procedural devices to deny hearings to those who plainly do not meet the criteria set forth in the rules. See generally United States v. Storer Broadcasting Co., 351 U.S. 192 (1956); pp. 277–79 infra. However, it is doubtful that the *Citizens* opinion can support such a broad reading. There was some dispute as to whether the FCC's policy statement should be considered a substantive or a procedural rule, and also a convincing argument that the agency was trying to adopt the functional equivalent of a legislative proposal to limit challengers' hearing rights which the Congress had failed to enact. Thus, the legislature had not modified the strong presumption in favor of a comparative hearing, which was acknowledged in the *Ashbacker* decision. In situations where the congressional intent to protect hearing rights is not so firmly established, or the agency's reliance on substantive rulemaking power is more carefully explained, the *Ashbacker* doctrine may not apply.

B. DISCOVERY

In most civil cases brought in federal and state courts, the litigants routinely have the right to conduct extensive discovery through a variety of devices such as oral depositions, written interrogatories, bills of particulars, and requests for admissions and stipulations. The advantages of liberal pretrial discovery are widely acknowledged: it assures fairness to the litigants and prevents "trial by surprise"; it encourages settlements; and it can improve the efficiency of the trial and the quality of the decision. Despite its general acceptance in the courts, however, pretrial discovery is not always available in administrative adjudications. Apart from the Freedom of Information Act, the APA does not have any provisions relating to discovery, and few agency enabling acts deal explicitly with the subject. Agency practice appears to be highly varied; a few agencies such as the Federal Trade Commission have adopted broad discovery provisions modeled on those used in the federal courts, but other agencies like the NLRB provide only limited opportunities for a respondent to discover the evidence against him before the hearing.

There are several reasons why agencies may be reluctant to follow the courts' lead and expand the discovery rights available to litigants. Without a specific delegation of power from the legislature to compel discovery from unwilling parties, the agency may lack the power to implement a liberal discovery policy. Compare FMC v. Anglo-Canadian Shipping Co., 335 F.2d 255 (9th Cir. 1964) (grant of general rulemaking power to Commission did not imply authorization to adopt discovery rules), with FCC v. Schreiber, 381 U.S. 279 (1965) (grant of authority to conduct proceedings empowers Commission to resolve "subordinate questions of procedure," including rules governing public disclosure of information received in investigations). Agencies may also be sensitive to the growing body of experience in antitrust and other fields of complex litigation which demonstrates that "discovery wars" can produce great cost and delay. One study found that the FTC's liberal discovery rules "caused significant delays" in agency adjudications "as respondents have sought to depose dozens if not hundreds of third persons on matters which the deponents often insisted deserved confidential treatment"; moreover, Administrative Law Judges' "rulings granting or denying applications for depositions have prompted many interlocutory appeals." Tomlinson, *Report of the Committee on Compliance and Enforcement Proceedings in Support of Recommendation No. 21 of the Administrative Conference of the United States*, 1 A.C.U.S. 577, 600 (1970). Perhaps the major reason why discovery is limited in many agencies, however, is the availability of alternative methods for disclosing information necessary to assure a fair hearing and a decision based on the best available evidence.

Most formal agency adjudications are preceded by a staff investigation, which is usually backed by the supoena power. In contrast to a private litigant who is primarily concerned with gathering and presenting information to support his own "theory of the case," the agency staff typically has a broader obligation to collect all relevant information that might be of use to the decisionmakers. If the staff is diligent in performing its duties, it may cover much of the ground that would be relegated to discovery in civil litigation. Moreover, the Freedom of Information Act, 5 U.S.C.A. § 552, is a powerful "discovery" tool which private parties can use to learn what information is available in the agency's files. See generally pp. 51–53 supra. Since bureaucracies typically commit most significant information to writing, a carefully drafted request under FOIA can often give a comprehensive picture of the agency's "case." [6] Another source of discovery is the "*Jencks* rule." First developed in criminal prosecutions, see Jencks v. United States, 353 U.S. 657 (1957), and later codified in 18 U.S.C.A. § 3500, the rule requires government attorneys who are acting in a prosecutorial capacity to disclose prior statements made by prosecution witnesses after the witness has testified. See, e. g., NLRB v. Adhesive Products Corp., 258 F.2d 403 (2d Cir. 1958).

Finally, a potentially important safeguard in the administrative process is the tentative nature of the

---

6. There are, however, some limitations on the use of FOIA as a discovery device. Exemption 7 authorizes agencies to refuse disclosure of information which would interfere with law enforcement proceedings, and this language has been interpreted as authorizing a blanket exemption to the disclosure of all witness statements prior to the hearing—in effect, limiting the respondent to the *Jencks* disclosure after direct testimony. 5 U.S.C.A. § 552(b)(7); NLRB v. Robbins Tire & Rubber Co., 437 U.S. 214 (1978). In addition, exemption 5 permits the withholding of "inter-agency or intra-agency memorandums or letters which would not be available by law to a party other than an agency in litigation with an agency." 5 U.S.C.A. § 552(b)(5). This provision has been interpreted as encompassing some of the government privileges applicable to civil discovery, such as attorney-client communications or trade secrets. See generally Federal Open Market Comm. v. Merrill, 443 U.S. 340 (1979); NLRB v. Sears, Roebuck & Co., 421 U.S. 132 (1975).

Administrative Law Judge's initial decision. In court adjudication, the appellate tribunal has only limited power to review and revise the facts found by the trial court. However, in the common situation where an ALJ's initial decision is reviewed by the agency heads, the APA provides that "the agency has all the powers which it would have in making the initial decision, except as it may limit the issues on notice or by rule." 5 U.S.C.A. § 557(b). This means that a litigating party may be able to present additional data and argument to the final agency decisionmakers, and that they will be able to consider it and revise the findings and conclusions in the initial decision. With these safeguards, a respondent may have the functional equivalent of the protections afforded by a formal discovery system.

C. EVIDENCE

1. PRESENTATION OF CASE

In broad outline, the form of many agency adjudications resembles that of a court trial. After the prehearing stage of pleadings, motions, and prehearing conferences is completed, an oral hearing is held before an official who is called a judge.[7] The agency and the respondent are represented by counsel who introduce testimony and exhibits. Witnesses may be cross-examined, objections may be raised, and rulings issued. At

---

7. If the agency seeks to compel testimony from an unwilling witness, or attempts to use evidence obtained in violation of constitutional safeguards, claims of privilege may arise. As previously noted, agencies generally follow the constitutional and common law evidentiary privileges observed in the courts. See pp. 92–97. Supra.

the conclusion of the testimony, the parties submit proposed findings and conclusions and legal briefs to the presiding officer. The Administrative Law Judge then renders his initial decision, which may be appealed to the agency heads. Beneath these surface similarities, however, there are some significant differences between judicial and administrative adjudications.

Administrative practice generally follows the judicial model in allocating burdens of proof. The APA adopts the customary common law rule that the moving party—that is, the proponent of a rule or order—has the burden of proof, including both the burden of going forward and the burden of persuasion. 5 U.S.C.A. § 556(d). Normally, the burden of persuasion is met by the familiar civil case standard of "a preponderance of the evidence." When Congress has not prescribed the degree of proof, courts have felt at liberty to establish higher standards in administrative adjudications affecting important private interests. Thus, the clear and convincing evidence standard has been applied to adjudications which threaten personal liberty and security, such as a deportation proceeding. Woodby v. Immigration & Naturalization Service, 385 U.S. 276 (1966). See generally Steadman v. SEC, 101 S.Ct. 999 (1981) (holding that the APA, 5 U.S.C.A. § 556(d), establishes the minimum quantity of evidence and the preponderance-of-the-evidence standard of proof for administrative adjudications).

Perhaps the most distinctive feature of many administrative adjudications is the substitution of written evidence for direct oral testimony. The APA explicitly authorizes this practice in formal rulemaking proceedings and in adjudications "determining claims for money or benefits or applications for initial licenses," by providing that "an agency may, when a party will not be prejudiced thereby, adopt procedures for the submission of all or part of the evidence in written form." 5 U.S.C.A. § 556(d). Use of written direct testimony can take several forms. One of the simplest and least productive is the use of "canned dialogue"—previously written questions and answers that are read into the record in place of live testimony. More effective and efficient is the practice originally developed by the ICC, in which verified written statements are prepared by witnesses and submitted to adverse parties for rebuttal. There are also some intermediate methods, such as the practice developed by the FTC in rulemaking hearings. Witnesses in those proceedings are required to submit advance texts of their testimony; then, at the hearings, they are requested to provide a brief oral summary of the principal points in their statements, much as witnesses in congressional hearings are encouraged to do. The bulk of hearing time can then be devoted to questioning and cross-examination designed to clarify and test the witnesses' conclusions.

One reason why written evidence plays such a significant role in administrative practice is the nature of the issues involved in many agency adjudications. In court proceedings, the crucial evidence is frequently eyewitness testimony relating to a particular transaction or event. To assess this type of testimony, the factfinder must make judgments about the witness' perception, memory, and sincerity as well as the inherent plausibility of his narrative. The witness' demeanor in testifying provides useful guidance in making this assessment. In administrative adjudications, however, the crucial evidence is usually opinion testimony. Sometimes the opinion of laymen is relevant, as in the situation where residents of a community want to testify in an NRC hearing to determine the location of a proposed nuclear power plant—some to support the grant of the license because they believe that the plant will bring new employment to the region, others to oppose it because they are concerned about the plant's effect on property values or environmental amenities. More commonly, however, agencies require expert opinion testimony on matters such as the medical diagnosis of the injuries suffered by a claimant for disability benefits, the economic justification for a proposed merger of two regulated companies, the impact of a proposed utility power line on wildlife habitat, or the perceptions of a random sample of consumers who responded to a survey questionnaire regarding their understanding of certain sales representations. The demeanor of the witness usually contributes little to the assessment of such evidence; more important are the qualifications and background of the expert, the adequacy of his data base and methodology, and the soundness of the inferences he has drawn from available information. Cross-examination may occasionally be useful in illuminating these matters, but direct oral testimony using the courtroom question-and-answer format is of little value, particularly when the administrator has some expertise in the subject matter of the expert's testimony.

2. CROSS–EXAMINATION

Few issues in Administrative Law have proven as controversial as the proper role of cross-examination in formal adjudications and rulemakings. The APA is deceptively simple; it merely provides that a party to an evidentiary hearing is entitled "to conduct such cross-examination as may be required for a full and true disclosure of the facts." 5 U.S.C.A. § 556(d). The Act's legislative history indicates that Congress was seeking to draw a line between an unlimited right of cross-examination, with all the cost, delay, and waste that unrestricted questioning can produce, and a reasonable opportunity to test opposing evidence. However, this does not provide much guidance in determining when cross-examination is "required for a full and true disclosure of the facts."

A helpful starting point is to recognize that the utility of cross-examination can vary according to the purpose for which it is used, the nature and importance of the testimony that is being attacked, and the skills and backgrounds of the hearing participants. In general, cross-examination can be used to challenge the credibility of the witness or to test the accuracy and completeness of his testimony. Credibility attacks usually fall into several broad categories. A questioner can challenge the witness' veracity or memory; he can explore factors that might compromise the witness' objectivity, such as a financial stake in the outcome or a strong ideological belief; he can suggest that the testimony is not really the witness' own product, but rather the result of coaching by counsel or some other influence; he can attack the witness' competence, by showing that he lacks the background and formal credentials to speak with authority or does not fully understand the issues; and he can show that the witness' testimony is inconsistent with prior practice or statements, or with recognized authorites. Substantive attacks on the accuracy of testimony also tend to repeat some common themes. A cross-examiner may try to show that the witness has a weak or insufficient basis for conclusions reached in his testimony, by exposing limitations in the witness' data or experience or opportunity to observe the events he has described; he may try to bring out points that were not discussed or not emphasized in the direct testimony; he may attempt to separate valid factual inferences from policy preferences or value judgments; and he may use cross-examination to clarify technical concepts or other unfamiliar matters for the decisionmakers.

When the direct testimony is based upon eyewitness observations, cross-examination which is directed at witness credibility, veracity, and perception may be useful means of testing the truth of the specific factual assertions. However, most observers seem to agree that credibility attacks are rarely successful when the witness is an expert. Questioning which is designed to clarify expert testimony or expose its substantive limitations may sometimes be useful, particularly when the decision-maker is unfamiliar with the subject matter of the testimony. More frequently, however, it can be a waste of time. Few cross-examiners have sufficient technical sophistication to meet an expert on his own ground and challenge his methodology or analysis convincingly. Too often counsel follows the path of least resistance and simply reads passages from treatises or reports, asking the witness whether he agrees or disagrees with the authority quoted—an exercise which is usually both pointless and tedious. In other instances, the cross-examiner may adopt a "shotgun" strategy in which his questions skip rapidly from one topic to another, in the hope of uncovering a useful bit of information or at least of making the witness appear confused. "Shot-gunning" is easier than careful preparation, but it may generate a choatic record and actually impede the decisionmakers' understanding of the testimony.

From the presiding officer's perspective, the major difficulty in controlling cross-examination is that these multiple factors affecting the utility of questioning cannot be reduced to a set of simple rules which can be easily and fairly applied in the heat of an adversary hearing. Without clear standards to guide his rulings, the ALJ may be under considerable pressure to allow relatively unconstrained questioning: the attempt to cut off a line of inquiry may invite a reversal and remand by the higher levels of the agency or by the courts, and the hearing time spent in disputes over the permissible scope of cross-examination may well be greater than the time the examination itself would consume. Thus, there are few authoritative rulings here and the practical situation in the agencies often seems to approach the unrestricted cross-examination that the drafters of the APA sought to avoid.

3. ADMISSIBILITY AND EVALUATION OF EVIDENCE

In comparison to court trials, administrative adjudications generally are governed by liberal evidentiary rules that create a strong presumption in favor of admitting questionable or challenged evidence. This difference between courts and agencies is reflected in the ways that the two tribunals deal with the problem of hearsay evidence—that is, statements which were made outside the hearing and are subsequently offered in evidence to prove the truth of the matter asserted. The Federal Rules of Evidence, which govern hearings before federal courts and magistrates, adopt the rule that hearsay is inadmissible, and then proceed to carve out more than twenty technical exceptions to that general standard. Rules 802–03. By contrast, the APA establishes a much simpler standard for administrative trial-type hearings. Section 556(d) provides that "[a]ny oral or documentary evidence may be received, but the agency as a matter of policy shall provide for the exclusion of irrelevant, immaterial, or unduly repetitious evidence." This provision opens the door to *any* evidence which the presiding officer admits and only *suggests* that insignificant or redundant evidence should be rejected.[8] Moreover, the APA pointedly omits hearsay or other "incompetent" evidence from the list of evidence which should not be received. As a result, the exclusion of evidence in a formal administrative adjudication may be reversible error, even though the material would be inadmissible in a court, if a party is prejudiced by the ruling. See, e. g., Samuel H. Moss, Inc. v. FTC, 148 F.2d 378, 380 (2d Cir. 1945) (agency admonished for rigidly adhering to common law admissibility rules, even though error in excluding evidence was not prejudicial).

The reasons for the APA's liberal rules of admissibility can be traced to basic differences in the nature of courts

8. See generally Gellhorn, *Rules of Evidence and Official Notice in Formal Administrative Hearings*, 1971 Duke L.J. 1, 13.

and administrative agencies. Judicial rules of evidence are formulated with the understanding that a significant proportion of cases will be tried to a jury. It is generally assumed that lay jurors tend to overestimate the probative value of hearsay testimony, particularly when the litigants are deprived of the opportunity to cross-examine a declarant who is not a witness in the proceeding. Thus, admitting such evidence in the absence of reliable circumstantial guarantees that it is trustworthy could be prejudicial to the party against whom it is offered. However, there is much less risk of unfairness or error when the factfinding is performed by expert administrators. In the administrative context, it makes sense to save the time and effort that would be spent ruling on questions of admissibility, and let the decisionmakers take account of the lesser probative value of hearsay or other questionable evidence in making their findings. In other words, the fact that a particular bit of evidence is hearsay should go to its *weight*, but not to its *admissibility*, in a formal agency adjudication.

Thus, in administrative hearings, the crucial question often is whether the ALJ or agency heads should rely on hearsay and other "tainted" evidence in reaching their decisions. It has long been recognized that hearsay can vary greatly in its reliability, ranging from "mere rumor" to "the kind of evidence on which responsible persons are accustomed to rely in serious affairs." NLRB v. Remington Rand, Inc., 94 F.2d 862, 873 (2d Cir.), cert. denied, 304 U.S. 576 (1938), rev'd on other grounds, 110 F.2d 148 (2d Cir. 1940). Several criteria can be extracted from this common sense notion, and used to determine whether a particular item of hearsay is sufficiently trustworthy to support a finding of fact.

(a) Are there circumstantial guarantees that the evidence is trustworthy? Some forms of hearsay are generically more reliable than others, because the circumstances surrounding the statements in question give some assurance that the declarants have been careful and accurate in their representations. Business records, agency reports to Congress or the public, and vital statistics are examples of information that is technically hearsay, but likely to be highly accurate; thus, these documents usually fall within an exception to the hearsay rule, even in a jury trial. In other situations, different kinds of information from a single source may have varying degrees of reliability. For example, factual newspaper accounts of significant events are likely to be accurate, because reporters normally do not fabricate news. However, newspaper quotations or summaries of statements made by particular individuals may be much less reliable. The process of hearing, understanding, and summarizing another's oral statements accurately can be very difficult, as any student knows who has reviewed class notes before an important examination. Thus, a newspaper report that an accident took place may be sufficient support for an administrative decision, whereas a summary of a speech given by a public official might not be. See, e. g., Montana Power Co. v. FPC, 185 F.2d 491, 498 (D.C.Cir. 1950), cert. denied, 340 U.S. 947 (1951).

(b) Is better evidence available? If the party against whom hearsay is offered has easy access to better information, but fails to produce it, then it may be reasonable to infer that the hearsay is reliable. See, e. g., United States ex rel. Vajtauer v. Commissioner, 273 U.S. 103 (1927) (deportation order upheld when alien produced no evidence to refute hearsay indicating that he had advocated forcible overthrow of the government); cf. Interstate Circuit, Inc. v. United States, 306 U.S. 208, 225–26 (1939).

(c) Would the cost of acquiring better evidence be justified in relation to the importance of the subject matter? If the hearsay declarant is readily available and the hearing is likely to have a major effect upon an individual's liberty or livelihood—as in a deportation proceeding—then hearsay may not be adequate to support an adverse finding. However, when the subject is a routine disability compensation claim in a program handling thousands of cases annually, and the declarant is a physician who prepared a diagnostic report, then the additional cost and delay of requiring live testimony may not be justified. See Richardson v. Perales, 402 U.S. 389 (1971) (physicians' written reports sufficient to support denial of disability claim even though opposed by live expert testimony on behalf of the claimant).

(d) How precise must the agency's factfinding be? If the agency needs only to make an approximation of the relevant facts, or can support a finding on the basis of a few documented instances, then hearsay evidence may be adequate. Thus, if the Federal Trade Commission can conclude that advertisements are unlawfully deceptive whenever a particular representation has the capacity to deceive even the most vulnerable consumers, it may be sufficient for the agency to produce a hearsay survey showing that a substantial proportion of the consumers interviewed were misled by the advertisements in question. Since the agency could support its finding by weaker evidence—or even by applying its expertise to the text of the advertisements—it would be pointless to require that each of the survey respondents be made available for cross-examination.

(e) What is the policy behind the statute being enforced? In some instances, the structure or purpose of the agency's program may have a bearing on the kind of evidence required to support a decision. For example, social security and workers' compensation programs are designed to provide benefits quickly and at low cost. A refusal to rely upon affidavits and written reports in such hearings could defeat the basic purposes of the programs.

When focusing on these criteria, it is important to remember that evaluation of technically incompetent evidence cannot be accomplished in the abstract. Much depends upon the quantity and quality of the evidence that each side has placed on the record, the kinds of issues being decided, the impact of an adverse decision on the litigants, and other circumstances surrounding the case.

4. OFFICIAL NOTICE

In the same manner that courts can bypass the normal process of proof by taking judicial notice of facts, administrative agencies can sometimes take "official notice" of material facts that have not been proved on the record in a formal adjudication. However, the procedures and standards used by the agencies in taking notice of nonrecord facts are significantly different from those followed by the courts.

The judicial practice is exemplified by the Federal Rules of Evidence, which limit judicial notice to facts that are beyond reasonable dispute: the facts noticed in federal courts must be either "generally known within the territorial jurisdiction of the trial court," or "capable of accurate and ready determination by resort to sources whose accuracy cannot readily be questioned." Rule 201(b). Under the APA, agencies are not so limited; section 556(e) simply refers to "official notice of a material fact not appearing in the evidence in the record," without regard to the disputability of the fact in question.

In addition to the requirement that the noticed facts be indisputable, the judicial practice is more restrictive than the APA in the limited opportunities it affords the parties to challenge noticed facts. The APA stipulates that "[w]hen an agency decision rests on official notice of a material fact . . . a party is entitled, on timely request, to an opportunity to show the contrary." 5 U.S.C.A. § 556(e). Similar rights exist in the federal courts, see Rule 201(e), but the more limited coverage of the Federal Rules of Evidence can operate to deprive a party of the opportunity to contest some kinds of facts that are judicially noticed. The Advisory Committee note to Rule 201 indicates that judicial notice applies only to "adjudicative facts"—those relating to the particular transaction or occurrence which gave rise to the litigation. Judicial notice of more general "legislative facts" which serve to inform the court's judgments on matters of law, policy, or discretion lie wholly within the court's control; the trial judge may decide them without any input from the parties. Under this provision, a trial judge may decide without considering any evidence, argument, or briefs that the marital privilege is a sound rule because testimony by one spouse against another will destroy the marriage relationship. If a similar question of legislative fact arose in an agency adjudication, a party could argue that the broader language of the APA afforded him an opportunity to contest the noticed matters.

This seems an anomalous result; presumably a specialized administrative agency should have at least as much latitude as a nonspecialist judge to take notice of policy or judgmental facts that fall within its area of expertise. By the same token, there appears to be little reason why a party in court litigation should not have an opportunity to contest important legislative facts that are being noticed by the court. See, e. g., 3 K. Davis, *Administrative Law Treatise* §§ 15:11–15:13 (2d ed. 1980). So long as the applicable rule affords parties an opportunity to challenge the tribunal's decision to take notice of extra-record facts, as the APA and the Federal Rules both provide, there seems little reason to distinguish between "disputable" and "indisputable" facts, or between those that are "legislative" and those that might be considered "adjudicative."

Instead of using these rigid and somewhat artificial distinctions among different kinds of facts to determine when official notice is proper, it may be more useful to focus on the basic policy considerations underlying the procedure for taking notice of extra-record facts. A liberal system of official notice can contribute to the convenience and efficiency of the process, by avoiding the need for repetitive, time-consuming proof on matters that have already been thoroughly investigated. However, the effect of a presiding officer's decision to take official notice is to shift the burden of proof to the opposing party on that issue: the APA procedure imposes an obligation on the opponent to challenge the noticed facts. Thus, the basic issue is whether it is fair for the agency to impose this burden on the respondent or other challenging party.

Several decisions involving official notice reflect this approach. In Manco Watch Strap Co., 60 F.T.C. 495 (1962), the Federal Trade Commission saw no fairness problem in taking official notice of more than two dozen prior proceedings in which agency counsel supporting the complaint had successfully proved that consumers were deceived when sellers failed to disclose that goods had been manufactured in foreign countries. However, the Commission's attempt to take official notice in more questionable circumstances brought a judicial reversal in Dayco Corp. v. FTC, 362 F.2d 180 (6th Cir. 1966). The respondent in that proceeding was a manufacturer whose officer had been a witness in a prior FTC case brought against one of its customers. The Commission sought to take notice of the characteristics and effects of the distribution system used by the manufacturer, which had been the subject of the charges in both proceedings. This was unfair, the court concluded, and not within the ambit of the APA's official notice provision. As a witness in the prior hearing, the company had not had a full chance to contest the facts which the agency had noticed; moreover, the agency could have used other procedural techniques to avoid the burden of repetitive hearings. It could have joined the respondent as a party in the first proceeding, or it even could have introduced the prior hearing record in the second proceeding and offered to make the witnesses available for cross-examination if necessary. Thus there was no real justification for the agency's use of official notice; it appeared to be merely an attempt to avoid the requirement in section 556(d) of the APA that the moving party has the burden of proof.

Judging from the small number of reported cases, the doctrine of official notice has apparently not been used extensively or creatively by many agencies. This reluctance may be partly a result of uncertainties in the applicable legal standards; without clear tests indicating when official notice is proper, agencies may be unwilling to risk reversal by taking notice of nonrecord facts. It remains a potentially useful device for simplifying and expediting hearings.

D. THE INSTITUTIONAL DECISION

In court litigation, decisions are essentially personal: the trial judge who issues findings and conclusions has heard the presentation of evidence and has also reviewed the relevant points of law personally, perhaps with the aid of one or two clerks. Even on appeal, the judges who make the decision and the clerks who assist them listen to arguments and review records and briefs themselves. Administrative agencies are not designed to function like courts, however, and even in formal adjudications the process of decision may be much different from the judicial model. The administrative decisionmaking process is often described as an "institutional decision," in recognition of the fact that it is the product of a bureaucracy rather than of a single person or a small group of identifiable people.

Most regulatory agencies are hierarchies, headed by political appointees who have the responsibility for establishing general policies. Technical expertise is found primarily at the lower levels of the protected civil service employees, and the expertise needed to decide a particular case may be spread among several bureaus or divisions within the agency. Thus, a central problem of the institutional decision is when and how the officials responsible for making the decision can take advantage of this reservoir of expertise without violating the requirements of fairness to the litigating parties. Conversely, issues may arise as to whether an agency head can properly delegate the power to decide a particular controversy or class of cases to subordinate officials instead of personally hearing and deciding.

This latter question (which is technically known as the "subdelegation" problem because it involves a redelegation by the agency heads of powers originally delegated to them by the legislature) has generally been resolved by recognizing a broad power in top administrators to assign responsibilities to their subordinates. This was not always the prevailing view. In a few early cases, courts strictly construed statutory delegations and concluded that powers had to be exercised personally by the agency heads. See, e. g., Cudahy Packing Co. v. Holland, 315 U.S. 357 (1942) (agency head must sign subpoenas). The culmination of this line of decisions was the first *Morgan* case, where the Supreme Court held that a statute which gave a private party the right to a "full hearing" required a personal decision by the agency head. Chief Justice Hughes, writing for the majority, reasoned that the duty to decide "cannot be performed by one who has not considered evidence or argument. . . . The one who decides must hear." Morgan v. United States, 298 U.S. 468, 481 (1936).

However, this principle was too broad to be taken literally, and the Court soon began to cut back on the *Morgan I* decision. The case returned for a second round of Supreme Court review after a trial had been held on the details of the agency's decisionmaking process, and the Court made clear that the administrator was not required to be physically present at the taking of testimony. Rather, it was sufficient that he "dipped into [the record] from time to time to get its drift," read the parties' briefs, and discussed the case with his assistants. The Court went on to note that "it was not the function of the court to probe the mental processes of the Secretary in reaching his conclusions if he gave the hearing that the law required." Morgan v. United States, 304 U.S. 1, 18 (1938). This latter point was stated even more forcefully when the *Morgan* controversy came before the Court for a fourth (and last) time several years later. Just as a judge cannot be deposed or cross-examined about his decisions, "so the integrity of the administrative process must be equally respected." United States v. Morgan, 313 U.S. 409, 422 (1941).

The practical effect of the *Morgan IV* decision is to make it virtually impossible for a challenging party to show that an administrator has failed to give sufficient personal attention to a decision. In any event, subsequent developments in the law have made the *Morgan* issues largely irrelevant. But see *Overton Park*, supra p. 76. Contemporary statutes and reorganization plans usually contain broad grants of authority to subdelegate decisions. The price control statute which was upheld against a delegation attack in Amalgamated Meatcutters v. Connally, 337 F.Supp. 737 (D.D.C.1971), discussed supra pp. 21–27, illustrates how broad a modern subdelegation can be: it provided that "[t]he President may delegate the performance of any function under this title to such officers, departments, and agencies of the United States as he may deem appropriate." 84 Stat. 800 § 203 (1970).

Although this may be an extreme example, it seems clear that the top administrators of a major regulatory agency or program need considerable discretion to assign tasks to their subordinates. The number of formal adjudications heard in many agencies, and the size of the records compiled in major contested proceedings, make it physically impossible for agency heads to conduct more than a selective policy review of staff recommendations.[9] In any event, it is not clear that they should do more than that. Agency heads and top program administrators are typically political appointees who are selected primarily on the basis of their ability to manage a complex bureaucracy and to make policy consistent with the goals of the Administration. They are not normally skilled at presiding over trial-type hearings or sifting through volumes of detailed evidence. In the contemporary

9. An interesting description of the workload pressures confronting a regulatory commissioner during a "typical" day of decisions is provided in Johnson & Dystel, *A Day in the Life: The Federal Communications Commission*, 82 Yale L.J. 1572 (1973).

administrative agency, those functions have been largely taken over by the Administrative Law Judge.

1. THE PRESIDING OFFICER

One of the significant changes that accompanied the passage of the Administrative Procedure Act in 1946 was the enhancement of the status and independence of the hearing officer. These officials, which were formerly known as "trial examiners" or "hearing examiners" and are now called "Administrative Law Judges" or ALJs, have several statutory protections. They are appointed through a professional merit selection system, which requires both high performance on a competitive examination and, in many instances, experience in the particular regulatory program; they may not be assigned to perform duties inconsistent with their judicial functions; and they are tenured employees who may be removed or disciplined only for good cause. 5 U.S.C.A. §§ 1305, 3105, 3344, 5362, 7521.

In a formal trial-type hearing, the ALJ has two primary functions: to conduct the hearing, and to render an initial or recommended decision. Both responsibilities are governed by detailed provisions of the APA. Section 556(b) requires that an ALJ preside at the taking of evidence in a formal adjudication, unless one or more of the agency heads personally conducts the hearing. Another section of the Act delegates broad power to the ALJ to control the proceeding. When authorized by statute and agency rules of practice, the ALJ may issue subpoenas and administer oaths, rule on offers of proof, dispose of procedural requests, and otherwise "regulate the course of the hearing." APA § 556(c). As a practical matter, the ALJ may have greater affirmative responsibility than a trial judge to assure that a full and accurate record is developed at the hearing. Most agencies have been given a statutory mission to accomplish, and they have the duty to develop the facts needed to carry out that mandate. Thus, the hearings need not be structured as pure adversary contests in which the presiding officer serves as a passive referee. In some programs, particularly those involving welfare or disability benefit claims, the hearings may be largely "inquisitorial," with the ALJ taking an active part in questioning witnesses and eliciting relevant facts.

After the hearing has concluded, the parties normally submit proposed findings of fact and conclusions of law, see APA § 557(c), and then the ALJ prepares a decision. Under section 557(b), this may be either an *initial* or a *recommended* decision. The distinction lies in the effect of the ALJ's determination: an initial decision becomes the final agency action unless it is reviewed by an appeal board or the agency heads, while a recommended decision must be considered and acted upon by the agency leadership before it takes effect. See 5 U.S.C.A. § 557(b). The existence of these two forms of ALJ decisions may be viewed as a recognition of the fact that agency adjudications have a widely varying policy content. If the proceeding involves routine application of settled principles to a particular fact situation, then it may be efficient to let the ALJ's initial decision become final without review by the agency heads. On the other hand, when a proceeding has been brought as a "test case" to develop policy in an area that is currently unsettled, the use of a recommended decision assures that the top leadership will consider the policy implications of the case. Finally, the APA acknowledges that some agency actions are virtually pure policy choices, even though they may have been preceded by a trial-type hearing. In these situations, a tenured ALJ may have much less to contribute to the ultimate determination than the political appointees who head the agency. Thus, section 557(b) provides that in initial licensing cases and formal rulemaking proceedings, the presiding officer may simply certify the record to the agency heads, and they in turn may issue a tentative decision for comment by the parties.

Regardless of whether it takes the form of an initial or a recommended decision, the ALJ's determination in a formal adjudication is likely to carry considerable weight with the ultimate agency decisionmakers. The ALJ has seen and heard the witnesses personally, and he has usually devoted more time and effort to mastering the issues than the higher level officials who will review his determination. However, the APA makes clear that the agency heads are not *required* to defer to the ALJ's factfinding in the same way that an appellate court must defer to the trial judge's factual determinations. Section 557(b) states that "[o]n appeal from or review of the initial decision, the agency has all the powers which it would have in making the initial decision, except as it may limit the issues on notice or by rule." One reason for this difference between judicial and administrative practice may be the importance of factual matters in the formulation of agency policy. When the agency makes policy through adjudicative decisions, the key policy issues may have a substantial factual component. In this situation, the agency heads who have the primary responsibility for formulating policy should not be bound by the factual conclusions of a tenured ALJ, particularly on doubtful issues of general or "legislative" fact. Policymakers should have some accountability to the political process, and the statutory provision giving them plenary authority to find facts may be one way of preserving this allocation of responsibility. However, the power of the agency to find facts *de novo* may cause practical and conceptual problems for a reviewing court when the agency heads and the examiner have reached different conclusions; see pp. 235–36 infra.

2. EX PARTE CONTACTS

Like a court trial, a formal agency adjudication is supposed to be decided solely on the basis of the record evidence. This principle is embodied in section 556(e) of the APA, which provides that "[t]he transcript of testimony and exhibits, together with all papers and requests filed in the proceeding, constitutes the exclusive record for decision." The primary reason for requiring this "exclusiveness of the record," as it is sometimes called, is fairness to the litigating parties. If the right to a trial-type hearing is to be meaningful, a participant must be able to know what evidence may be used against him, and to contest it through cross-examination and rebuttal evidence. These rights can easily be nullified if the decisionmakers are free to consider facts outside the record, without notice or opportunity to respond.

The most common problem of extra-record evidence occurs when there are ex parte contacts—communications from a litigating party to a decisionmaking official that take place outside the hearing and off the record. There are several reasons why ex parte contact issues arise more frequently in agency proceedings than in court trials. Judicial decisions are almost always made on the record, after an adversary proceeding; the few exceptions, such as applications for a temporary restraining order, are clearly defined and relatively well understood. In this setting, litigants and their attorneys generally assume that it is improper to discuss the merits of pending cases with the judge outside of the formal proceedings. However, on-the-record proceedings comprise only a small part of the workload in most administrative agencies.

The great bulk of agency decisions are made through informal action, or through public proceedings like notice-and-comment rulemaking where ex parte contacts may be not just permissible but affirmatively desirable. Frequently, regulated companies or interest group representatives will be involved in several pending proceedings before an agency, perhaps involving related issues. In this continuing course of dealing, it is easy for even the most careful person to slip and touch upon issues that are under consideration in a formal adjudication. When this happens, public information laws like the Freedom of Information Act and the Government in the Sunshine Act, discussed pp. 51–54 supra, provide a means for adverse parties to document the indiscretion. This is not to suggest that all improper ex parte contacts between regulators and regulated are innocent; but it does seem clear that regulatory officials function in a complex environment where the line between "responsive government" and "backroom dealing" is often indistinct.

The APA as originally enacted did not deal explicitly with ex parte contacts, and as a result claims of improper ex parte influence were generally evaluated under the due process clause of the Constitution. See, e. g. WKAT v. FCC, 296 F.2d 375, 383 (D.C.Cir.), cert. denied, 368 U.S. 841 (1961); see also Massachusetts Bay Telecasters, Inc. v. FCC, 261 F.2d 55, 65–67 (D.C.Cir. 1958) (APA separation of function provisions used by analogy to invalidate decision where ex parte contacts occurred). In 1976, however, the APA was amended (90 Stat. 1247) and it now has detailed provisions governing ex parte contacts in formal adjudications. Section 557(d)(1) prohibits any "interested person outside the agency" from making, or knowingly causing, "any ex parte communication relevant to the merits of the proceeding" to any decisionmaking official. It also imposes similar restraints on the agency decisionmakers, who are defined to include any "member of the body comprising the agency, administrative law judge, or other employee who is or may reasonably be expected to be involved in the decisional process." 5 U.S.C.A. § 557(d)(1)(B).

When an improper ex parte contact does take place, the APA requires that it be placed on the public record; if it was an oral communication, a memorandum summarizing the contact must be prepared and incorporated into the record. 5 U.S.C.A. § 557(d)(1)(C). Finally, the APA amendments impose a potentially severe sanction on parties who improperly try to influence the agency: an outside party who made or caused the improper contact can be required to show cause "why his claim or interest in the proceeding should not be dismissed, denied, disregarded, or otherwise adversely affected on account of such violation." 5 U.S.C.A. § 557(d)(1)(D). The prohibitions on ex parte contacts come into force when a proceeding has been noticed for hearing, unless the agency has designated some earlier time. 5 U.S.C.A. § 557(d)(1)(E).

The 1976 amendments have clarified the ground rules for formal adjudications and formal rulemaking proceedings governed by the APA. In other types of proceedings, however, questions concerning the propriety of off-the-record communications may still arise. Informal and "hybrid" rulemaking proceedings have been a continuing source of difficulty; see the discussion at pages 259–61 infra.

3. SEPARATION OF FUNCTIONS

When an agency is conducting a formal adjudication, a variant of the ex parte contacts problem often arises within the agency. Usually, agency staff members are assigned to act as advocates in trial-type hearings. For example, staff attorneys may be designated "counsel supporting the complaint" in a disciplinary proceeding, and instructed to act as prosecutors presenting the case against the respondent. When the proceeding is structured in this fashion, the question may arise as to whether the staff attorneys may consult with the decisionmakers outside the record of the proceeding.

From the perspective of the accused respondent, this sort of consultation is likely to seem just as unfair as any other ex parte communication by an adverse party. On the other hand, there are some valid policy reasons for permitting free communications within the agency. Many administrative decisions, including those made in formal adjudications, involve highly technical issues. The expertise necessary to understand those issues is usually found at the staff levels of the agency rather than among the ALJ's and the agency heads; thus, insulating the decision-makers from expert staff may undermine the quality of the decision.

The APA seeks to resolve this tension by defining a limited class of agency staff members who may not consult with decisionmakers in a formal adjudication. This ban on internal communications is generally referred to as "separation of functions."   Section 554(d) provides that any employee who is "engaged in the performance of investigative or prosecuting functions" may not participate in the decision or advise the decision-makers in that case or any factually related case. Any input from the prosecuting staff must come "as a witness or counsel in public proceedings." Id. Thus, the APA acknowledges that a staff member who acts as an advocate is likely to have strong views on the merits, and that it would be unfair to the respondent to give such persons preferential access to the decisionmakers. However, agency employees who have not taken on an adversary role in the particular hearing will be more objective, and the agency heads should be free to call upon them when they need assistance in interpreting the record evidence. Finally, the APA recognizes that the risk of unfairness is likely to be small when the proceedings do not have an accusatory or adversary tenor. Section 554(d) stipulates that the separation of functions requirements do not apply to initial licensing or ratemaking—proceedings which are designed to decide policy questions rather than to impose sanctions for past conduct.

Although the agency decisionmakers may consult with nonprosecuting staff members when they are evaluating the record of a formal proceeding, this does not mean that they are free to obtain additional, nonrecord evidence from these agency employees. The principle of section 556(d) that the transcript, exhibits, and other formal filings constitute the "exclusive record for decision" still applies, and consideration of nonrecord evidence may be reversible error. A decision by the Administrator of the Environmental Protection Agency authorizing the construction of a nuclear power plant was reversed on this ground in Seacoast Anti-Pollution League v. Costle, 572 F.2d 872 (1st Cir. 1978). The Administrator had established a "technical review panel" of agency scientists to assist him in reviewing an initial decision involving the thermal pollution that would result from the proposed reactor. The court held that this review panel had not merely analyzed the record, but rather had supplemented it with additional scientific material which should have been introduced as evidence. Since the Administrator had relied on their assessments, the error was prejudicial and reversal was required.

In addition to the internal separation of functions required by section 556(d) of the APA, it has sometimes been argued that agencies should have a structural separation of functions. That is, some commentators have contended that the system of administrative adjudication is inherently unfair because a single agency often investigates, decides to issue a complaint, conducts the hearing, reviews the initial decision, imposes the sanctions, and checks compliance with its orders. In extreme form, this line of criticism concludes that an independent system of "administrative courts" should be established solely for the purpose of hearing and deciding cases brought by the agencies. Congress has occasionally responded to these concerns by enacting statutes which require strict separation of prosecuting and deciding functions. The National Labor Relations Board is perhaps the best example. In 1947, Congress separated the responsibility for investigating violations and issuing complaints from the Board, and conferred it on an independent General Counsel. The Board members who ultimately hear and decide these cases have no control over the General Counsel or the decision to prosecute.

Litigants have also attacked the institutional combination of functions, claiming that the mixture of prosecuting and deciding powers in a single agency was so unfair as to constitute a denial of due process of law. This argument was unanimously rejected by the Supreme Court in Withrow v. Larkin, 421 U.S. 35 (1975). The Court pointed out that even in criminal trials, judges make a variety of preliminary determinations that are analogous to the agency's decision to issue a complaint: arrest and search warrants are issued by judges who may later preside at the trial, and "[j]udges also preside at preliminary hearings where they must decide whether the evidence is sufficient to hold a defendant for trial." 421 U.S. at 56. Moreover, trial judges who are reversed in civil appeals and administrators who have had their decisions remanded by the courts for further consideration are not considered incapable of giving fair and impartial consideration to the merits of the case. Thus, the due process claim fails unless the protesting party can demonstrate some particular bias which goes beyond the mere combination of prosecuting and adjudicating functions in a single agency.

This concern for the potential unfairness of combining multiple powers in a single agency is not wholly insubstantial. It is probably true, at least in some instances, that an agency head who has reviewed an investigative file and concluded that there was enough evidence to issue a complaint will be more likely to find the respondent guilty when he later reviews the initial decision. But the price of total insulation of the adjudicators could often be high. When issues are technically complex and there is a need for a coherent national regulatory policy in a particular field, the case for combining functions in a single agency is strong. If it were possible to create equal expertise in two separate institutions, it would certainly be costly to do so. More troublesome than the cost is the likelihood that separate bureaucracies would work at cross purposes, resulting in even less coherent policy than the agencies currently produce. Adjudicating cases under a vague "public interest" standard or other broad delegation of power is an important part of the policymaking process; so also is deciding which cases to bring, against which respondents, under what theories. If different bureaucracies were performing these functions in a single regulatory area, the possibilities for policy stalemate or confusion could increase markedly.

4. BIAS AND PREJUDGMENT

The right to an administrative trial-type hearing would have little meaning if the decisionmaker held a personal grudge against one of the litigants, or had already made up his mind about the facts of the case before any evidence was taken. Thus in agency adjudications as in court trials, due process combines with statutory provisions to assure that the decisionmaker is impartial. See, e. g., Goldberg v. Kelly, 397 U.S. 254 (1970), discussed pp. 159–67 supra (due process requires impartial decisionmaker in welfare eligibility determination, even though adjudication procedures were informal); 5 U.S.C.A. § 556(b) (procedures for ruling on claims that decisionmakers are biased or otherwise disqualified from participating in formal adjudications).

However, the task of determining when an administrator has violated the requirement of impartiality is sometimes more difficult than deciding when a judge should recuse himself from hearing a case. Courts generally perform only one function, the resolution of disputes in adversary proceedings, while agencies typically have been delegated a variety of managerial and policymaking responsibilities in addition to the power to adjudicate particular cases. The actions taken and the statements made by administrators in the course of these nonadjudicative duties may create the appearance that a particular case has been prejudged, if not the reality. On the other hand, stringent prohibitions on the appearance of prejudgment in formal adjudications could make it difficult for administrators to perform their nonjudicial functions adequately. In addition, most agencies have a statutory mandate to fulfill; rather than simply resolving disputes that are presented to them, agencies are supposed to implement important social policies such as protecting consumers from dangerous foods and drugs or preventing unscrupulous practices in the sale of securities.

To this extent, at least, most agencies have what might be considered a "built-in bias."

In light of these conflicting pressures to assure fairness to the litigating parties in formal adjudications while preserving the agencies' flexibility to carry out their mandates, it is not surprising that reviewing courts have had a difficult time determining when an administrator's statements and actions constitute impermissible bias or prejudgment. In considering this issue, it is useful to distinguish among three kinds of potentially biasing factors: ideological commitment, personal or pecuniary interest, and prior exposure to the evidence.

1. *Ideological Commitment.* The requirement of impartiality implies that the agency decisionmaker will be open minded, but not necessarily empty headed. The political appointees who head the agencies are chosen in large measure because of the policy positions they have publicly taken, and it would be absurd to require that the Secretary of Transportation have no ideas on the subject of auto safety or that the Administrator of the Environmental Protection Agency be indifferent to the problems of pollution. Thus, an administrator who has taken public positions on controversial matters of law or policy generally is not disqualified from deciding cases which raise those issues. The same rule generally applies to judges who have spoken out on matters that are at issue in pending cases. In Laird v. Tatum, 409 U.S. 824 (1972), Justice Rehnquist refused to disqualify himself from participating in a case concerning the constitutionality of government surveillance of political activity, even though he had testified on behalf of the Administration in congressional hearings dealing with the same activities and had made

other public statements in support of the government's position before being appointed to the Court. Since virtually all of the justices had expressed public opinions on constitutional issues before their appointment to the Court, and had written opinions on these questions as part of their judicial duties, a rule which required disqualification for prior statements on issues of law and policy would prevent the Court from functioning.

Similar reasoning was applied to administrative adjudicators in FTC v. Cement Institute, 333 U.S. 683 (1948). There, the Federal Trade Commission had issued public reports and given testimony in Congress concluding that a particular system of pricing which was widely used in the cement industry violated the antitrust laws. When the agency later issued a complaint against one of the companies using the pricing system, the respondent claimed that the agency's prior reports showed impermissible prejudgment of the issues. The Court disagreed; the commission's release of the investigative reports "did not mean that the minds of its members were irrevocably closed on the subject," and the respondent had a sufficient opportunity in the formal hearing to prove that the reports were erroneous. As in the *Tatum* case, the Court was concerned that a rigid rule of disqualification would mean that no tribunal would be able to adjudicate the case: there was no provision for substituting commissioners, and it was not clear that a court case could be brought if the agency was unable to act. This latter consideration is sometimes called the "doctrine of necessity." Since many regulatory functions are unique to particular agencies, it may be necessary for the agency heads to decide a pending matter even though there are serious questions of bias or prejudgment.

An exception to the general rule that a publicly stated position on matters of law or policy is not grounds for disqualification was applied in Pillsbury Co. v. FTC, 354 F.2d 952 (5th Cir. 1966). The issue in *Pillsbury* arose out of congressional hearings which were held after the FTC had reversed an initial decision on a point of law and remanded the case to the ALJ for further hearings. Several of the congressmen participating in the oversight hearings were extremely critical of the Commission's ruling, and they subjected the FTC Chairman and some agency staff members to detailed, hostile questioning. Despite the fact that the Chairman disqualified himself from participating in the case when it returned to the Commission for review, the court held that the entire agency was disqualified. In the court's view, the congressional pressure had so interfered with the agency's process of decision that the respondent could not get a fair hearing. However, the passage of time and the consequent changes in agency personnel had diluted the risk of prejudgment, and so the court remanded the case for further proceedings.

Pillsbury is difficult to reconcile with the Supreme Court's approach in *Cement Institute*. A possible means of harmonizing the decisions is to view intense external pressure like that involved in *Pillsbury* as different in kind from a voluntarily taken policy position. Under this approach, the congressional hostility may have been sufficient to give the Commissioners a personal rather than an ideological commitment to a particular result; they may well have concluded that powerful congressmen were prepared to retaliate against the agency and its leadership if they persisted in their prior view of the legal issues.

2. *Personal or Pecuniary Interest.* While ideological commitments are usually not sufficient to disqualify adjudicators, the opposite is true when administrators have a financial or other personal stake in the decision. In this situation disqualification is required not only by due process, see pp. 159–61 supra, but also by statutes, executive orders, and agency regulations prohibiting conflicts of interest. Most of these provisions follow the general approach taken in the federal judicial disqualification statute: a judge must recuse himself "in any case in which he has a substantial interest, has been of counsel, is or has been a material witness, or is so related to or connected with any party or his attorney as to render it improper" to participate in the decision. 28 U.S.C.A. § 455. Troublesome questions regarding the applicability of these standards may arise, particularly when an agency adjudicator comes to government service from private practice and his law firm has been active in representing clients before the agency. However, the general principle is well established: a personal stake in the outcome, however small, constitutes grounds for disqualification.

3. *Prior Exposure to the Evidence.* Some of the most difficult questions about the disqualification of adjudicators arise when a litigant claims that agency decisionmakers have prejudged the issues as a result of their exposure to the evidence outside the record of the proceeding. Many statutes permit or require agency heads to consider nonrecord evidence at the preliminary stages of a proceeding when they are deciding whether to authorize an investigation or issue a complaint, and this combination of functions has been upheld against due process attack.

See pp. 162–64 supra. On the other hand, an adjudicator who has become personally familiar with the evidence by serving in an adversary capacity as an investigator or advocate is disqualified from participating in the decision. Thus, in American Cyanamid Co. v. FTC, 363 F.2d 757 (6th Cir. 1966), a commissioner who had investigated the respondent's practices in his prior job as staff counsel to a congressional committee was held ineligible to participate in an adjudication where the same practices were alleged to be violations of the antitrust laws.

A more common problem is the public statement by a regulatory commissioner which suggests that he may have already made up his mind on facts that are at issue in a pending case. Speeches, articles, and interviews are useful means of informing the public about agency policy and activities, but they can cast doubt on the fairness of the hearing process if the administrator makes careless comments about the merits of pending cases. In this situation, reviewing courts have been concerned that public statements will tend to entrench the commissioner in his views, making it difficult for him to consider the evidence impartially when the case comes before the agency for final decision. The test applied in this situation emphasizes both actual and apparent fairness: the reviewing court will inquire whether a disinterested observer would conclude that the administrator has in some measure prejudged the facts of the case. Texaco, Inc. v. FTC, 336 F.2d 754 (D.C.Cir. 1964), vacated and remanded on other grounds, 381 U.S. 739 (1965); Cinderella Career & Finishing Schools, Inc. v. FTC, 425 F.2d 583 (D.C.Cir. 1970) (*Cinderella II*).

E. FINDINGS, CONCLUSIONS, AND REASONS

A formal adjudication concludes with the issuance of a written decision, and the APA has detailed provisions governing the contents of the agency's final product. Section 557(c) requires that the parties be given an opportunity to submit proposed findings and conclusions, or "exceptions" to the proposed decision (usually in the form of briefs), before the agency renders a recommended, initial, or final decision. The APA then directs that "[a]ll decisions" in formal adjudications, whether preliminary or final, "shall include . . . findings and conclusions, and the reasons or basis therefor, on all the material issues of fact, law, or discretion presented on the record." Id.

There are several reasons for requiring agencies to state in detail the factual, legal, and policy bases of important decisions. Exposure of the agency's reasoning helps to assure that administrators will be publicly accountable for their decisions, and that interested persons will have better guidance on the agency's current policy. The need to prepare a detailed analysis of the evidence and arguments can also exert some discipline on the decisionmaking process, by forcing the responsible officials to deal with each party's points carefully and systematically. Finally, statements of findings, conclusions, and reasons make meaningful judicial review possible: without them, a reviewing court will likely find it very difficult to determine whether the agency has exceeded the bounds of the power conferred by the legislature, or has abused its discretion by taking account of factors not properly relevant to its decision, or has found facts without a sufficient evidentiary basis.

Unfortunately, much of the value of the APA require-ments governing findings and statements of reasons is lost when the opinions are not prepared, or at least carefully considered, by the responsible decisionmakers. Traditional-ly, top administrators in some agencies which have a large volume of adjudications have delegated most of the responsibility for documenting their decisions to special-ized opinion writing staffs. The opinions prepared by these staffs may rely heavily on standard "boilerplate" passages, and they may be written with a view toward minimizing the discussion of points that might cause problems on judicial review. In these circumstances, the opinion-writing process does not really impose any disci-pline on the decision, and a reviewing court cannot be sure that it is considering the actual bases for the agency action; the opinion becomes more of a rationalization for the decision than an explanation.

F. SUBSTANTIAL EVIDENCE REVIEW

Since the APA establishes a liberal rule for admissi-bility of evidence in formal adjudications, see pp. 202–07 supra, the principal check on the quality of the evidence relied upon by agencies is judicial review of the factual support for agency action. In formal adjudica-tions, the reviewing court will evaluate the agency's factual basis under the substantial evidence test, 5 U.S.C.A. § 706(2)(E), unless some other standard of fact review is specified by statute. The language of this provision is deceptively simple; it merely states that reviewing courts should set aside agency action which is "unsupported by substantial evidence" in a case governed by the formal hearing requirements of the APA "or otherwise reviewed on the record of an agency hearing provided by statute." Id. Over the years, courts and commentators have struggled to give more precise content to this broad statutory standard, with only partial success.

The substantial evidence test generally is regarded as falling somewhere between the other two fact review provisions contained in section 706. It does not permit the court to find the facts de novo as the "unwarranted by the facts" test of section 706(2)(F) allows; a court applying the substantial evidence test is supposed to assess the reasonableness of the agency's factfinding, and not find the "right" or "true" facts itself. On the other hand, the substantial evidence test is supposed to be less deferential to the agency's factual findings and conclusions than the "arbitrary and capricious" test of section 706(2)(A). Substantial evidence review of formal adjudications is sometimes analogized to appellate review of jury verdicts; in this approach, substantial evidence is "enough to justify, if the trial were to a jury, a refusal to direct a verdict when the conclusion sought to be drawn from it is one of fact for the jury." NLRB v. Columbian Enameling & Stamping Co., 306 U.S. 292, 300 (1939). Another frequently quoted formulation states that substantial evidence is "such relevant evidence as a reasonable mind might accept as adequate to support a conclusion." Consolidated Edison Co. v. NLRB, 305 U.S. 197, 229 (1938). These verbal glosses on the text of the APA are admittedly not very helpful in applying the substantial evidence test to particular cases. Perhaps the most that can be said is that a court reviewing agency action under the substantial evidence test should make sure that the agency has done a careful, workmanlike job of collecting and evaluating the available data—or, as Judge Leventhal put it, that the agency has taken a "hard look" at the important factual issues.

In reviewing agency findings under the substantial evidence test, the court is obliged to consider the "whole record." Universal Camera Corp. v. NLRB, 340 U.S. 474 (1951). That is, the court is not supposed to look only for evidence that supports the agency's decision; it is required to consider all of the relevant evidence for and against the agency's findings, and determine whether they are within the zone of reasonableness. In the federal system, and in many states as well, uncorroborated hearsay is generally sufficient to constitute substantial evidence. See, e. g., Richardson v. Perales, 402 U.S. 389 (1971) (hearsay reports of examining physicians were substantial evidence for denial of disability claim, even though opposed by live testimony on behalf of the claimant). The old "legal residuum rule", which required that there be a residuum of legally competent evidence to support agency findings, is now generally regarded as an overly technical doctrine which can work substantial injustice when hearsay is the only, or best, available evidence. See Carroll v. Knickerbocker Ice Co., 218 N.Y. 435, 113 N.E. 507 (1916) (workers' compensation claim denied because the only evidence that the injuries had been sustained on the job were statements by the injured worker, who had died as a result of his injuries).

Another problem which can occur when courts review agency findings under the substantial evidence test is how the court should treat an agency's reversal of an ALJ's initial decision. As previously noted, the APA gives the agency heads broad power to find the facts de novo when they are reviewing an initial decision. See pp. 216–18 supra. At the same time, however, section 557(c) stipulates that the initial decision is part of the official record of the proceeding, and the substantial evidence test requires the reviewing court to consider the "whole record." Moreover, the fact that the ALJ actually heard the witnesses testify suggests that his findings should be given some deference by the reviewing court. While these potentially conflicting directives of the APA have never been completely harmonized, the *Universal Camera* decision suggests a useful approach for evaluating the ALJ's decision. Since the ALJ's decision is part of the record, the reviewing court must consider it in evaluating the evidentiary support for the final agency decision. Thus, a contrary initial decision may undermine the support for the agency's ultimate determination. However, the weight to be accorded the ALJ's findings may depend upon the kind of issues that are involved in the proceeding. When the case turns on eyewitness testimony, as the *Universal Camera* case did, the initial decision should be given considerable weight: the ALJ was able to observe the demeanor of the witnesses and assess their credibility and veracity first hand. On the other hand, if the decision depends primarily upon expert testimony or policy considerations, the ALJ's decision may deserve little deference; the agency heads may be the best equipped to deal with this kind of testimony, and the reviewing court should be less concerned about their reversal of the ALJ.

CHAPTER IX
RULES AND RULEMAKING

One of the most significant developments in **Administrative** Law during the 1970's was the growing importance of agency rulemaking as a means of formulating policy. Administrative rulemaking is not a recent invention; the Administrative Procedure Act as originally passed in 1946 had several provisions dealing with rulemaking procedures, and examples of rules issued by the executive departments can be found in the earliest history of our national government. What has changed in recent years is the number and significance of decisions being made in agency rulemaking proceedings and, as a consequence, the procedures that agencies must follow in adopting rules.

There are probably several reasons why rulemaking has recently become a major factor in administrative practice. For many years, commentators have urged agencies to make greater use of their rulemaking powers, arguing that the rulemaking process can be both fairer and more efficient than case-by-case adjudication. Rulemaking proceedings can put all affected parties on notice of impending changes in regulatory policy, and give them an opportunity to be heard before the agency's position has crystallized. A rule can also resolve in one proceeding issues which might remain unclear for years if the case-by-case approach were followed. A clear general rule can produce more rapid and uniform voluntary compliance among the affected firms or individuals than standards which are linked to the facts of a particular case; the scope of an adjudicative precedent is often less

[237]

clear than the scope of a rule. General rules also serve the goal of equal treatment for parties who are similarly situated. For example, if the Federal Trade Commission elects to attack a fraudulent selling practice by bringing a series of cease-and-desist adjudications against companies that are using the questionable sales technique, the first firm to be subjected to an order will be forced to operate at a competitive disadvantage until the agency completes subsequent proceedings against rival sellers. Finally, administrative rules can serve as a substitute for the legislative standards which were formerly required by the delegation doctrine. As the courts have become increasingly reluctant to strike down broad delegations of quasi-legislative power, see pp. 13–27 supra, agency rules have become more important as a source of law for reviewing courts to apply. An administrative decision which violates the agency's own rules is an abuse of discretion and can be reversed on judicial review, unless the agency can state good reasons for departing from its own standards; see pp. 77–78 supra.

Despite these advantages of rules over individual adjudications, the agencies probably would not have embraced rulemaking so eagerly without some external pressures. From the agency's perspective, writing a general rule is often more difficult than deciding a particular case, and the likelihood of producing an undesirable or unintended result is correspondingly greater. Moreover, general rules are more likely to inspire concerted opposition from those who will be covered by them. An individual case isolates one respondent, generally selected because of questionable actions, for possible sanction, but a general rule can inspire the whole industry (whose members may or may not have engaged in similar actions) to fight—not only before the agency but in the courts, the Congress, and the media as well. In short, promulgating a rule can be more costly to the agency in time, effort, and good will than deciding a series of cases.

The major impetus for agencies to make greater use of their rulemaking authority has come from the legislature and, to a considerable degree, from the nature of the tasks that they have been given to perform. Many programs created during the wave of health, safety, and environmental regulation that was enacted during the 1970's required the responsible agencies to promulgate general rules, and some of these statutes contained judicially enforceable deadlines by which rules had to be issued. In addition, some of the older agencies like the FTC were given new grants of rulemaking authority which they interpreted as a congressional mandate to make more agressive use of the rulemaking power. The nature and scope of the tasks given to agencies under the new programs of health, safety, environmental, and consumer protection regulation also made rulemaking a more logical form of proceeding. Instead of receiving a mandate to regulate a few hundred railroads, or a few thousand commercial broadcasters, the agencies implementing new programs of "social regulation" were directed to control hundreds of thousands of workplaces or pollution sources, or millions of consumer transactions. They could not hope to accomplish their statutory missions unless they were prepared to make use of their rulemaking authority.

As administrative rulemaking expanded in volume and significance through the 1970's the provisions for rulemaking procedures and judicial review of rules contained in the Administrative Procedure Act began to show signs of stress. Courts and legislatures became more willing to experiment with new variations on the APA models, as they sought to accommodate the old procedures to the new kinds of decisions that agencies were making. That process is not yet completed, but it is possible to draw some tentative conclusions from the experience of the past decade. First, however, it is necessary to review the rulemaking procedures established in the Administrative Procedure Act.

A. THE TYPES OF ADMINISTRATIVE RULES

At first glance, the APA's definition of "rule" seems almost as broad as its definition of "order." Under section 551(4), a rule is "the whole or a part of an agency statement of general or particular applicability and future effect designed to implement, interpret, or prescribe law or policy" or to establish rules of practice. This formulation is probably more confusing than it needs to be. The reference to rules of "particular applicability," which seems contrary to the very idea of a rule, is something of an historical anomaly. It is designed to preserve the traditional understanding that ratemaking proceedings (that is, those concerned with the approval of "tariffs" or rate schedules filed by public utilities and common carriers) should generally be regarded as rulemaking proceedings rather than adjudications. In most instances, the characteristic features of rules are their *general* application to all parties and fact situations which fall within their ambit, and their *prospective* effect. They are designed to establish future standards of conduct rather than to assess past acts or practices under an existing standard. Some common characteristics of rules are that (a) they apply to groups rather than to named individual respondents (and usually the affected groups are defined so that they may later include new members), (b) they result in sanctions against an individual party only after a further adjudicative proceeding, and (c) they are based upon general, "legislative" facts rather then on specific, "adjudicative" facts. In other words, rules are the administrative equivalent of statutes.

The APA's procedural requirements for rulemaking vary depending upon the kind of rules that the agency is promulgating. One basic distinction recognized by the APA is the difference between *legislative* and *interpretative* rules. Conceptually, these two types of rules are fairly easy to distinguish. If the Food and Drug Administration has a specific statutory delegation of power to issue rules prescribing the contents of common food products, and the statute imposes fines or other penalties on those who violate the standards, that is a clear exercise of legislative rulemaking authority: like a legislature, the agency writes standards of conduct which are backed by legal penalties. On the other hand, an agency may issue rules which simply interpret an existing provision of law. Thus, the Federal Trade Commission has the power to issue complaints, conduct formal adjudications, and issue cease and desist orders against companies which are engaged in "unfair methods of competition." The agency might issue rules stating that it interprets this statute to mean that certain kinds of agreements among competitors—for example, shopping center leases which prohibit discount sales—are sufficiently anticompetitive to warrant the issuance of complaints against those who have signed such contracts. This interpretative rule would not foreclose an accused party in a subsequent adjudication from presenting evidence or argument designed to show that the agency's reading of the statute was misguided; nor would it preclude a reviewing court from construing the statute differently. Rather, this rule would merely serve as a warning to affected parties that the FTC had taken a formal position on a legal issue that falls within its jurisdiction.

One practical difficulty that often arises is that neither the relevant statutes nor the agency rules themselves indicate very clearly whether a particular exercise of the rulemaking authority should be considered "legislative" (the APA uses the term "substantive") or "interpretative." The statute may provide in general terms that the agency can "issue rules to carry out the provisions of this title," and the agency may simply issue rules defining the prohibited conduct, without explaining the consequences of a violation. Since the APA establishes different procedural requirements for issuing legislative and interpretative rules, see pp. 246–47 infra, a reviewing court may have to decide what kind of a rule it is dealing with. The type of rule under consideration may also affect the scope or intensity of judicial review. In reviewing a legislative rule, the court is supposed to defer to the agency's judgment concerning the wisdom or propriety of the rule's content, so long as the rule is within the agency's jurisdiction, was issued through proper procedure, and is not arbitrary or contrary to constitutional right. However, an interpretative rule is more analogous to a litigant's brief: it may be followed by the reviewing court if it is based upon persuasive reasoning, but the court is technically free to substitute its own interpretation of the applicable law.

Courts confronting this problem have generally used two tests in determining whether a particular rule is legislative. The most common and widely accepted test is whether the Congress has delegated to the agency power to make rules having the force and effect of law. An agency may interpret the statutes it administers, even though it lacks power to make rules which are legally binding on those it regulates; but it cannot issue rules which have the force and effect of law without an express delegation of authority.[1] In applying this test, the reviewing court would look primarily to the text of the statutes administered by the agency, their legislative history, and other aids to statutory construction which might clarify the nature and scope of the powers conferred by the legislature. Some courts have also applied a second test for distinguishing legislative from interpretative rules: if the rule has a "substantial impact" on affected private parties, then it is legislative. See, e. g., Pickus v. United States Bd. of Parole, 507 F.2d 1107 (D. C.Cir. 1974) (Parole Board regulations listing and weighting factors to be considered in acting upon applications

---

1. See Addison v. Holly Hill Fruit Prods., Inc., 322 U.S. 607 (1944); National Petroleum Refiners Ass'n v. FTC, 482 F.2d 672 (D.C.Cir. 1973), cert. denied, 415 U.S. 951 (1974).

for parole deemed legislative rules because they would
have a major impact on an inmate's chances for parole).[2]

The "substantial impact" test has been criticized because it fails to acknowledge the primary importance of
the legislative delegation, and because virtually any significant rule—whether legislative, interpretative, or procedural—can have a substantial impact on private rights.
See generally 2 K. Davis, *Administrative Law Treatise*
76–78 (2d ed. 1979). However, the Supreme Court seemed
to rely on both tests in Chrysler Corp. v. Brown, 441 U.S.
281 (1979), where it was faced with the question whether
an agency regulation governing disclosure of records supplied by private parties was substantive or interpretative.
The Court noted that the test of whether the rule was "one
'affecting individual rights and obligations'" was "an
important touchstone for distinguishing those rules that
.   .   .   have the 'force of law.'" Id. at 302. However, it also stated that even a significant impact on
private rights, standing alone, was not sufficient to support a conclusion that the rule was legislative. The
statutory delegation also had to be examined carefully,
because "the exercise of quasi-legislative authority by
governmental departments and agencies must be rooted in
a grant of such power by the Congress and subject to
limitations which that body imposes." Id.

B. RULEMAKING PROCEDURES

Agency rulemaking proceedings can take on several
different procedural forms under the APA: they may be
formal, informal, or exempted completely from the Act's

---

2. See also Morton v. Ruiz, 415 U.S. 199 (1974).

procedural requirements. In addition, the basic APA procedural models have often been supplemented or modified by Congress in particular grants of rulemaking authority, and reviewing courts have occasionally required agencies to use procedures additional to those specified in the APA. Before discussing these latter "hybrid" rulemaking approaches, however, it is necessary to examine the three kinds of rulemaking procedures contemplated by the APA.

1. *Exempted Rulemaking.* The general rulemaking provision of the APA, section 553, contains several exemptions which give agencies discretion to determine how much public participation—if any—will be permitted before a final rule is issued. Section 553(a) completely exempts from public notice and opportunity to comment all rulemaking proceedings relating to "a military or foreign affairs function" or "agency management or personnel or to public property, loans, grants, benefits, or contracts." The policy behind these exemptions is not entirely clear. In some areas of military or foreign policy formulation, there is undoubtedly a need for secrecy or fast action that conflicts with the notice and public comment requirements of the APA informal rulemaking procedures. However, there are other exceptions in section 553 that seem adequate to deal with these situations. For example, section 553(b)(3)(B) permits the agency to omit notice and opportunity for comment when it finds that public proceedings "are impracticable, unnecessary, or contrary to the public interest." The exemption for personnel, grant, and contract matters seems even more difficult to justify. When it was originally enacted, there was a general assumption that private parties had few

procedural rights when the government action affected a "privilege" or a "mere gratuity" rather than private property. That distinction has now been rejected as unsound and unworkable in contemporary due process analysis; see pp. 140–49 supra. In recent years the government has sought to accomplish a wide variety of social objectives through the spending power, and the effect of the section 553 exemption for subsidy and personnel matters is to immunize a wide range of important policy decisions from public participation. The sweeping exemptions of section 553(a) have been criticized by commentators, and the Administrative Conference of the United States has recommended that the military and foreign affairs exemption be repealed. 1 CFR § 305.73–5.

Another set of exceptions to the APA's public participation requirements for rulemaking is contained in section 553(b)(3). One of these exemptions is based on the kinds of rules being promulgated: the agency may avoid notice and comment and simply issue a final rule when it is developing "interpretative rules, general statements of policy, or rules of agency organization, procedure, or practice." The rationale for this exemption appears to be twofold. Interpretative or procedural rules and policy statements (which are functionally similar to interpretative rules) often have a less substantial impact on private rights than a legislative rule, and they are generally subjected to more intensive judicial review. Thus, the need for public participation during the formulation of the rule may often be less than when the agency is considering rules that will have the force of law. Moreover, the agencies usually have discretion over whether they will clarify their policies by issuing interpretative rules or general statements of policy; few statutes compel them to use these forms of rulemaking. In this situation, any procedural formalization—even the simple requirements of notice-and-comment rulemaking—might deter the agencies from informing the public of important policy decisions through interpretative rules and formal policy statements. Notwithstanding these factors, however, many important decisions which have a substantial social and economic impact appear to be exempted unnecessarily from the APA's public participation requirements. For example, the FCC issued a major change in the standards it used in renewing television and radio broadcast licenses without any public participation by styling it as a policy statement rather than a legislative rule. See Citizens Communications Center v. FCC, 447 F.2d 1201 (D.C.Cir. 1971) (setting aside the policy statement because it deprived challengers of the comparative hearing required by statute), discussed supra p. 191.

The final exemption to the APA's notice-and-comment procedures applies to any kind of substantive rule, and requires a particularized showing that public participation would be useless or counterproductive. Section 553 (b)(3)(B) permits the agency to issue a rule in final form when "notice and public procedure . . . are impracticable, unnecessary, or contrary to the public interest." In practice, this exception applies primarily when delay would frustrate the rule's purpose, or the subject matter is so routine or trivial that public participation would be negligible. To invoke this exemption, the APA also requires that the agency make a "good cause" finding and incorporate a brief statement of its reasons for avoiding public participation in the final rule. This finding is subject to judicial review, and the rule can be set aside if the court concludes that the agency did not have an adequate justification for cutting off the public's right to participate. See, e. g., Texaco, Inc. v. FPC, 412 F.2d 740 (3d Cir. 1969) (rule establishing requirement that regulated companies pay compound interest on refunds ordered by the FPC was not "minor" or "emergency" in nature, and therefore the agency's failure to allow public comment was erroneous).

While these exemptions from public participation are quite broad, they are permissive rather than mandatory. The APA establishes minimum procedural requirements, and the agency is usually free to give affected persons more opportunities to participate than the Act requires. Thus an agency could use notice-and-comment procedures, or confer informally with affected interest groups, or hold public hearings on important rules that are technically exempt from the APA. The Administrative Conference has recommended that agencies provide such opportunities for public participation when an interpretative rule or general policy statement "is likely to have a substantial impact on the public." 1 CFR § 305.76–5.

2. *Informal Rulemaking.* The basic rulemaking procedure prescribed by section 553 of the APA is generally called "informal" or "notice-and-comment" rulemaking. In the absence of directives to the contrary in an agency's enabling legislation, the APA's informal rulemaking procedures will apply whenever the agency issues substantive rules. Thus, if the statute merely authorizes the agency to issue regulations and those regulations affect the legal

rights of private parties, they have the effect of law and the agency will be required to follow the notice-and-comment procedure of section 553.

The APA's informal rulemaking process is simple and flexible. There are only three procedural requirements which an agency must meet when it issues rules under section 553. First, it must give prior *notice,* which is usually accomplished by publication of an item in the Federal Register. The notice is required to contain "either the terms or substance of the proposed rule or a description of the subjects and issues involved," as well as a reference to the legal authority for issuing the rule and information about the opportunities for public participation. 5 U.S.C.A. § 553(b). After publication of the notice of rulemaking, the agency must "give interested persons an opportunity to participate" through *submission of written comments* containing data, views, or arguments. 5 U.S.C.A. § 553(c). The agency is not required to hold any oral hearings under this section; it has discretion to decide whether interested persons will be allowed to submit testimony or to present oral argument to the decisionmakers. Finally, after the agency has considered the public comments, it must issue with its final rules "a concise general *statement of . . . basis and purpose."* Id. In recent years reviewing courts have begun to demand a more careful articulation by the agency of its reasons for issuing a rule, but it still seems to be true that the statement of basis and purpose in an informal rulemaking proceeding can be far less detailed than the findings, conclusions, and statements of reasons required in a formal adjudication. See pp. 232–33 supra; Automotive Parts & Accessories Ass'n v. Boyd,

407 F.2d 330, 338 (D.C.Cir. 1968) (function of statement of basis and purpose in informal rulemaking is to enable the reviewing court "to see what major issues of policy were ventilated by the informal proceedings and why the agency reacted to them as it did").

The simple procedures of notice-and-comment rulemaking provide an efficient means for informing the administrators and reaching a prompt decision. From the point of view of a party who opposes a particular rule, however, the procedures may seem much less fair than trial-type hearings where parties enjoy extensive rights to know and challenge opposing evidence. Moreover, the APA informal rulemaking procedures do not require the agency to expose its factual, legal, and policy support to public criticism. Unless a challenging party is able to obtain internal agency documents under the Freedom of Information Act, see pp. 51–52 supra, he may not be able to discover all of the supporting evidence and analysis that the agency has relied upon until the rule has been issued and an action is brought in court to challenge its validity. Because the agency's premises have not been examined in a public adversary proceeding, informal rulemaking may produce inaccurate or misguided decisions if the agency is not sufficiently rigorous or self-disciplined in gathering and analyzing information. In other words, notice-and-comment rulemaking is an excellent technique for gathering information and educating the agency; but it is not as well suited to testing the factual or legal basis for a proposed rule. For these reasons, regulated industries and other constituency groups have often sought additional procedural safeguards in administrative rulemaking. These more elaborate forms of rulemaking can be divided into formal and hybrid rulemaking procedures.

3. *Formal Rulemaking.* Section 553(c) of the APA contains an exception to the general rule that an agency need only permit an opportunity to comment and then prepare a statement of basis and purpose after it has published notice of a proposed rule. It states that "[w]hen rules are required by statute to be made on the record after opportunity for an agency hearing," the APA's formal adjudication procedures must be used. Thus, when some other statute (usually the one which delegates rulemaking authority) directs the agency to do so, it must conduct a trial-type hearing and provide interested persons with an opportunity to testify and cross-examine adverse witnesses before issuing a rule. This process is generally called "rulemaking on a record" or "formal rulemaking."

Since legislative draftsmen are often not attuned to the nuances of the APA, the relevant statutes may be ambiguous with respect to whether Congress intended the agency to use formal or informal rulemaking. This was the situation that the Supreme Court encountered in United States v. Florida East Coast Ry., 410 U.S. 224 (1973). The statute merely provided that the Interstate Commerce Commission "may, after hearing" issue rules establishing incentive per diem charges for the use of freight cars. The protesting railroad argued that this language required the ICC to follow the APA's formal rulemaking procedures. The Supreme Court disagreed: the term "hearing," standing alone, has "a host of meanings," and the legislative history of the statute did not clearly indicate that Congress wanted the ICC to use formal rulemaking. A statute did not have to track verbatim the APA phrase "on the record after opportunity for an agency hearing" in order to trigger the formal rulemaking requirements, but a clear expression of congressional intent was necessary. In effect, the *Florida East Coast* decision creates a strong presumption in favor of informal rulemaking.

Although the point was not discussed at length in the opinion, the *Florida East Coast* decision may be based upon the Court's assumption that trial-type hearings are generally not desirable in rulemaking. Commentators have criticized formal rulemaking on the ground that it is a costly, cumbersome process which contributes little to the quality of decision. The FDA, which is required to use formal rulemaking in some of its regulatory programs, is often cited to illustrate the costs and delays that can result from formal rulemaking procedures. In the notorious Peanut Butter rulemaking, for example, the parties consumed weeks of hearing time and hundreds of pages of transcript cross-examining experts on issues such as whether peanut butter should contain 87 or 90 percent peanuts. See generally Hamilton, *Rulemaking on a Record by the Food and Drug Administration*, 50 Texas L.Rev. 1132 (1972). Another FDA formal rulemaking dealing with vitamin supplements was an even longer exercise in futility. After it had held 18 months of hearings, the agency was reversed on appeal because it had unduly restricted cross-examination of a government expert. National Nutritional Foods Ass'n v. FDA, 504 F.2d 761, 792–99 (2d Cir. 1974), cert. denied, 420 U.S. 946 (1975). In other agencies, the costs and delays associated with formal rulemaking have led to the virtual abandonment of regulatory programs. Hamilton, *Procedures for the Adoption of Rules of General Applicability: The Need for Procedural Innovation in Administrative Rulemaking,* 60 Calif.L.Rev. 1276, 1283–1313 (1972). Against the background of this experience, the Supreme Court's reluctance to conclude that an ambiguous statute required formal rulemaking is understandable.

Even when the statute does plainly require formal rulemaking, the APA permits some departures from the procedures used in formal adjudications. See generally pp. 180–236 supra. Section 556(d) allows the agency to substitute written submissions for oral direct testimony in rulemaking. However, the proviso in the same section that a party is entitled "to conduct such cross-examination as may be required for a full and true disclosure of the facts" still applies, so the agency must make available for cross-examination the persons who supplied the information contained in the written submissions if it intends to rely on the evidence they provided. If the agency has relied on technical studies or survey research, it may be required to produce the raw data so that the parties can use it in cross-examination. Thus, in Wirtz v. Baldor Elec. Co., 337 F.2d 518 (D.C.Cir. 1963), the Labor Department had conducted a survey of manufacturers to determine the prevailing wages in the electrical equipment industry. When the agency used statistics derived from this survey in a formal rulemaking to set minimum wages for government contractors in the industry, it made available for cross-examination the statistician who had tabulated the figures from the questionnaires. However, the Department refused to disclose individual companies' responses, because it had given them assurances that their replies would be kept confidential. The reviewing court concluded that the industry representatives opposing the rule needed access to the raw data in order to cross-examine effectively, and since the agency was unwilling to retract its promises of confidentiality, the rule had to be set aside. This data disclosure requirement can cause considerable delay and expense in proceedings where the agency needs to rely on surveys or other technical reports: in addition to the time spent in hearings, the agency may have to resort to compulsory process to obtain the necessary data when the persons or companies supplying it are not willing to have it disclosed to the public. If any of the subpoenaed parties resists, as is likely to happen when sensitive commercial information is involved, there may be lengthy litigation over the legality of the agency's demand before the data can be collected. See generally pp. 82–102 supra.

Another potential difference between formal adjudication and formal rulemaking is the process of decision followed within the agency. Under section 557 of the APA, the agency may omit the presiding officer's initial or recommended decision in formal rulemaking, and instead issue a tentative agency decision for public comment. In addition, the strict separation of functions requirements of section 554 do not apply; decisionmakers in a formal rulemaking are free to consult with staff experts throughout the agency, including those who were responsible for presenting the agency's position at the hearing. Unlike adjudications, rulemaking proceedings are generally not accusatory; consequently, there is less need to isolate the decisionmakers from a potentially adversary staff in order to assure fairness to the accused.

However, the ban on ex parte contacts with outside parties contained in section 557(d) does apply to formal rulemaking proceedings.

Rules issued after a formal rulemaking proceeding are also subjected to more intensive judicial review than those which are the products of informal rulemaking. Section 706(2)(E) provides that the substantial evidence test applies to proceedings "subject to sections 556 and 557 . . . . or otherwise reviewed on the record of an agency hearing"—language which includes formal rulemaking proceedings. Informal rulemaking proceedings do not fit within this section, and so their factual basis is reviewed under the more lenient arbitrary and capricious test. The application of these standards to rulemaking records is discussed in more detail below. See pp. 265–74.

4. *Hybrid Rulemaking.* In the late 1960's, as rulemaking became an increasingly important form of administrative decisionmaking, dissatisfaction with the rulemaking procedures provided by the APA began to spread. Informal rulemaking was simple and efficient, but it gave interested persons few rights to know and contest the basis of a proposed rule. Formal rulemaking, on the other hand, provided abundant opportunities to participate and to challenge the agency's proposal, but at the cost of near paralysis. As these shortcomings became more apparent, courts, commentators, and legislators attempted to develop intermediate procedural models that would permit effective public participation in rulemaking while avoiding the excesses of trial procedure. These compromise rulemaking procedures are generally described as "hybrid rulemaking."

Reviewing courts were some of the most active exponents of hybrid rulemaking procedures. Several distinct lines of legal analysis can be traced in the judicial development of hybrid rulemaking. One of the earliest doctrinal bases was procedural due process, which was invoked in the "blocked space case," American Airlines, Inc. v. CAB, 359 F.2d 624 (D.C.Cir.) (en banc), cert. denied, 385 U.S. 843 (1966). Several airlines had claimed that the CAB could not use informal rulemaking to issue rules limiting the classes of cargo they could transport, because the statute assured them a trial-type hearing before their certificates (licenses) could be amended. The court rejected this argument and held that informal rulemaking was a proper procedure for making this sort of general determination. However, the majority did note that if a participant could make a convincing showing that an important contested issue needed to be explored in an evidentiary hearing, then due process might require the agency to provide some trial-type procedures within the general context of informal rulemaking.

The due process basis for hybrid rulemaking was ultimately rejected by the Supreme Court in the *Florida East Coast* case, discussed pp. 251–53 supra. Following the distinction established in the two early cases of Londoner v. Denver, 210 U.S. 373 (1908) and Bi-Metallic Investment Co. v. State Board of Equalization, 239 U.S. 441 (1915), the Court held that there was no constitutional right to oral proceedings in rulemaking. Due process sometimes required the opportunity for a hearing in "proceedings designed to adjudicate disputed facts in particular cases," but there was no such right when the purpose of the proceeding was to develop "policy-type rules or standards." 410 U.S. at 224. Thus, for questions of policy or general "legislative facts," the APA's informal rulemaking procedures are constitutionally adequate.

By the time the *Florida East Coast* case was decided, the courts had developed other legal bases for hybrid rulemaking procedures. Inartful or ambiguous legislative drafting provided some occasions for creative judicial interpretation. Thus, a general grant of rulemaking authority accompanied by a requirement that the rules be subject to substantial evidence review (which is the standard normally applicable to formal rulemaking) was construed to require hybrid procedures, including evidentiary hearings on some contested issues, in Mobil Oil Corp. v. FPC, 483 F.2d 1238 (D.C.Cir. 1973) (rules setting rates charged by pipelines transporting certain kinds of hydrocarbon products). In other instances, the courts reinterpreted the APA provisions governing informal rulemaking to enhance the opportunities for meaningful public participation. This approach is illustrated by United States v. Nova Scotia Food Products Corp., 568 F.2d 240 (2d Cir. 1977), where the court concluded that the APA's right to comment in informal rulemaking had been violated when the agency had not made a key scientific study available to potential commenters. "To suppress meaningful comment by failure to disclose the basic data relied upon," the court reasoned, "is akin to rejecting comment altogether." Finally, some of the hybrid rulemaking opinions have little direct basis in the texts of the relevant statutes or constitutional provisions. In essence, the courts created

[257]

a judicial common law of rulemaking procedure. See generally Davis, *Administrative Common Law and the Vermont Yankee Opinion*, 1980 Utah L.Rev. 3.

In light of their diverse legal bases and divergent procedural requirements, the hybrid rulemaking decisions cannot be easily summarized. However, some examples of the procedural requirements imposed in these cases may illuminate the underlying problems that the courts were trying to resolve.

a. *Disclosure of Methodology.* In International Harvester Co. v. Ruckelshaus, 478 F.2d 615 (D.C.Cir. 1973), the court reversed the Environmental Protection Agency's refusal to suspend the effective date of new emissions standards for light trucks because the agency had failed to disclose the methodology it had used in predicting that compliance with the standards would be feasible. Disclosure was considered necessary both to assure fairness to the commenting parties, and to permit meaningful judicial review of the agency's decision.

b. *Record Management and "Notice of Intent to Rely."* In several of the new programs of health, safety, and environmental rulemaking that came into existence during the 1970's, proceedings often produced records that ran into tens of thousands of pages, and sometimes into the hundreds of thousands. These massive records contained a diverse collection of materials, ranging from highly technical scientific studies to consumer postcards expressing a general opinion about the proposed rule. Reviewing courts occasionally prodded the agencies to use greater care in assembling and analyzing these records. See, e. g., Texas v. EPA, 499

F.2d 289, 297 (5th Cir. 1974). In Ethyl Corp. v. EPA, 541 F.2d 1 (D.C.Cir.) (en banc), cert. denied, 426 U.S. 941 (1976), the dissenters argued that the agency should be required to give notice of its intent to rely upon important materials in the voluminous record, so that interested persons would be able to prepare effective comments. 541 F.2d at 85, 91. The majority stopped short of imposing such a requirement, but indicated that they might do so in a future case if a participant showed that the record was so disorganized as to be unusable. 541 F.2d at 49 n.102; see generally Pedersen, *Formal Records and Informal Rulemaking*, 85 Yale L.J. 38 (1975).

c. *Response to Cogent Comments.* On occasion the statements of basis and purpose which agencies issued after informal rulemaking proceedings were too "concise" and "general" to give the reviewing court a clear picture of the administrator's reasons for accepting some contentions and rejecting others. To fill this gap, the court could remand the proceeding for a more complete statement of the reasons for the decision. See, e. g., Kennecott Copper Corp. v. EPA, 462 F.2d 846, 850 (D.C.Cir. 1972). Alternatively, the court might direct the agency to respond to "cogent comments"—that is, those which were "significant enough to step over a threshold requirement of materiality." Portland Cement Ass'n v. Ruckelshaus, 486 F.2d 375, 393–94 (D.C.Cir. 1973).

d. *Prohibitions on Ex Parte Contacts.* Even before the recent hybrid rulemaking decisions, courts had on one occasion reversed a rule issued in notice-and-comment proceedings because the decisionmakers had engaged in off-the-record discussions with an interested party. In Sangamon Val. Television Corp. v. United States, 269 F.2d 221 (D.C.Cir. 1959), the court set aside a rule reallocating a television channel from one city to another because a corporate official of an interested license applicant had met informally with the FCC commissioners to discuss the merits of the proceeding. The court distinguished the *Sangamon* case from other informal rulemaking situations by noting that the proceeding involved conflicting private claims to a valuable privilege. Although the rule appeared to make only a general determination of the number of stations that would be available in the two cities, in fact it was likely to determine which of several competing applicants would get a license. In this respect, the proceeding was functionally similar to a comparative licensing adjudication.

The situation was less closely analogous to adjudication when the D.C. Circuit set aside another FCC rule on ex parte grounds in Home Box Office, Inc. v. FCC, 567 F.2d 9 (D.C.Cir. 1977) (per curiam), cert. denied, 434 U.S. 829 (1978). In the course of developing a rule regulating pay cable television, the commissioners had held a number of private meetings with interested participants. The court felt that it would be "intolerable" if there were one rulemaking record for insiders, and another for the general public. In addition to this concern for the fairness of the process, the court reasoned that non-record communications would undermine the effectiveness of judicial review, since the reviewing judges would not have access through the rulemaking record to all of the material considered by the agency.

Another panel of the same court reached a different result when the ex parte issue arose again in Action for Children's Television v. FCC, 564 F.2d 458 (D.C.Cir. 1977), which involved a proposed FCC rule governing television advertising and programming directed at children. The commissioners had privately negotiated a compromise voluntary compliance agreement with industry representatives after the public comment period had closed, and then had terminated the proceeding. The court held that since the Children's Advertising proceeding was already underway when *Home Box Office* was decided, the novel doctrine of that case should not be applied retroactively to invalidate the agency's decision; and in well-considered *dictum* the court stated that the ban on ex parte contacts should be limited to *Sangamon* rules involving conflicting claims to valuable privileges. Id. at 474, 477. See also United States Lines, Inc. v. FMC, 584 F.2d 519 (D.C.Cir. 1978) (statute directing Maritime Commission to hold a hearing before approving an agreement among competing companies did not require compliance with 5 U.S.C.A. §§ 556–57, but improper ex parte contacts were grounds for reversal); United Steelworkers v. Marshall, 48 Ad.L.2d 1007 (D.C.Cir. 1980) (ex parte contacts by agency staff allowed; *HBO* rule said to be limited to contacts by persons with a financial interest in the outcome). See Gellhorn & Robinson, *Rulemaking Due Process: An Inconclusive Dialogue*, 48 U.Chi.L.Rev. 201 (1981).

e. *Cross-Examination.* In a few hybrid rulemaking cases, reviewing courts indicated that cross-examination on particular issues might be necessary even though the proceeding was generally governed by the APA's informal rulemaking provisions. Thus, in the *International Harvester* case, discussed p. 258 supra, the court upheld rulemaking procedures in which the EPA permitted participants at an oral hearing to submit written questions to the hearing officer, who had discretion as to whether to ask the witness the suggested questions. In the course of its opinion, however, the court stated that a claim of the right to cross-examine might be upheld "on critical points where the general procedure proved inadequate to probe 'soft' and sensitive subjects and witnesses." 478 F.2d at 631. When a case arose in which the D.C. Circuit took this next step and directed an agency to permit cross-examination on a crucial issue in an informal rulemaking proceeding, the Supreme Court reversed in an unusually strong opinion which seems likely to halt the judicial development of hybrid rulemaking procedures.

Vermont Yankee Nuclear Power Corp. v. Natural Resources Defense Council, Inc., 435 U.S. 519 (1978), arose out of a Nuclear Regulatory Commission rulemaking which was designed to decide how the "fuel cycle" effects of nuclear energy, such as radioactive waste, should be factored into licensing adjudications involving individual power plants. The agency was authorized to use informal rulemaking in issuing this kind of rule, but it had agreed to hold an oral hearing at which witnesses would be questioned by agency representatives. On judicial review, the District of Columbia Circuit held that this procedure was insufficient: some testimony on key matters such as the agency's plans for radioactive waste disposal must be subjected to cross-examination.

The Supreme Court reversed, describing the D.C. Circuit's cross-examination requirement as "Monday morning quarterbacking." A major premise of the *Vermont Yankee* opinion is the Supreme Court's belief that reviewing courts have a very limited role in creating a common law of administrative procedure to supplement or modify the procedures prescribed by the Administrative Procedure Act. In the Court's view, the APA enacted "'a formula upon which opposing social and political forces have come to rest'" (435 U.S. at 547, quoting Wong Yang Sung v. McGrath, 339 U.S. 33, 40 (1950)), and it is not the province of the judiciary to alter that legislative judgment. Moreover, the Court was skeptical that additional procedures such as cross-examination would achieve the objective of providing a more adequate record for agency decision and judicial review. On the other hand, the Court was convinced that judicially imposed hybrid rulemaking requirements would impose real costs. If the courts were free to devise procedural requirements on an ad hoc basis, "judicial review would be totally unpredictable" and the agencies would probably gravitate toward using the slow and cumbersome formal rulemaking procedures in order to avoid reversal. 435 U.S. at 546–47.

These policy rationales underlying the *Vermont Yankee* opinion have been questioned by commentators and its future seems uncertain. Compare Scalia, *Vermont Yankee, the APA, the D.C. Circuit, and the Supreme Court,* 1978 Sup.Ct.Rev. 345, with Stewart, *Vermont Yankee and the Evolution of Administrative Procedure,* 91 Harv.L.Rev. 1805 (1978). The Court's assumption that the judiciary has a very limited role to play in devising doctrines of administrative procedure may not take sufficient account of the language and history of the APA, the longstanding practices of reviewing courts, or the changes in the scope and importance of administrative rulemaking that have taken place since 1946 when the APA was enacted. While some procedural devices like cross-examination appear to have questionable utility in rulemaking, it seems clear that the lower courts were responding to legitimate concerns in trying to develop intermediate forms of rulemaking procedure. Informal rulemaking procedures often seem to give inadequate assurances of rationality and fairness, and some extremely important questions of social policy have been decided in rulemaking proceedings in recent years. It is true that the hybrid rulemaking decisions had not generated a set of uniform, understandable tests for determining when procedures additional to notice and comment would be required, but the law was evolving rapidly and greater predictability might have emerged in a reasonably short time.

Regardless of the soundness of the *Vermont Yankee* opinion, it seems clear that it has shifted the primary focus of procedural innovation from the judiciary to the other branches of government. Congress has shown considerable willingness to experiment with variations on the APA procedural models, and many of the recent grants of rulemaking authority incorporate approaches that were first developed in the hybrid rulemaking cases. See, e. g., 42 U.S.C.A. § 7607(d) (EPA approval of state implementation plans under the Clean Air Act); 15 U.S.C.A. § 57a (FTC consumer protection rulemaking). The executive branch has also been active in trying to improve rulemaking procedures as part of its regulatory reform efforts. In the Carter Administration, for example, an executive order was issued directing the cabinet departments to go beyond the APA in providing opportunities for public participation in rulemaking and to prepare a detailed cost-benefit analysis of the basis for major rules. E.O. No. 12044, 43 Fed.Reg. 12,661 (1978); see also E. O. No. 12291, 46 Fed.Reg. 13193 (Feb. 19, 1981) (similar order by President Reagan). Thus, despite the *Vermont Yankee* decision, hybrid rulemaking now appears to be an established feature of the administrative process.

C. FORM AND SCOPE OF JUDICIAL REVIEW OF RULES

Since the passage of the Administrative Procedure Act in 1946, there have been substantial changes in the form of judicial review of rules. These shifts have also affected the substance of review, and they undoubtedly contributed to the development of hybrid rulemaking described on pp. 255–62 supra. The primary issue has been the scope of review of the factual basis for a proposed rule. Rules, like all other forms of agency action reviewed under the APA, must be within the agency's jurisdiction (§ 706(2)(C)), based on consideration of proper factors (§ 706(2)(A)), and not in violation of constitutional rights (§ 706(2)(B)) or procedural requirements (§ 706(2)(D)). While these questions of law are sometimes difficult to resolve in particular cases, they have not caused the practical and conceptual difficulties that have arisen over judicial review of the facts in rulemaking.

When the APA was enacted in 1946, a party wishing to challenge an agency rule usually had two choices: he could bring an action to enjoin enforcement, or he could wait until the agency tried to impose a penalty on him for violations and then assert the rule's invalidity as a defense. Both actions were brought in the district court, where a trial could be held to determine disputed issues of fact when the challenging party wished to contest the factual support for the rule. See generally, Nathanson, *The Vermont Yankee Nuclear Power Opinion: A Masterpiece of Statutory Misinterpretation*, 16 San Diego L. Rev. 183, 190–91 (1979). Normally, the ripeness doctrine, discussed pp. 318–20 infra, prevented the challenging party from obtaining review until agency enforcement of the rule was imminent, if not already begun. Gradually, however, this system of "enforcement review" began to change.

In 1950, the Administrative Orders Review Act (the Hobbs Act), 64 Stat. 1129, 28 U.S.C.A. §§ 2341–51, shifted a substantial portion of judicial review of administrative action from the district courts to the courts of appeals. Since the appellate courts could not conduct trials, disputes over the factual basis for an administrative rule might require a transfer of the case to the district court for a hearing. Then, in 1967, the Supreme Court's decision in Abbott Laboratories v. Gardner, 387 U.S. 136 (1967), expanded the possibilities for pre-enforcement judicial review of rules. The Court effectively reversed the presumption that rules were not ripe for judicial review until they were enforced against a particular party. The *Abbott Laboratories* decision held that a rule could be challenged as soon as it was issued unless there was some special reason for the court to refuse review, such as the existence of factual questions that needed to be clarified in the context of a particular enforcement proceeding.

Finally, the decision in Citizens to Preserve Overton Park, Inc. v. Volpe, 401 U.S. 402 (1971), discussed pp. 75–76 supra, made clear that even an informal administrative decision like notice-and-comment rulemaking could be reviewed on the basis of an administrative "record" consisting of the memoranda, letters, reports, and public comments that were available to the administrator when the rule was issued. This shift toward review of rules on the administrative record rather than on the basis of evidence introduced in a court proceeding meant that the primary opportunity to contest the factual basis of the rule was in the administrative proceeding. Realization of this fact undoubtedly contributed to the development of hybrid rulemaking procedures.

Pre-enforcement review on the administrative record also created some problems for the reviewing courts, because an informal rulemaking record was fundamentally different from the adjudicative records that the judges were accustomed to reviewing. As Judge McGowan noted, an informal rulemaking record "is indistinguishable in its content from [materials collected in] the proceedings before a legislative committee hearing on a proposed bill—letters, telegrams, and written statements from proponents and opponents, including occasional oral testimony not subjected to adversary cross-examination." In reviewing this kind of record, there is a risk that the judges will "vote their policy preferences in the same

[267]

manner as does the legislator" and "thereby risk nullification of the principle that democracies are to be run in accordance with the majority will." McGowan, *Congress and the Courts*, 62 A.B.A.J. 1588, 1589–90 (1976). Thus, the basic problem in prescribing the scope of review for the factual basis of rules is to develop and apply a standard that will enable the courts to set aside arbitrary or irrational rules, yet not permit them to make essentially legislative or political judgments.

In the absence of any legislation defining the proper scope of judicial review, the rationality of administrative rules would be tested against the standards of substantive due process, in much the same way that statutes can be reviewed for arbitrariness or irrationality. This form of fact review is very limited: "if any state of facts reasonably can be conceived that would sustain [the rule], there is a presumption of the existence of that state of facts." Pacific States Box & Basket Co. v. White, 296 U.S. 176, 185 (1935), quoting Borden's Farm Products Co. v. Baldwin, 293 U.S. 194, 209 (1934). The APA and other statutes prescribing the scope of review of administrative rules generally provide for more intensive and skeptical judicial scrutiny of the facts than the deferential standard of substantive due process. However, translating those less deferential standards of review into operational terms has proven difficult.

The APA provides different fact review standards for formal and informal rulemaking. As previously noted, regulations issued after formal rulemaking proceedings are measured against the substantial evidence test. Since informal rulemaking is not conducted "on the record after opportunity for an agency hearing" within the meaning of the APA, rules which are issued after notice-and-comment proceedings fall within the residual "arbitrary and capricious" fact review standard of section 706(2)(A). This is most deferential of the three fact review standards contained in the Act.

It seems clear that a reviewing court applying the arbitrary and capricious standard will consider both the data available to the agency and the reasoning processes by which the administrator drew inferences and conclusions from the data. It is also well established that the court is supposed to determine whether the agency's factual analysis is reasonable, not whether that analysis is correct. In other words, the court cannot substitute its judgment for the agency's. In practice, however, these principles are not easy to apply, and judges have differed over the degree of administrative uncertainty or guesswork they will tolerate.

This issue sharply divided the judges of the District of Columbia Circuit in Ethyl Corp. v. EPA, 541 F.2d 1 (D.C.Cir.) (en banc), cert. denied, 426 U.S. 941 (1976), which involved a rule reducing the use of lead additives in gasoline on the ground that the additives created a health hazard. The majority was willing to defer to the agency's decision, so long as it was not based on "hunches" or "wild guesses." Judge Wright, the author of the majority opinion, concluded: "where a statute [delegating rulemaking authority] is precautionary in nature, the evidence difficult to come by, uncertain, or conflicting because it is on the frontiers of scientific knowledge, . . . and the decision that of an expert administrator, we will not demand rigorous step-by-step proof of cause and effect." 541 F.2d at 28. The four dissenters, however, were much less deferential. In their view, the administrator could not perform a rational risk assessment unless he established a chain of causation by which lead compounds moved from the gas tanks of automobiles through the environment and into the bodies of humans in sufficient concentrations to create a demonstrable risk to health. Since they did not believe that the administrator had collected sufficient data to establish this chain of causation, the dissenters would have reversed. 541 F.2d at 94–112. Judge Bazelon, while generally concurring with the majority, felt that judicial review of the facts should be extremely restrained, because "substantive review of mathematical and scientific evidence by technically illiterate judges is dangerously unreliable." At most, reviewing courts could assure rationality indirectly, by making sure that the agency had strictly complied with applicable procedural requirements and had exposed its factual support to public scrutiny. 541 F.2d at 66–67.

The difficulty of defining the proper approach to judicial review of the facts in rulemaking is compounded when the substantial evidence test is applied to rules. The APA contemplates that the substantial evidence test will apply only to rules issued after a formal rulemaking proceeding; however, in recent years the Congress has increasingly required that regulations developed through informal or hybrid rulemaking be supported by substantial evidence.

The application and meaning of the substantial evidence test may vary depending upon the kinds of issues that are involved in the rulemaking. The simplest situation is when the rule is based almost entirely upon findings of fact, like the prevailing wage determination in Wirtz v. Baldor Elec. Co., discussed pp. 253–54 supra. In that case, the agency supported the proposed rule by presenting tabulations of the data it had collected from manufacturers. However, industry representatives had conducted their own survey of some of the same companies, and had obtained markedly different results. The agency produced no credible evidence to rehabilitate its survey from the industry's attack, and it was unwilling to produce the individual company responses from which it had tabulated the prevailing wage rates. In this situation, the court concluded that there were serious questions about the reliability of the agency's factfinding, and therefore the rule was not supported by substantial evidence on the whole record.

It is fairly unusual for the results of a rulemaking to depend as heavily on findings of fact as did the minimum wage rule in the *Wirtz* case. More commonly, factual issues are mixed with policy considerations. In addition, it may not be possible for the agency to gather reliable evidence to support findings of fact, either because the state of scientific knowledge has not developed to the point where confident answers can be given, or because it would be too slow and costly to collect the necessary data. In these situations, reviewing courts have often tried to adjust the intensity of review to take account of the quality of information that is reasonably available to the agency.

An example of this approach is Industrial Union Dept., AFL–CIO v. Hodgson, 499 F.2d 467 (D.C.Cir. 1974), where the court distinguished between issues which were predominantly factual and those which were basically policy judgments. The Occupational Safety and Health Administration had issued a standard limiting workers' exposure to asbestos dust, and the record revealed considerable technical dispute over both the feasibility of industry compliance with the rule and the nature and magnitude of the risks to workers. In applying the substantial evidence test to this rule, the court noted that some of the factual determinations involved matters on which ample information was available, and the agency's task "consisted primarily of evaluating the data and drawing conclusions from it." These findings were reviewed in the normal manner under the substantial evidence test. On the other hand, some of the issues in the proceeding were "on the frontiers of scientific knowledge, and consequently as to them insufficient scientific data is presently available to make a fully informed factual determination." Id. at 474. For these issues, the agency was required to exercise a considerable measure of policymaking discretion. "[W]here the facts alone do not provide the answer," the court observed, the administrator "should so state and go on to identify the considerations he found persuasive." The reviewing court would then examine this decision "to see whether the agency, given an essentially legislative task to perform, carried it out in a manner calculated to negate the dangers of arbitrariness and irrationality." Id. at 475, 476.

A plurality of the Supreme Court took a similar approach in reviewing another occupational health rule, this time involving the chemical benzene, in Industrial Union Department, AFL–CIO v. American Petroleum Institute, 100 S.Ct. 2844, 2871 (1980). The plurality concluded that the substantial evidence test did not permit the administrator to make a pure policy judgment, wholly unsupported by fact. On the other hand, he was not required to support his finding "with anything approaching scientific certainty"; it would be sufficient under the substantial evidence test if the finding of risk was supported by "a body of reputable scientific thought."

If reviewing courts adjust the intensity of judicial review to take account of the quality of the information that is reasonably available to the administrator, then as a practical matter the substantial evidence test and the arbitrary and capricious standard tend to converge. See generally DeLong, *Informal Rulemaking and the Integration of Law and Policy*, 65 U.Va.L.Rev. 257, 284–89 (1979). In rulemaking, as in other areas of judicial review, the attitude with which the court approaches the administrative record may have more practical significance than the verbal formulas defining the scope of review. The trend in recent years seems to be away from judicial deference toward a much closer and more skeptical probing of the basis for administrative rules.

Judicial review of the factual support for agency rules has increasingly been supplemented by executive branch review. During the Carter Administration the Regulatory Analysis Review Group in the White House and the Regulatory Council, which was composed of the heads of several executive departments and agencies, began reviewing major rules to make sure that the agency had adequately analyzed the costs and benefits of the proposed regulation. Congress has also shown increasing interest in reviewing particular rules through the legislative veto mechanism, discussed pp. 38–39 supra. However, this form of review would be more concerned with the political acceptability of the rule than with its factual basis. The development of these new review mechanisms, along with the trend toward increased judicial scrutiny of the basis for administrative rules, indicates that agencies may be held to higher standards of rationality and accountability as the scope and impact of their delegated powers increase.

CHAPTER X

PROCEDURAL SHORTCUTS

Statutes frequently confer broad rights to a trial-type hearing on those who are subject to regulation, particularly when the agency seeks to modify a license or certificate. Administrative hearings can be costly in time, manpower, and other resources, and they sometimes make only a marginal contribution to the quality of information available or to the acceptability of the final decision. Thus, agencies often have an incentive to develop procedural techniques for avoiding unnecessary hearings or of minimizing the issues that will be considered in a formal adjudication. One method of accomplishing this to to issue detailed substantive rules, and then deny a hearing to anyone who fails to raise a disputed issue under the amended standard in the same manner that federal courts grant summary judgment when there is no disputed issue of material fact. For example, the Federal Trade Commission might issue a rule stating that it is a deceptive practice to sell gasoline without posting the octane rating on the pump. In later adjudications brought against alleged violators, the only triable issue would be whether the respondent had failed to post the required information; the deceptiveness of a failure to disclose would already have been established by the rule.

In other situations, the agency may take a different kind of procedural shortcut by making policy in an individual adjudication rather than in a rulemaking proceeding. There may be a variety of practical reasons for this seemingly anomalous choice. The agency may not want to take on the whole industry at one time in a general rulemaking proceeding, or it may fear public and congressional criticism if it establishes a clear general policy. It may feel the need for considering the policy first in a concrete fact situation, building rules only incrementally in the fashion of common law courts. Alternatively, the agency may not have focused on the policy question until the final stages of an adjudication, when the cost and delay of starting a new proceeding would be considerable.

When the agency attempts to use either kind of procedural shortcut, an adversely affected party may feel that he is being treated unfairly because he has been denied the kind of proceeding contemplated by the Administrative Procedure Act. The general structure of the APA implies that rules of general applicability and future effect should be developed in rulemaking proceedings, while trial-type hearings should be held when statutes require formal hearings before an order is issued against an individual party. Yet the APA does not compel an administrator to use one form of proceeding rather than the other; this matter is left to the more particular statutes delegating authority to the agency. When those statutes simply give the administrator authority both to issue rules and to adjudicate particular cases, then the general rule is well established: "the choice between proceeding by general rule or by individual, ad hoc litigation is one that lies primarily in the informed discretion of the administrative agency." SEC v. Chenery Corp., 332 U.S. 194, 203 (1947) (*Chenery II*). In the years since the *Chenery* decision, however, the courts have added a considerable gloss to that general principle.

A. USE OF SUBSTANTIVE RULES TO FORECLOSE HEARINGS

Early experiments in using the rulemaking power to streamline adjudications were initiated by licensing agencies operating under broad public interest standards. The Federal Communications Commission, for example, is authorized to grant broadcast licenses as "the public interest, convenience, and necessity" may dictate, and the agency is required to hold a "full hearing"—a formal adjudication under the APA—before refusing a license application. In United States v. Storer Broadcasting Co., 351 U.S. 192 (1956), the Commission had issued multiple ownership rules reducing the number of television outlets that could be controlled by one licensee. Storer, which exceeded the new maximum limit, had applied for an additional license before the rule became final, but the FCC nonetheless dismissed the application as not conforming to the new rule. Storer claimed that this procedure was a denial of its statutory right to a full hearing, but the Supreme Court held that the rule was valid and therefore the denial of a trial-type hearing was proper.

Apart from the particular statutes at issue in the *Storer* opinion, there are strong functional arguments supporting the result. The decision to impose the multiple ownership limitation on licensees was essentially a policy judgment to foster diversity in programming by avoiding overconcentration of broadcast facilities in a few powerful companies. This issue is not peculiarly suited to determination in oral hearings where witness testimony and documentary exhibits are introduced and subjected to cross-examination. Rulemaking procedure provides adequate assurance that all interested parties will be given notice and an opportunity to submit relevant data, views, and arguments. If there is a need to accommodate unique factual circumstances, the rule may include a waiver provision, as the multiple ownership rule did. The use of the rulemaking power to give content to a vague statutory standard clearly serves the interests of efficiency and predictability, with no real loss to the accuracy of decision or fairness to the regulated parties.

Subsequent decisions made clear that the *Storer* principle was not limited to the communications field. In FPC v. Texaco, Inc., 377 U.S. 33 (1964), the Court held that a statutory hearing requirement did not prevent the FPC (predecessor to the Federal Energy Regulatory Commission) from using rulemaking to impose conditions on the grant of gas pipeline certificates and then "barring at the threshold those who neither measure up to them nor show reasons why in the public interest the rule should be waived." The D.C. Circuit suggested a possible qualification to the *Storer* principle in the "blocked space case," American Airlines, Inc. v. CAB, 359 F.2d 624 (D.C.Cir.) (en banc), cert. denied, 385 U.S. 843 (1966). The CAB had issued a rule that effectively modified some air carriers' certificates specifying the kinds of cargos they could transport. Despite a statutory requirement that trial-type hearings be held before certificates were modified, the court held these rulemaking procedures acceptable. The majority placed considerable emphasis on the fact that the protesting airlines had made no showing of a particular need for trial procedures. If such a showing had been made, the court indicated, then due process might require that some trial procedures be incorporated into the rulemaking proceeding. However, subsequent decisions of the Supreme Court have sharply limited, if not completely rejected, this gloss on the *Storer* principle. See pp. 256–64 supra. For the time being, at least, the principal limitations on the agencies' power to use rulemaking to simplify or avoid adjudications are the statutory delegations of authority in particular regulatory programs.

B. SUMMARY JUDGMENT

Once an agency has established clear standards governing individual adjudication, it may seek to avoid unnecessary hearings by adopting a summary judgment procedure. For the most part, administrative summary judgment rules are similar to Rule 56 of the Federal Rules of Civil Procedure: a judgment on the merits may be rendered without hearing when there is no genuine issue of material fact to be tried.[1]

The Food and Drug Administration has been the most active agency in experimenting with the summary judgment device, largely because of workload pressures created by statutory amendments.[2] Since 1938, the FDA has been empowered to evaluate the safety of therapeutic drugs before granting a "new drug approval" (NDA) or license to market the product. In 1962, the statute was amended to require that the manufacturer demonstrate the drug's effectiveness as well as its safety. The drug

1. See generally Gellhorn & Robinson, *Summary Judgment in Administrative Adjudication*, 84 Harv.L.Rev. 612 (1971).
2. See R. Merrill & P. Hutt, *Food and Drug Law* 415–25 (1980).

efficacy amendments directed the FDA to withdraw approval of an NDA if the manufacturer failed to produce "substantial evidence" of the drug's effects; however, it also required the agency to give "due notice and opportunity for hearing" before withdrawing approval. When these amendments were passed, NDA's had been granted to approximately 4,000 drugs involving more than 16,000 claims of effectiveness.

To cope with this large backlog, the FDA set up a series of scientific advisory panels to review the available studies on each drug, and to prepare a report on its effectiveness. The agency also issued rules defining "substantial evidence" narrowly to mean only adequate and well controlled clinical studies using standard experimental methodology; anecdotal reports from sources such as practicing physicians were not considered. Finally, FDA promulgated a summary judgment rule which stipulated that an applicant desiring a hearing had to submit an analysis of the factual matters he was prepared to prove. If it appeared that there was no "genuine and substantial issue of fact," the request for hearing would be denied.

This procedure was challenged by drug companies who wanted a full evidentiary hearing before their products were removed from the market. In Weinberger v. Hynson, Westcott & Dunning, Inc., 412 U.S. 609 (1973), the Supreme Court generally upheld the FDA's summary judgment practice. A primary factor in the Court's rationale was the common sense notion that it would be pointless to hold a hearing if the challenging party had no chance of succeeding on the merits. It was also clear that the FDA could not accomplish its statutory mission of getting ineffective drugs off the market if it were required to grant a trial-type hearing on every claim, however insubstantial. However, the Court imposed some significant limitations on the use of summary judgment. It suggested that the regulations had to be "precise" in order to cut off an applicant's hearing rights. Thus, the Court distinguished between a study that was "totally deficient" in proper scientific controls, and one in which the agency had to exercise "discretion or subjective judgment" in determining whether the controls were adequate. In the latter case, "it might not be proper to deny a hearing." 412 U.S. at 621 n. 17. In addition, the Court held, without any discussion or analysis, that the drug company's submissions had been sufficient to warrant a hearing. The result of these qualifications was considerable uncertainty about the proper scope of administrative summary judgment. Some lower courts have taken the Supreme Court's reference to "precision" in the applicable standards to mean that the agency must give adequate notice specifying the nature of the facts on which it proposes to take action, and give the affected party an opportunity to respond, before it grants summary judgment. Hess & Clark v. FDA, 495 F.2d 975 (D.C.Cir. 1974).

Apart from the FDA, it appears that the agencies generally have not made extensive use of the summary judgment device. One reason may be the uncertainties resulting from the Supreme Court's decision in *Hynson, Westcott.* Without better guidance, it remains difficult to determine when a standard is sufficiently "precise," and it is doubtful that many agencies would be able to frame their standards as exactly as the FDA, which relies on generally accepted scientific principles of proof. It may also be significant that most of the adjudicating agencies have extensive informal mechanisms for resolving cases by voluntary compliance or consent settlement. When a case is reasonably clear on the facts, these mechanisms may often serve the same functions that summary judgment does in court litigation.

C. FORMULATION OF POLICY IN ADJUDICATION

Administrative agencies have frequently been criticized for relying too heavily on case-by-case adjudication to formulate policy, rather than using their rulemaking powers. The National Labor Relations Board has been one of the most reluctant to resort to rulemaking, and in several instances court challenges have been brought seeking to compel the Board to use rulemaking procedures when it is contemplating a major shift in policy. The Board's adjudicative powers extend to disputes between labor and management over union elections to select a collective bargaining representative. In NLRB v. Wyman-Gordon Co., 394 U.S. 759 (1969), the Board had ordered an election, and also had ordered the company to provide the union organizers with a list of the names and addresses of employees eligible to vote in the election. The list was known as an "Excelsior list," in reference to an earlier agency adjudication where the Board had established this requirement, but made it applicable only in future cases. Wyman-Gordon claimed that this "rule" was invalid because it had not been adopted in accordance with the APA rulemaking procedures. The NLRB then resorted to the subpoena power to procure a list, and when the company still resisted, it brought an enforcement action.

When the case reached the Supreme Court, the Justices were openly criticial of the NLRB's failure to use rulemaking to establish the Excelsior list requirement. The majority noted that the APA's rulemaking procedures "were designed to assure fairness and mature consideration of rules of general application. They may not be avoided by the process of making rules in the course of adjudicatory proceedings." Notwithstanding this strong language, however, the Court's holding supported the NLRB. A key factor was whether the Excelsior rule was immediately binding upon the affected companies, in the sense that a violation of the rule would accrue penalties; this was what distinguished a rule from a precedent. Since the obligation to obey did not come into play until after the agency had issued its order backed by the subpoena power, the administrative order was upheld.

This concern with the policy's effect upon private conduct was reiterated when the issue of choice between adjudication and rulemaking returned to the Court in *NLRB v. Bell Aerospace Co.*, 416 U.S. 267 (1974). The agency had changed its policy by expanding the category of "managerial employees" who were protected by the Act's rights to organize and bargain collectively. As in *Wyman-Gordon*, the company argued that a significant policy change of this nature had to be made in rulemaking rather than in an individual adjudication. Once again, the Supreme Court disagreed. The company had not shown any retroactivity problem with the policy change; no fines or damages were being imposed "for past actions taken in good faith reliance on Board pronouncements," and no other industry reliance interest was apparent. Thus, the general *Chenery II* principle that agencies have discretion to proceed by adjudication or rulemaking governed. See also p. 276 supra.

In recent years, the NLRB's insistence on making policy solely through case-by-case adjudication has become increasingly aberrational among federal agencies generally. Some agencies have been required by statute to use rulemaking procedures for important policy decisions; others have found it necessary to rely heavily on rulemaking in order to accomplish their statutory objectives; and some have apparently been convinced that rulemaking is a fairer and more efficient method of formulating general policy. See generally pp. 237–40 supra. Thus, unless rulemaking procedures become unduly cumbersome or difficult for the agencies, the traditional tendency to use individual cases as the vehicle for major policy decisions may be largely a thing of the past.[3]

3. But see Note, *NLRB Rulemaking: Political Reality versus Procedural Fairness,* 89 Yale L.J. 982 (1980) (suggesting that the NLRB's practice of using adjudication rather than rulemaking to decide sensitive issues where there is no consensus has limited agency exposure to political attack).

CHAPTER XI

OBTAINING JUDICIAL REVIEW

A party seeking court reversal of an administrative decision may be met at the threshold with a series of technical defenses that will bar the court from reaching the merits of his claim. This complex and often overlapping set of doctrines is intended primarily to define the proper boundaries between courts and agencies—that is, to keep the courts from exceeding the limits of their institutional competence and intruding too deeply into the workings of the other branches of government. For example, administrators often make political or bargained decisions which are not confined by legal standards. When this happens, a court may have no law to apply, and review would be inappropriate. Another question as to the propriety of review may arise when a party tries to obtain a judicial reversal of a preliminary agency decision, such as the opening of an investigation or the issuance of a complaint. In this situation, premature judicial review could frustrate or delay the administrative process, and waste judicial resources. To deal with these kinds of problems, doctrines such as ripeness, exhaustion of admininstrative remedies, and nonreviewability have been developed. These doctrines are partly statutory and partly judge-made; in addition, some of the rules limiting judicial review are based upon constitutional limitations on the power of the courts.

A. JURISDICTION: THE METHODS OF REVIEW

Any decision that a court cannot reach the merits of a litigant's claim could be described as "jurisdictional," and occasionally a loose reference to "lack of jurisdiction" will be found when the real basis of the decision is lack of standing to sue, or failure to exhaust administrative remedies, or one of the other technical defenses to judicial review. This lax usage can be misleading: particularly in the federal system, the concept of jurisdiction is more properly confined to questions concerning the power of the court to hear and decide a particular type of case. The federal courts are courts of limited rather than general jurisdiction; under Article III of the Constitution, Congress has broad power to establish lower federal courts and define the kinds of cases they may hear. Thus, the preliminary inquiry in any attempt to obtain judicial review in the federal system is what statutory basis should be invoked.

1. "NONSTATUTORY" REVIEW

One common form of judicial review is generally referred to as "nonstatutory" review. Technically this is a misnomer because all judicial review must be based upon some statutory or constitutional grant of subject matter jurisdiction. The term "nonstatutory" does, however, suggest the distinctive features of this mode of review: it grew out of the old common law system of writs, and it exists outside the system of "statutory" review which Congress normally creates when it delegates power to an agency. In other words, nonstatutory review is based on some general grant of jurisdiction to the federal courts; by contrast statutory review is tailored to the particular regulatory program or even to a particular kind of decision within a regulatory program.

Before the modern system of civil procedure was developed, much judicial review of administrative action took place through the common law writs of mandamus, certiorari, and the like. That tradition persists in the Mandamus and Venue Act, 28 U.S.C.A. § 1361, which permits the federal district courts to hear suits "in the nature of mandamus to compel an officer or employee of the United States or any agency thereof to perform a duty owed to the plaintiff." Since this provision applies only when the agency decision is "ministerial" or nondiscretionary, its utility is fairly limited. Other nonstatutory review provisions do not suffer from this defect. The general federal question statute, 28 U.S.C.A. § 1331, grants the federal courts jurisdiction to hear cases "arising under" the Constitution and laws of the United States. A 1980 amendment to this provision wholly eliminated the requirement that the "amount in controversy" be $10,000 or more.[1] Now, any action involving a federal question (including those brought against the United States or its officers or agencies) may be brought without regard to the dollar value of the plaintiff's

---

1. Pub.L. 96–486 (Dec. 1, 1980), amending 28 U.S.C.A. § 1331. (However, the legislation amended the Consumer Product Safety Act to retain the $10,000 amount in controversy requirement for suits based on knowing violations of consumer product safety rules. See 15 U.S.C.A. § 2072(b).) This completes the change made in 1976 creating an exception to the $10,000 requirement in cases where the United States or its officers or agencies are defendants.

claim. In addition to actions to compel, enjoin, or set aside agency action, a litigant may seek to recover damages for harm inflicted by an administrative agency. This form of nonstatutory review is discussed separately below; see pp. 290–300 infra.

Until recently, there was a question as to whether the Administrative Procedure Act itself provided a basis for nonstatutory review. Section 704 of the APA broadly proclaims that "final agency action for which there is no adequate remedy in a court [is] subject to judicial review," and section 702 states without qualification that a person who is "adversely affected or aggrieved by agency action . . . is entitled to judicial review thereof." Despite this promise of judicial redress for bureaucratic wrongs, however, the Supreme Court has held that the APA is not an independent grant of jurisdiction; it merely tells the reviewing court what to do after it has obtained jurisdiction under some other statute. Califano v. Sanders, 430 U.S. 99 (1977). With the elimination of the amount in controversy requirement from the federal question statute, however, this restrictive interpretation no longer has practical effect on the availability of review.

2. ENFORCEMENT OF ADMINISTRATIVE ORDERS

At one time administrative orders were not self-operative. If the respondent did not comply voluntarily, the agency had to bring a suit for enforcement. Even then the order was not binding until judicially enforced. In every instance, the respondent was assured judicial scrutiny of the order—whether it was properly made and within the scope of the agency's authority.

This two-step procedure—requiring proof before the agency of the violation and before the court of the regularity of the agency's proceeding—proved cumbersome and unnecessarily time-consuming. It required that an agency seek judicial enforcement and meet the standards of judicial review even though the parties did not seriously object to the order. It also allowed the respondent which the agency had found to be violating the rule or regulation to continue the objectionable practices until the judicial order was issued. Once the agency's order was judicially approved, however, the court's order could be enforced by contempt procedures. Thus, enforcement was both too late and too harsh when it finally occurred. Reforms have now eliminated automatic judicial review. Except for the NLRB, most federal administrative orders are final unless appealed within a set time period (usually 60 days). In addition, failure to comply with an order is subject to statutory penalty. In other words, the order is self-executing unless the respondent takes immediate action to appeal.

3. OTHER "STATUTORY" REVIEW

Since they are individually enacted as part of the legislation prescribing the powers of an agency, special statutory review proceedings can take a variety of forms. Most commonly, however, they follow the pattern set by the Federal Trade Commission Act in 1914: after the agency's decision becomes final, an interested person may file a petition to review in a federal court of appeals. The court reviews the decision on the basis of the record compiled by the administrator, and if the agency action has violated the APA, some other statute, or the Constitution, the reviewing court may vacate the decision or remand it for further proceedings.

4. DAMAGE ACTIONS

Litigants often seek more than a simple reversal of an agency's decision. They may want compensation from the government for injuries suffered as a result of illegal actions by public officials, or they may claim that a private party is liable in damages for violating laws or rules administered by a regulatory agency. Defendants also may inject questions of Administrative Law into a damage action, by claiming that an issue must be referred to an expert agency for decision before the court imposes liability. Several distinct bodies of doctrine have arisen to deal with these kinds of claims.

a. *The Federal Tort Claims Act.*

One of the oldest forms of nonstatutory review of administrative action is a tort suit against the official who allegedly committed a violation of law. In this form of action, the plaintiff must allege that the official took action which was not justified by his legal authority, and which would be compensable in damages if it had been committed by a private party. To succeed in such a claim, the plaintiff must avoid the bar of the sovereign immunity doctrine.

Sovereign immunity, which has been criticized as an archiac and unjust principle of law, holds that the government cannot be sued without its consent. The primary justification for the retention of the sovereign immunity doctrine is that it prevents the courts from interfering unduly with the operations of the executive branch. While there is some force to this point, it is doubtful that a blanket exemption of all government actions from liability is necessary to accomplish that goal. This kind of analysis has increasingly persuaded legislatures to expand the range of claims for which injured persons can seek redress against the government. In the federal system, the most important of these statutory waivers of sovereign immunity is the Federal Tort Claims Act, 28 U.S.C.A. § 2860(h).

As originally enacted in 1946, the Federal Tort Claims Act contained broad exceptions that left much of the sovereign immunity doctrine intact. One of these exceptions denied tort liability for a wide variety of intentional torts, including assault, battery, false arrest, libel, and malicious prosecution. In 1974, this exclusion was narrowed considerably to permit recovery for intentional torts committed by law enforcement officers. 88 Stat. 50. Actions for defamation, misrepresentation, deceit, and interference with contract rights are still barred, however. The second broad exception to the Act is potentially more significant in terms of the number and importance of unlawful agency actions that may be immunized from review: suits are barred if the responsible officials are exercising a "discretionary function," regardless of whether thay have abused their discretion. 28 U.S.C.A. § 2680(a). This vague exemption has proved difficult to apply, though the more recent decisions seem to have restricted the definition of "discretionary functions" somewhat. Compare Dalehite

v. United States, 346 U.S. 15 (1953) (decision to produce explosive substance for use as fertilizer in foreign aid program, and negligence in producing, packaging, and handling the materials, not actionable under discretionary function exemption), with Indian Towing Co. v. United States, 350 U.S. 61 (1955) (suit for shipwreck caused by Coast Guard's negligent failure to maintain a beacon light not barred by discretionary function exemption) and Rayonier, Inc. v. United States, 352 U.S. 315 (1957) (plaintiff suffering property damage as a result of the Forest Service's negligence in fighting a fire not barred from recovery by discretionary function exemption).

b.   *Violations of Constitutional Rights.*

A separate (and quite extensive) body of doctrine dealing with compensation for governmentally inflicted injuries applies when the plaintiff claims that an agency or official has violated his constitutional rights. Although most of the damage litigation has been brought against state officials under the Civil Rights Act of 1871, 42 U.S.C.A. § 1983, the Supreme Court has held that comparable claims against federal officials arise directly under the Constitution. This right was recognized in Bivens v. Six Unknown Named Agents of the Federal Bureau of Narcotics, 403 U.S. 388 (1971), where the Court held that an individual could bring a suit under the Fourth Amendment to recover for injuries resulting from the actions of federal narcotics agents during an unlawful search of his apartment. However, the Court in *Bivens* left open the question of whether there was some residual immunity for official action taken in good faith within the scope of the officer's authority.

When that issue was finally decided in Butz v. Economou, 438 U.S. 478 (1978), the Court adopted the same "privileges" or immunity defenses it has applied to state officials in damage actions under the Civil Rights Act. Balancing the injustice of denying redress to an injured plaintiff against the injustice of imposing liability on an official who had exercised his discretion in good faith, and taking account of the risk that liability would make administrators overly cautious in reaching important decisions, the Court concluded that the scope of official immunity depended upon the kind of function the official was performing. Executive officers exercising discretion were accorded only a qualified immunity: an official would be protected from liability only if he had a good faith belief that his conduct was lawful, and the belief was reasonable. However, administrators exercising quasi-judicial powers were given a broader immunity. Both the decisionmakers and the prosecuting staff in agency adjudications were given absolute immunity for actions taken in the course of their quasi-judicial functions. The Court felt that this complete immunity was necessary to assure that "judges, advocates, and witnesses can perform their respective functions without harassment or intimidation." Adjudications decide conflicting claims of rights and liabilities, and therefore create winners and losers; as a result, "[t]he loser in one forum will frequently seek another, charging the participants in the first with unconstitutional animus." 438 U.S. at 512. With the losing party thus motivated to pursue litigation, the responsible officials might become wary of prosecuting cases vigorously or ruling against alleged violators if they knew that they could be subjected to damage liability. At the same time, absolute immunity for officers exercising judicial functions would not be likely to cause many unredressed injuries, because adjudicative proceedings are less likely to give rise to constitutional violations than other forms of administrative action. Because trial-type hearings are designed to assure the fairness of the process and the accuracy and impartiality of the result, "there is a less pressing need for individual suits to correct constitutional error." Id.

c. *Rights of Private Action.*

In some areas of law, regulation by government agencies and systems of private liability overlap. One of the oldest and most familiar examples of the use of private remedies to supplement a regulatory program is the antitrust laws: both the Federal Trade Commission and the Department of Justice can take administrative action or bring cases in court to prohibit anticompetitive activities, and at the same time private parties can bring actions to recover treble damages for injuries they may have suffered as a result of illegal conduct. In addition, a few regulatory statutes contain "citizen suit" provisions which authorize a private person to enforce agency rules or standards. Section 304 of the Clean Air Act, 42 U.S.C.A. § 7604, adopts this approach. It permits any person to bring a civil suit against any government official or private party who is claimed to be violating air pollution standards established under the Act. The purpose of such private actions to enforce regulatory statutes is twofold: it provides redress for injured parties who were supposed to be protected by the regulatory program, and it supplements government resources by increasing the chances that a violator will be detected and sanctioned. However, there is risk that private enforcement actions will be used to harass defendants, or will interfere with the responsible agency's efforts to develop a coherent program of enforcement. The Clean Air Act deals with this latter problem in part by requiring that a party must give EPA 60 days prior notice of his intent to bring a citizen suit. If EPA then initiates an enforcement action of its own, the citizen suit is barred; if the private action goes forward, then EPA has a right to intervene; but it does not allow the EPA to bar the private suit without bringing its own enforcement action.

Statutory provision for citizen suits is relatively new and fairly uncommon. More frequently, the statute simply declares certain kinds of conduct illegal, and then gives an agency power to enforce the prohibition. In this situation, an intended beneficiary of the program may seek a private damage remedy under the statute, claiming that there is an "implied right of private action." Thus, in J. I. Case Co. v. Borak, 377 U.S. 426 (1964), the Court was called upon to interpret a statute which provided that "it shall be unlawful for any person" to solicit shareholder proxies in violation of SEC rules. A stockholder who had suffered financial losses as a result of a merger which had been effected through a misleading proxy statement—which allegedly violated the SEC's rules—brought a damage action against the company. Even though the relevant section of the statute made no provision for private damage remedies, the Court held that an action could be implied because the statute was designed to protect investors like the plaintiff and the availability of damage remedies would contribute to the SEC's enforcement effort.

The opposite result was reached in Cort v. Ash, 422 U.S. 66 (1975), where stockholders sought to imply a private action against the corporation under a criminal statute prohibiting corporations from making campaign contributions in presidential elections. In contrast to the system of regulation involved in *Case v. Borak*, the language and legislative history of the campaign finance law did not reflect any congressional intent to protect shareholders; rather, the Act was designed to reduce the influence of monied interests in election campaigns. Moreover, the Court felt that the implication of private remedies would not necessarily contribute to this goal. Damages would not cure the harm that might have been done in the election, and it would not necessarily deter management from making illegal contributions, since the damage remedy "would only permit directors in effect to 'borrow' corporate funds for a time." 422 U.S. at 84. Thus, the plaintiff was limited to whatever remedies for breach of fiduciary duty or ultra vires action by the corporation's board of directors existed under state law. As these two cases suggest, the criteria for implying private rights of action under regulatory statutes are amorphous, and it is too early to predict how they will be applied in future cases. See also Cannon v. University of Chicago, 441 U.S. 677 (1979) (private right of action implied under Education Amendments of 1972 for female applicant allegedly denied admission to medical school because of her sex).

d. *Primary Jurisdiction.*

When a private party brings a private damage action against a regulated person or company based on activities that are also subject to control by the agency, the question may arise as to whether the court should refrain from deciding the case until the agency has had a chance to review the controversy. The primary jurisdiction doctrine is designed to define the situations when the court should refer the matter to the agency for an initial determination.[2]

There are two principal reasons for requiring a private litigant to resort to the administrative process before pursuing his damage claim: the litigation may involve issues of fact which are beyond the conventional experience and expertise of judges, or the decision may require the exercise of administrative discretion under broad statutory standards. See Far East Conference v. United States, 342 U.S. 570 (1952). The requirement of preliminary decision by the agency also serves the goal of national uniformity in regulatory programs. If the courts were free to decide unresolved matters of law and policy without benefit of the agency's position, the possibilities of inconsistent or wrong decisions might increase. See, e. g., Texas & Pac. R. R. Co. v. Abilene Cotton Oil Co., 204 U.S. 426 (1907) (dispute over rates charged by a regulated carrier was within the primary jurisdiction of the ICC, in part because a major objective of the statute creating the ICC was to achieve national uniformity of rates).

2. While the doctrine of primary jurisdiction generally arises in private damage actions, it is not so confined. For example, it has been applied to government action under the antitrust laws to require that the case be submitted first to the Federal Maritime Commission which has general regulatory authority over rate agreements among ocean shipping lines. Far East Conference v. United States, 342 U.S. 570 (1952).

On the other hand, if an issue raised in the action falls outside the ambit of the agency's special expertise or unique authority, the claim will not be barred by the primary jurisdiction doctrine. An airline which had the bad luck or bad judgment to "bump" Ralph Nader from a flight on which he held a confirmed reservation learned this lesson in Nader v. Allegheny Airlines, Inc., 426 U.S. 290 (1976). Nader brought a damage action for fraudulent misrepresentation, claiming that the airline had deceptively failed to disclose that it might "overbook" its flights and deny boarding to passengers with confirmed reservations. One of the airline's defenses was that the question fell within the primary jurisdiction of the Civil Aeronautics Board because that agency had power to issue cease and desist orders against regulated carriers which had engaged in "unfair or deceptive practices." The Supreme Court disagreed. The CAB's statutory power to abate deceptive practices was not synonymous with common law fraud and misrepresentation, and the Board had no power to immunize carriers from this kind of liability. More significantly, the issue was not one on which an accurate decision "could be facilitated by an informed evaluation of the economics or technology of the regulated industry"; rather, the common law fraud standards "are within the conventional competence of the courts, and the judgment of a technically expert body is not likely to be helpful in the application of these standards to the facts of this case." Id. at 305–06.

These cases suggest several facets of the doctrine of primary jurisdiction. First, it is most likely to be applied in the intensively regulated industries where agencies control entry, price, and nature and quality of service than in industries that are subject to less extensive controls. Even in these intensively regulated industries, however, not all questions which arise in private litigation will fall within the doctrine: primary jurisdiction is most likely to apply when the questions are factual rather than legal, or discretionary rather than governed by detailed rules. In these areas, the need for administrative expertise is most pressing. Second, primary jurisdiction is a one-way doctrine protecting only the agency's jurisdiction. It is applied by a court to stay or dismiss a proceeding before it until the agency can act upon the matter; it is not applied by agencies or courts to defer or dismiss agency action until a court has decided a question—even if the doctrine ordinarily would not be invoked if the case had been presented first to a court. Third, the doctrine only allocates jurisdictional priority. Once the agency renders its decision, recourse to the courts—that is, judicial review of agency action— is still available. Primary jurisdiction, in brief, does not assign exclusive jurisdiction between courts and agencies; it is only one of several techniques used to set an appropriate time for judicial review. Fourth, the principal justification for the doctrine of primary jurisdiction is to coordinate the work of agencies and courts. Their activities are most likely to come into conflict where the agency's regulation is pervasive and coordinated, and uniform interpretations are necessary to assure effective regulation. However, application of the doctrine does not assure uniformity or prevent agency inconsistency. Reviewing courts do not always interpret legal questions or identify fact questions identically.

Nor does the Supreme Court resolve every conflict among the circuits. Primary jurisdiction serves merely to avoid major conflicts, not to eliminate every possible conflict or inconsistency. The doctrine of primary jurisdiction is designed to take advantage of whatever contribution the agency can make within its area of specialization. It also seems true that allowing the agency the first opportunity to decide an issue (or case) will in practice give it the final voice in most cases.

B. NONREVIEWABILITY: STATUTORY PRE-CLUSION AND "COMMITTED TO AGENCY DISCRETION"

Statutes giving courts the jurisdiction to review administrative action are frequently drafted in very broad terms. The general federal question statute, 28 U.S. C.A. § 1331, for example, permits the courts to hear any claim "arising under" the Constitution or laws of the United States. This language literally seems to make every decision made by an agency pursuant to its delegated authority susceptible to judicial review. Yet in some instances there are good reasons to deny judicial review altogether, despite the broad sweep of the jurisdictional statutes. Two such exceptions to the general availability of judicial review are codified in section 701 of the APA. Under this provision, judicial review is not available when "statutes preclude review" or the decision is "committed to agency discretion by law." The first of these doctrines is primarily concerned with formal expressions of legislative intent, while the latter deals primarily with functional reasons why review would be impossible, or harmful.

1. STATUTORY PRECLUSION OF REVIEW

Since Congress controls the jurisdiction of the federal courts, it is free to write into statutes particular exceptions to the general availability of judicial review— in other words, to "preclude" judicial review by statute. Courts are bound to follow these congressional directives so long as they are constitutional, but statutory preclusions run counter to a strong modern trend toward making judicial review freely available. In Abbott Laboratories v. Gardner, 387 U.S. 136 (1967), the Supreme Court formally acknowledged this presumption of reviewability. It held that judicial review of final agency action "will not be cut off unless there is persuasive reason to believe that [this] was the intention of Congress." Congressional intent to preclude review had to be demonstrated by "clear and convincing evidence." In the contemporary administrative state, judicial review serves two important social functions: it provides redress for persons who have been harmed by arbitrary or illegal government action, and it serves to keep the agencies faithful to the policy objectives and procedural safeguards established by the legislature.

The strength of the presumption of reviewability is reflected in the extraordinary feats of statutory constuction that courts have performed to avoid a conclusion that statutes had precluded judicial review. For example, veterans' benefits have long been administered under statutes which provided varying degrees of insulation from judicial scrutiny. In Tracy v. Gleason, 379 F.2d 469 (D.C.Cir. 1967), the court held that a statute which barred review of "any question of law or fact concerning a claim for benefits or payments under any law administered by the Veterans Administration" did not bar a suit by a veteran's estate alleging that the VA had wrongfully terminated the decedent's benefits. The court reached this result by narrowly interpreting the word "claim" in the preclusion statute: despite the fact that the custom within the agency was to call any request for benefits a "claim," the statutory term was interpreted as covering only initial applications for benefits and not forfeitures of adjudicated awards. Congress responded to this decision by amending the statute to state its intention to prevent review of VA determinations in even clearer terms. The amended statute directed that "the decisions of the Administrator on any question of law or fact under any law administered by the Veterans Administration providing benefits for veterans and their dependents or survivors shall be final and conclusive and no . . . court . . . shall have power or jurisdiction to review any such decision." 84 Stat. 790 (1970). Despite this extraordinarily clear expression of Congressional intent, the Supreme Court nevertheless found a way to grant limited review in Johnson v. Robison, 415 U.S. 361 (1974). The claimant Robison was a conscientious objector who had performed alternative service, as required by the Selective Service law. The VA had concluded that he was ineligible for assistance under a statute which provided educational assistance to veterans who had "served on active duty." Robison asserted that this interpretation denied his constitutional rights to equal protection of the laws and free exercise of religion. The Court held that he escaped the statutory preclusion because he was not seeking review of an administrative decision under the statute, but rather was challenging the constitutionality of the statute itself.

The *Robison* opinion reflects a tendency of contemporary reviewing courts to seek a functional or institutional reason for prohibiting review, and to bar litigants only when there is a valid policy justification. The legislative history of the statutory preclusion for VA decisions seemed to serve two policy goals: preventing burdens on the courts and the agency, and assuring national uniformity in the application of VA standards and policies. The Court reasoned that neither justification applied to constitutional claims like Robison's: the number of constitutional attacks was likely to be small, and the VA admittedly had no special competence in determining constitutional rights. See generally Rabin, *Preclusion of Judicial Review in the Processing of Claims for Veterans' Benefits: A Preliminary Analysis*, 27 Stan. L.Rev. 905 (1975).

A different, and perhaps more common, type of statutory preclusion is legislation which imposes a time limit on actions to review an administrative decision. A provision of this kind was at issue in Adamo Wrecking Co. v. United States, 434 U.S. 275 (1978). The petitioner had been prosecuted for violating an air pollution emission standard for asbestos dust while demolishing a building, and in defense he attempted to raise a variety of objections to the validity of the rule. However, the relevant section of the Clean Air Act required that challenges must be brought within 30 days of the date when the rule was issued, and the petitioner had missed that deadline. The Court nevertheless granted limited review by directing the court hearing the enforcement action to determine whether the asbestos rule was the kind of emissions standard authorized by the Clean Air Act. At the same time, the court was precluded from deciding claims that the standard lacked factual support or was issued through defective procedures. The reasoning of the *Adamo Wrecking* opinion is rather obscure, but the case does show a reluctance to cut off all access to judicial review unless there is a persuasive reason for doing so. It also reflects the courts' willingness to make fine adjustments in the availability or scope of review in order to strike a balance between the risk of unfairness or injustice to the complaining party and impairment of the regulatory program.

Whether Congress could cut off all judicial review—either indirectly as in the *Adamo* case by setting short time limits or other restrictive conditions on the agency's decision, or directly by explicitly forbidding any challenge to the rule—remains an open question. See Harrison v. PPG Indus., Inc., 100 S.Ct. 1889, 1898 (1980) (Powell, J., concurring). This question was the subject of a famous dialogue by Professor Hart on the power of Congress to limit the jurisdiction of the federal courts. See Hart, *The Power of Congress to Limit the Jurisdiction of the Federal Courts: An Exercise in Dialectic*, 66 Harv.L.Rev. 1362 (1953). Professor Hart concluded that as long as some court, state or federal, was open to hear claims that the action was not legal, Congress could close off access to other forums. However, as Professor Mashaw and Dean Merrill have pointed out, the Hart theory "is so riddled with exceptions" that they almost swallow the rule. J.

Mashaw & R. Merrill, *The American Public Law System* 885 (1975).

2. COMMITTED TO DISCRETION

While statutory preclusion is concerned primarily with the legislature's intent to bar review, the exception for actions "committed to agency discretion" is more directly concerned with functional reasons for limiting or denying review. Courts are designed to make and review reasoned decisions—those which result from finding facts, drawing inferences from them, and applying legal principles to them. Agencies perform similar functions in both adjudication and rulemaking, but they also make other kinds of decisions as well—including political judgments or bargained decisions that the courts may not be competent to review. In addition, some areas of administration have a compelling need for speed, flexibility, or secrecy in decisionmaking which is inconsistent with the open and deliberate processes of judicial review. When the court finds that there is some compelling practical justification for avoiding review, it may conclude that the action is wholly or partly committed to the agency's unreviewable discretion. The effect of this determination is not only to prevent the normal judicial review for abuse of discretion under section 706(2)(A); it also prevents the court from examining other alleged defects in the agency decision, such as lack of adequate factual support or procedural error.

Administrative decisions affecting national defense and foreign policy are often committed to agency discretion, in part because of the need to preserve the secrecy of negotiations with foreign countries or to prevent disclosure of military plans. Thus, a decision by the Secretary of Defense to use foreign vessels to ship military supplies rather than reactivating the American "mothball fleet" has been held nonreviewable, Curran v. Laird, 420 F.2d 122 (D.C.Cir. 1969) (en banc) (Leventhal, J.), and so has the President's decision to approve or modify the CAB's grants of air routes between the United States and foreign countries, Chicago & So. Air Lines v. Waterman S. S. Corp., 333 U.S. 103 (1948). The *Waterman Steamship* opinion suggests a second policy rationale for the courts' reluctance to review decisions that involve negotiations with foreign countries: such foreign policy matters are "political, not judicial," and the Constitution confers the power to make political decisions solely on the legislative and executive branches of government.

Decisions have also been "committed to agency discretion" where the administrator is acting in a managerial capacity—that is, exercising continuing supervision over an area of responsibility through a series of small decisions which may have to be based on intuition or hunch rather than findings of fact and deductions from legal principles. Examples of regulatory areas where this rationale has been applied to preclude judicial review include supervision of rents charged by private landlords in subsidized housing (Hahn v. Gottlieb, 430 F.2d 1243 (1st Cir. 1970); cf. Langevin v. Chenango Court, Inc., 447 F.2d 296 (2d Cir. 1971)), and the decision by the administrator of a VA hospital to transfer a doctor who had "strained personal relationships" with his colleagues (Kletchka v. Driver, 411 F.2d 436 (2d Cir. 1969)).

The determination that an administrative decision is committed to agency discretion thus depends upon the

practical necessities of the situation. In applying this
exception to the general rule of reviewability, the court
will balance the harm to the party seeking judicial review
against the risk that review will have an adverse impact
on the regulatory program. It will also consider whether
the issues are appropriate for courts to resolve—that is,
whether there is some law to apply. The answers to
these questions are rarely apparent on the face of the
statute; instead the results often seem to depend on the
courts' unarticulated perceptions of the day-to-day workings of a particular regulatory program.

C. STANDING

A person bringing a court challenge to an administrative decision must have standing to seek judicial review.
The standing doctrine is a complex and frequently changing body of law which has both a constitutional and a
common law basis. The constitutional source of the
standing doctrine is Article III, § 2 of the Constitution
which limits the federal judicial power to "cases" and
"controversies." The American judicial process is an
adversary system, which depends upon the litigants to
gather and present the information needed for a sound
decision. The "case or controversy" limitation, as embodied in the standing doctrine, seeks to assure sufficient
opposition between the parties to make this system function properly. In addition, the law of standing may help
to keep the power of the judiciary within its proper
relationship to the political branches of government. If
the courts can decide issues of constitutional interpretation and statutory construction only when necessary

to resolve a concrete dispute, the risk of dominance by an "anti-majoritarian" judiciary is reduced.

The difficulty, however, is that these considerations of institutional competence and legitimacy conflict with other strongly held values. That is, while these institutional considerations may argue for a strict application of the standing doctrine, the individual plaintiff's demand for redress from illegal government action exerts a powerful counterclaim on the court's sense of justice. Moreover, institutional considerations do not always argue for limiting review. Judicial review of administrative action reflects competing claims of institutional value. As previously noted, restraint in the exercise of the reviewing function can be viewed as a socially valuable method of minimizing the judiciary's interference with political decisions; but judicial review can also be viewed as a method of assuring that bureaucratic actions are consistent with the legislative mandates established by the political branches. In light of these conflicting policy imperatives, it is perhaps not surprising that the law of standing has had an erratic pattern of development.

The early view was that a person seeking judicial scrutiny of agency action had to show that he had a legally protected interest—that is, one recognized by the Constitution, by statute or common law—which was adversely affected by the agency's decision. A personal or economic interest was not sufficient; the plaintiff had to show a legal right which was invaded. E. g., Alabama Power Co. v. Ickes, 302 U.S. 464 (1938); Tennessee Elec. Power Co. v. TVA, 306 U.S. 118 (1939); see Joint Anti-Fascist Refugee Committee v. McGrath, 341 U.S. 123, 151–52 (1951) (Frankfurter, J., concurring).

The "legally protected interest" test suffered from a number of deficiencies which led to its eventual rejection. Its circularity tended to confuse the threshold question of standing with the merits of the plaintiff's claim, because the court was required to consider the merits of the plaintiff's assertions of administrative illegality in order to determine whether he had a sufficient legal interest to confer standing. Moreover, it was excessively rigid because it depended more upon ancient common law concepts of "legal interest" than upon policy considerations such as the need for a judicial check on a growing federal bureaucracy. These defects led to a crumbling of the doctrinal barriers in the 1940's.

The first major breakthrough occurred in FCC v. Sanders Bros. Radio Station, 309 U.S. 470 (1940). The Court there held that the statutory language granting judicial review to "persons aggrieved" by an FCC license decision included not only disappointed applicants but also competitors facing potential economic injury from the agency's action. The test of an "aggrieved person," in other words, was not limited to the assertion of a personal legal wrong. The Court's rationale is significant. The Court concluded that Congress "may have been of the opinion that one likely to be financially injured by the issuance of a license would be the only person having a sufficient interest to bring to the attention of the appellate court errors of law in the action of the Commission." See also Scripps-Howard Radio, Inc. v. FCC, 316 U.S. 4 (1942) (private litigants "have standing only as representatives of the public interest"); Associated Indus. of New York v. Ickes, 134 F.2d 694, 704 (2d Cir.), vacated as moot, 320 U.S. 707 (1943) (private parties granted standing as "private Attorney Generals" to enforce statutory requirements). Thus, a complainant was required only to demonstrate some personal injury in order to assert the public interest in those situations where statutory provisions for review could be broadly construed. Once standing was granted, he was free to assert all available grounds for reversal, even though some of them might not be relevant to his personal interest.

The adoption of the APA in 1946, providing in section 702 that a person "adversely affected or aggrieved by agency action within the meaning of a relevant statute" could obtain judicial review, eventually contributed to the liberalizing trend. Litigants began to argue that the Act did not merely codify the existing "legal interest" theory but rather expanded the availability of standing by allowing judicial review whenever the complainant could prove that he was adversely affected in fact. Under this construction of the APA, the *Sanders* rationale (allowing anyone injured in fact to have standing on behalf of the public interest) would support standing for the plaintiff in all appeals from federal administrative action except when that action is committed to agency discretion or a statute otherwise precludes judicial review.

This construction was not initially accepted by most courts, however. They concluded that section 702 was merely declaratory of prior law and granted no new rights of judicial review. See, e. g., Road Review League v. Boyd, 270 F.Supp. 650, 660–61 (S.D.N.Y.1967); Norwalk CORE v. Norwalk Redevelopment Agency, 395 F.2d 920, 933 n.26 (2d Cir. 1968). In other words, under this view the APA could be relied upon as a grant of standing where the interest asserted by the plaintiff is one Congress otherwise recognized.

At first the Supreme Court merely tolerated this trend. In Hardin v. Kentucky Utilities Co., 390 U.S. 1 (1968), the Court held that "when the particular statutory provision invoked does reflect a legislative purpose to protect a competitive interest, the injured competitor has standing to require compliance with that provision." This holding was not novel doctrine, but some of the language and reasoning in the opinion suggested that the Court might be willing to re-examine the issue of standing under the APA. Two years later, the Court followed up with a complete revision of the law of standing.

In the companion cases of Association of Data Processing Service Organizations v. Camp, 397 U.S. 150 (1970) and Barlow v. Collins, 397 U.S. 159 (1970), the Court reduced the law of standing for judicial review of administrative action to two seemingly straightforward questions: (1) is the complainant "aggrieved in fact"; and (2) is the interest sought to be protected by the complainant "arguably within the zone of interests to be protected or regulated by the statute or constitutional guarantee in question?"

The first requirement of injury-in-fact rests upon an acknowledgement of Article III's constitutional limitation on the judicial power of the federal courts. However, as discussed below, it poses some difficult questions when the claimed injury is remote, small in size, or to a noneconomic interest. The second half of the Court's test—that plaintiff's interest is "arguably within the zone of interests to be protected or regulated by the statute"—is based on section 702 of the APA as well as prudential considerations of court time and undue interference in agency matters. Indeed, this test is more relaxed than either the text of APA or the prior decisions of the lower courts because the "relevant statute" need only "arguably" protect plaintiff's interest. The zone of interest test has provoked less litigation than the injury-in-fact portion of the standing doctrine, but there are some difficulties in applying the test to particular statutes.

One of the first problems to arise after the *Data Processing* and *Barlow* decisions was the applicability of the injury-in-fact test to noneconomic interests. The Sierra Club raised this issue when it brought suit to block the development of a ski resort in a wilderness area and the construction of a highway through federal lands. Sierra Club v. Morton, 405 U.S 727 (1972). The Supreme Court went part of the way toward granting standing on the basis of harm to noneconomic interests. It held that threats to aesthetic, recreational, and environmental interests could constitute sufficient injury in fact to satisfy the standing requirement. See also Scenic Hudson Preservation Conference v. FPC, 354 F.2d 608, 616 (2d Cir. 1965). However, the Sierra Club's pleadings were defective, because it had failed to allege that any of its members actually used the wilderness area that would be affected by the resort development; instead, its pleadings merely said that the Club "by its activities and conduct has exhibited a special interest in the conservation and the sound maintenance of the national parks, . . . regularly serving as a responsible representative of persons similarly interested." The Court distinguished this claim of a "mere 'interest in a

[*312*]

problem'" from a valid claim of harm to a noneconomic interest: "[T]he 'injury in fact' test requires more than an injury to a cognizable interest. It requires that the party seeking review be himself among the injured." The practical effect of this requirement seems slight. Since recreational and aesthetic interests are widely shared and highly subjective, it has not proved difficult for a broad based citizen group like the Sierra Club to find proper plaintiffs and draft pleadings that will satisfy the Court's requirements.

The second difficulty in applying the injury-in-fact test arises when the plaintiff asserts a remote or speculative threat of harm to a protected interest. The existence of a real or threatened injury can become extremely problematic when the government program uses indirect subsidies, tax credits, or other manipulation of market incentives to achieve a desired result, rather than providing for direct regulation or disbursements of benefits to claimants. This problem first came before the Supreme Court in United States v. Students Challenging Regulatory Agency Proceedings, 412 U.S. 669 (1973) (*SCRAP*). The plaintiffs in that action were a group of law students who wanted to contest the ICC's approval of a freight rate which they felt would discourage the use of recycled materials and thereby contribute to environmental pollution. To establish standing, they alleged that the rate increase would lead to increased litter and depletion of minerals and other natural resources in forests or parks where they engaged in recreational activities. The Court thought this an "attenuated line of causation," but it did not bar the students from maintaining their action. Instead, it noted that the plaintiffs must be prepared to prove the allegations of harm in their complaint, and it remanded to the district court for further proceedings.

The Court expanded on the causation requirement in two later cases involving subsidy programs. Simon v. Eastern Kentucky Welfare Rights Organization, 426 U.S. 26 (1976), involved tax exemptions for private hospitals providing medical care to indigents. When the IRS issued a Revenue Ruling reducing the amount of indigent care a hospital must provide in order to qualify for the exemption, the welfare organization and several indigent individuals sought judicial review. Despite allegations that the individual plaintiffs had been denied treatment as a result of the IRS ruling, the Court held that they did not have standing. Their harm was caused by the hospitals who denied them treatment, not by the Treasury Department officials who wrote the regulation; even in the absence of the Ruling, the plaintiffs might have been denied service. Moreover, it was not clear that a favorable decision on the merits would be likely to redress the claimed injury. "Absent such a showing," the majority observed, "exercise of its power by a federal court would be gratuitous and thus inconsistent" with the Article III case or controversy limitations.

These new tests of causation and redressability seemed likely to limit the availability of judicial review in a wide variety of subsidy or indirect benefit programs. However, the subsequent decision in Duke Power Co. v. Carolina Environmental Study Group, Inc., 438 U.S. 59 (1978), made clear that not every claim of indirect harm would be barred. The plaintiffs in that action sought to challenge the constitutionality of a statute which encouraged the development of nuclear power by limiting the

[*314*]

liability of utilities for damages caused by a "nuclear incident." They alleged that two nuclear power plants which were under construction near their residences would cause thermal pollution and health risks from radioactive discharges; in addition, they claimed that the plants would not be constructed and operated without the statute limiting liability. The District Court agreed, finding as fact that "but for" the subsidy, the plants would not have been built or operated. Since this finding was not clearly erroneous, the Supreme Court concluded that the plaintiffs had satisfied the causation and redressability requirements of the injury-in-fact test. Moreover, the Court rejected the argument that it should apply the requirement, first developed in the context of taxpayers' suits to prevent government expenditures, that the plaintiff show a "subject-matter nexus between the right asserted and the injury alleged." See, e. g., Flast v. Cohen, 392 U.S. 83 (1968). The lack of such a "nexus" could be taken into account as a "prudential" or discretionary factor by a court deciding a standing issue, but it is not required by Article III of the Constitution outside the area of taxpayers' suits.

Despite this extension of the law of standing far beyond the old legally protected interest test, it is still questionable whether the doctrine provides a coherent approach to defining the scope of judicial power. See generally J. Vining, *Legal Identity* (1978). When standing is granted on the basis of harm to small, remote, or noneconomic interests, the standing requirement does not assure vigorous adversary presentation of cases. It does impose some limits on the power of courts to hear and decide claims of administrative illegality, but these limits appear to be few and often unrelated to the policies underlying the doctrine. The evolution of the injury-in-fact test to incorporate causation and redressibility has injected potentially complicated factual inquiries into the standing calculus, and resolution of these threshold factual issues can be costly to both courts and litigants. See Scott, *Standing in the Supreme Court—A Functional Analysis,* 86 Harv.L.Rev. 645 (1973). The time may be ripe for another thorough reexamination of the doctrinal and practical bases for standing to seek judicial review of administrative action.

D. EXHAUSTION AND RIPENESS

Even though the agency's decision is reviewable and the plaintiff has standing to litigate, he may still be unable to get judicial review if he has brought the action at the wrong time. When the party seeking review has come into court prematurely, he is likely to be told that he has failed to exhaust his administrative remedies or that the matter is not yet ripe for judicial review. Ripeness and exhaustion are complementary doctrines which are designed to prevent unnecessary or untimely judicial interference in the administrative process.

If the agency proceeding is still at an early stage and the party seeking review has the right to an administrative hearing or review, the court will decline to hear his appeal on the ground that he has failed to exhaust his administrative remedies. Judicial intervention may not be necessary because the agency can correct any initial errors at subsequent stages of the process; moreover, the agency's position on important issues of fact and law may not be fully crystallized or adopted in final form. Myers

v. Bethlehem Shipbuilding Corp., 303 U.S. 41 (1938), illustrates one situation in which this principle applies. The company had been served with an NLRB complaint, alleging that it had engaged in unfair labor practices. Bethlehem Shipbuilding took the position that the complaint was invalid because the NLBR had no jurisdiction over the company, and it tried to obtain immediate judicial review of the complaint. Despite the company's claim that it would suffer irreparable harm if it were forced to participate in an unnecessary evidentiary hearing, Bethlehem was required to exhaust its administrative remedies: "Lawsuits also often prove to have been groundless," the Court observed, "but no way has been discovered of relieving a defendant from the necessity of a trial to establish the fact." See also FTC v. Standard Oil Co. of California, 101 S.Ct. 488 (1980) (issuance of an FTC complaint not "final agency action" subject to review before the final adjudicatory order is delivered).

In the years since the decision in *Bethlehem Shipbuilding,* courts have carved out some exceptions to the requirement that the plaintiff exhaust his administrative remedies before seeking judicial review. In McKart v. United States, 395 U.S. 185 (1969), further administrative appeal was not required of a draft registrant who had failed to appeal his Selective Service reclassification from an exempt category to one which made him eligible for induction. The Court balanced a number of factors in determining that his suit should not be barred by the exhaustion doctrine. Since the passage of time had foreclosed all further administrative remedies to the petitioner, the court saw no risk of impeding the agency's program through premature intervention in the administrative process. Moreover, the issues involved were straightforward questions of law which did not require the exercise of administrative expertise, and application of the exhaustion doctrine could inflict considerable hardship and injustice on the petitioner. The Court was reluctant to require exhaustion when criminal sanctions were at issue because "[t]he defendant is often stripped of his only defense; he must go to jail without having any judicial review of an assertedly invalid order." Finally, fairness seemed to demand an opportunity for review here since the statute did not give registrants adequate notice that they might forfeit their claims if they failed to take an administrative appeal. Weighing these considerations, and the likelihood that few registrants would try to bypass the administrative process since they would risk criminal penalties by doing so, the Court held that the exhaustion doctrine could not bar the defendant from asserting the invalidity of his classification as a defense to the criminal prosecution.

The ripeness doctrine looks to similar factors in determining the availability of review—that is, the fitness of the issues for judicial determination and the hardship to the parties that would result from granting or denying review—but it has a different focus and a different basis from exhaustion. The exhaustion doctrine emphasizes the position of the party seeking review; in essence, it asks whether he may be attempting to short circuit the administrative process or whether he has been reasonably diligent in protecting his own interests. Ripeness, by contrast, is concerned primarily with the institutional relationships between courts and agencies, and the competence of the courts to resolve disputes without further administrative refinement of the issues. In extreme cases, the ripeness doctrine serves to implement the policy behind Article III of the Constitution. Since the judicial power is limited to cases and controversies, federal courts cannot decide purely abstract or theoretical claims, or render advisory opinions. See, e. g., National Automatic Laundry & Cleaning Council v. Shultz, 443 F.2d 689 (D.C.Cir. 1971) (review of agency advisory opinions involving hypothetical rather than real fact situations would exceed the judicial power).

Apart from these relatively rare situations where ripeness takes on a constitutional dimension, the primary factors to be considered are defined by the leading case of Abbott Laboratories v. Gardner, 387 U.S. 136, 148–49 (1967): the court must "evaluate both the fitness of the issues for judicial decision and the hardship to the parties of withholding court consideration." Application of the test relating to the fitness of the issues is illustrated by Abbott Labs and its companion case, Toilet Goods Ass'n v. Gardner, 387 U.S. 158 (1967). The petition that was held ripe for review in Abbott Labs posed a purely legal question—that is, whether the statute gave the FDA authority to require the kind of labeling that the agency had mandated drug manufacturers to place on their products. By contrast, the rule at issue in Toilet Goods was held not ripe for review. It required companies using color additives in cosmetics to give FDA inspectors "free access" to their plants, on pain of losing their certification to market their products. In this instance the Court believed that further development of the facts in the context of a specific enforcement proceeding might aid judicial review. Matters such as "an understanding of what types of enforcement problems are encountered by the FDA, the need for various sorts of supervision in order to effectuate the goals of the Act, and the safeguards devised to protect legitimate trade secrets" could all be more fully explored on the basis of an evidentiary record. Thus, under the ripeness doctrine, as in exhaustion, judicial review is more likely to be available for issues of law than for questions of fact or policy or discretion. However, it should be noted that *Abbott Labs* and *Toilet Goods* were decided before the decision in *Overton Park* ushered in the concept of judicial review on the record of an informal rulemaking proceeding. See generally pp. 75–77, supra. Thus, it is possible that a contemporary agency promulgating a rule like the one at issue in *Toilet Goods* would compile a rulemaking record that would answer most of the questions that the court was asking, and therefore even that rule might be ripe for review.

While the availability of pre-enforcement review of substantive agency rules is well established today, difficult ripeness issues may still arise. One problematic situation involves an agency's refusal to provide preliminary relief to abate an alleged risk of injury pending a full hearing on the merits. An example is Environmental Defense Fund, Inc. v. Hardin, 428 F.2d 1093 (D.C. Cir. 1970). There an environmental group had petitioned the Secretary of Agriculture, who then had the responsibility for licensing pesticides, to initiate a formal hearing for the purpose of revoking the certification for the pesticide DDT; they also had requested that the Secretary use his power to suspend the marketing of DDT immediately as an "imminent hazard." The Secretary started the formal cancellation process, but he took no action in the request for suspension. His nonaction on the latter request was held ripe for review. The court ruled that in the circumstances the agency's failure to act "is the equivalent of an order denying relief." Moreover, in light of the allegations of imminent harm to the environment from DDT, even a temporary refusal to suspend marketing might cause "irreparable injury on a massive scale." Later, when the Secretary had considered and issued a decision refusing to suspend marketing, the court again granted review, and reversed because the administrator had erroneously interpretated the statutory standard. In dealing with the agency's argument that judicial review was premature, the court distinguished exhaustion cases like Myers v. Bethlehem Shipbuilding, discussed p. 317, supra, which had held that courts could not review an administrative decision to vote a complaint. In effect, the court viewed the suspension decision as a separate proceeding governed by different criteria and different practical considerations; it was not merely the first public step in a formal adjudication. Environmental Defense Fund, Inc. v. Ruckelshaus, 439 F.2d 584 (D.C.Cir. 1971). As in *Abbott Labs,* the court gave primary emphasis to the pragmatic finality of the agency decision and to the strong presumption in favor of judicial review. However, other courts have reached different results on similar facts; see, e. g., Nor-Am Agricultural Products, Inc. v. Hardin, 435 F.2d 1151 (7th Cir. 1970) (en banc), cert. dismissed, 402 U.S. 935 (1971) (suit by producers of a registered fungicide to enjoin administrator's decision suspending registration not ripe because the action was not final and merely started the cancellation process).

CONCLUSION

Throughout the twentieth century, as the regulatory state has grown and the focus of public concern has shifted, Administrative Law has experienced a pattern of shifting doctrinal bases for judicial review. This is perhaps most apparent at the level of constitutional doctrine, where a series of constitutional tests for the legality of legislative and administrative action have first come to prominence, and then been cut back, or fallen into disfavor. Judicial efforts to assure the rationality of economic regulation under the rubric of substantive due process enjoyed a brief prominence which is reflected in leading cases like *Lochner* and *Nebbia*; but by 1935, when the *Pacific States Box & Basket* case was decided, it had become clear that the courts were neither willing nor able to review the details of legislative and administrative regulatory policy on this basis. At that time the substantive due process doctrine was replaced briefly by the delegation doctrine in the New Deal cases such as *Panama Refining* and *Schechter*. However, this constitutional test for the legality of administrative regulation was also short-lived, and the delegation doctrine has survived only as theoretical foundation and rather remote threat of judicial intervention. It is, in any case, easily avoided by the exercise of minimal care in legislative drafting.

After the decline of the delegation doctrine, the focus of constitutional adjudication shifted from concern with the basic structure of the administrative process to assessing fairness in the implementation of regulatory programs. In the 1960's, the Warren Court's concern for the protection of individual rights produced a sweeping change in the application of procedural due process to agency action. The landmark case of Goldberg v. Kelly, which abolished the old right-privilege distinction and opened vast new areas of administrative practice to constitutional review, initiated a period of rapid constitutionalization of administrative procedure. However, the era of procedural due process review was also brief. By the late 1970's the Court had sharply limited the scope of procedural due process through restrictive definitions of protected liberty and property interests, while also becoming more skeptical of the ability of trial-type procedures to assure the fairness and accuracy of administrative decisions. At about the same time, the Court was undertaking a comparably rapid expansion and then a gradual retraction of the constitutionally based doctrines governing the availability of judicial review. Barriers of standing and ripeness, rooted in the case or controversy requirement of Article III, were reduced in the late 1960's and early 1970's, but occasionally raised in the later years as the Court struggled with limiting doctrines such as injury in fact and redressability in an effort to define the proper relationship between courts and agencies.

There are undoubtedly numerous reasons, including personnel changes in the Supreme Court, for the pattern of shifting constitutional grounds for controlling bureaucratic behavior. One significant consideration, however, may be the fact that constitutional decisions often cut too deeply or broadly into an increasingly complex network of administrative agencies and programs. Doctrines which affect the basic structure of regulation, such as substantive due process and the delegation doctrine, have an unpredictable but potentially severe impact on the government's ability to achieve desired social objectives. A holding of unconstitutionality requires new legislation to remedy the defect, and political consensus on the form and content of a regulatory program may be impossible to recapture. Even doctrines which affect the implementation rather than the validity of a regulatory program, such as procedural due process, can have broad, unforeseeable effects. Expansion of due process rights may not have produced the proverbial "flood" of litigation, but it did produce a steadily rising tide of cases, some of them petty or trivial, from all layers of the federal and state bureaucracies. In dealing with this diverse collection of agency decisions, the Court generally lacked reliable empirical information about either the effectiveness of particular procedural devices in assuring fairness and accuracy, or the impact of additional procedures on the operations of the affected agencies. Faced with these uncertainties, it is perhaps not surprising that the Court has become increasingly reluctant to write codes of administrative procedure for the agencies, backed by the finality of constitutional adjudication.

At the same time that the constitutional bases for judicial review have proven unsatisfactory as solutions to the problem of bureaucratic accountability, the statutory and common law doctrines governing the reviewing function have also fallen into some disarray. The simple system envisioned by the Administrative Procedure Act,[3] which assumes that judicial review will be invoked

---

3. For a summary of four issues that need to be considered when seeking to apply the APA to unfamiliar fact situations, see *Notes on Using the APA*, Appendix III, p. 411 infra.

primarily for major, formalized administrative decisions and which varies the scope of review according to the kind of procedure used, has been modified in several significant respects. The decision in *Overton Park,* holding that even an informal decision could be reviewed on the administrative record, injected the courts into broad areas of discretionary, unstructured decisionmaking which produced only fragmentary "records" for judicial review. As "hybrid" procedural forms came into vogue, statutes and judicial decisions began to blur, if not obliterate, the distinction between rulemaking and adjudication. At the same time, the substance of regulatory programs began to shift away from the familiar economic bases to highly technical assessments of risk and benefits, often at the frontiers of scientific knowledge.

All of these developments, and others as well, have placed a considerable strain on the reviewing function. Courts have tried several strategies to discharge these new responsibilitites on judicial review, with mixed results. Efforts to impose procedural requirements on agency decisions, in the hopes that more formal procedures would produce a better (or at least a more familiar) record for judicial review, brought a sharp rebuke from the Supreme Court in the *Vermont Yankee* decision. Within the lower courts, there has been an ongoing debate over whether the courts can or should immerse themselves in the technical intricacies of agency decisions, or merely check to see whether the administrators are taking account of the relevant factors in a plausible fashion. These difficulties, together with the efforts of the political branches of government to increase their own ability to review particular administrative decisions through mechanisms such as the legislative veto or regulatory analysis, raise the question whether judicial review itself may be declining in importance.

As a functional matter, judicial review has some considerable practical advantages over other methods of assuring bureaucratic accountability. Because judicial review operates at the level of individual decisions rather than at the more general level of policies or programs, it holds forth a greater promise of doing justice in particular cases. Moreover, in contrast to the political review mechanisms, judicial scrutiny is automatically triggered at the request of the injured party; the courts have relatively little discretion to refuse to hear a meritorious case. Judicial review also can improve the quality of government administration. The realization that their decisions will be subject to careful scrutiny by prestigious reviewers who are insulated from the political pressures of the moment can have a significant disciplining effect on administrators. In effect, judicial review is a primary quality control on the information and reasoning employed by the agencies. In the long run, however, the courts' ability to realize these benefits may depend upon their ability to find a workable middle ground between the extremes of ignoring arbitrary or unfair bureaucratic action on the one hand, and trying to re-do the work of the agencies without their technical expertise or institutional strengths on the other. This essential task of judicial review is difficult to capture in a verbal formula and even more difficult to implement in practice, but for the near future at least it seems much more important than the effort to control the administrative process through development of new constitutional doctrines.

APPENDIX I

SELECTED CONSTITUTIONAL AND STATUTORY PROVISIONS

UNITED STATES CONSTITUTION

Article I

Section 1. All legislative Powers herein granted shall be vested in a Congress of the United States, which shall consist of a Senate and House of Representatives.

Section 7. [1] All Bills for raising Revenue shall originate in the House of Representatives; but the Senate may propose or concur with Amendments as on other Bills.

[2] Every Bill which shall have passed the House of Representatives and the Senate, shall, before it become a Law, be presented to the President of the United States; If he approves he shall sign it, but if not he shall return it, with his Objections to that House in which it shall have originated, who shall enter the Objections at large on their Journal, and proceed to reconsider it. If after such Reconsideration two thirds of that House shall agree to pass the Bill, it shall be sent together with the Objections, to the other House, by which it shall likewise be reconsidered, and if approved by two thirds of that House, it shall become a Law. But in all such Cases the Votes of both Houses shall be determined by yeas and Nays, and the Names of the Persons voting for and against the Bill shall be entered on the Journal of each House respectively. If any Bill shall not be returned by the President within ten Days (Sundays excepted) after it

[*327*]

shall have been presented to him, the Same shall be a Law, in like Manner as if he had signed it, unless the Congress by their Adjournment prevent its Return in which Case it shall not be a Law.

[3] Every Order, Resolution, or Vote, to Which the Concurrence of the Senate and House of Representatives may be necessary (except on a question of Adjournment) shall be presented to the President of the United States; and before the Same shall take Effect, shall be approved by him, or being disapproved by him, shall be repassed by two thirds of the Senate and House of Representatives, according to the Rules and Limitations prescribed in the Case of a Bill.

Section 8. The Congress shall have Power .   .   .

[18] To make all Laws which shall be necessary and proper for carrying into Execution the foregoing Powers, and all other Powers vested by this Constitution in the Government of the United States, or in any Department or Officer thereof.

Article II

Section 1. [1] The executive Power shall be vested in a President of the United States of America. .   .   .

Section 2. [1] The President shall be Commander in Chief of the Army and Navy of the United States; .   .   .
he may require the Opinion, in writing, of the principal Officer in each of the executive Departments, upon any Subject relating to the Duties of their respective Offices
.   .   .   .

[2] He shall have Power, by and with the Advice and Consent of the Senate, to make Treaties, provided two

thirds of the Senators present concur; and he shall nominate, and by and with the Advice and Consent of the Senate, shall appoint Ambassadors, other public Ministers and Consuls, Judges of the supreme Court, and all other Officers of the United States, whose Appointments are not herein otherwise provided for, and which shall be established by Law; but the Congress may by Law vest the Appointment of such inferior Officers, as they think proper, in the President alone, in the Courts of Law, or in the Heads of Departments. . . .

Section 3.   He shall from time to time give to the Congress Information of the State of the Union, and recommend to their Consideration such Measures as he shall judge necessary and expedient; . . . he shall take Care that the Laws be faithfully executed, and shall Commission all the Officers of the United States.

Section 4.   The President, Vice President and all civil Officers of the United States, shall be removed from Office on Impeachment for, and Conviction of, Treason, Bribery, or other high Crimes and Misdemeanors.

Article III

Section 1.   The judicial Power of the United States, shall be vested in one supreme Court, and in such inferior Courts as the Congress may from time to time ordain and establish. . . .

Section 2.   [1]   The judicial Power shall extend to all Cases, in Law and Equity, arising under this Constitution, the Laws of the United States, and Treaties made, or which shall be made, under their Authority;—to all Cases affecting Ambassadors, other public Ministers and Consuls;—to all Cases of admiralty and maritime Jurisdiction;—to Controversies to which the United States shall be a Party;—to Controversies between two or more States;—between a State and Citizens of another State;—between Citizens of different States;—between Citizens of the same State claiming Lands under the Grants of different States, and between a State, or the Citizens thereof, and foreign States, Citizens or Subjects.

Amendment I [1791]

Congress shall make no law respecting an establishment of religion, or prohibiting the free exercise thereof; or abridging the freedom of speech, or of the press; or the right of the people peaceably to assemble, and to petition the Government for a redress of grievances.

Amendment IV [1791]

The right of the people to be secure in their persons, houses, papers, and effects, against unreasonable searches and seizures, shall not be violated, and no Warrants shall issue, but upon probable cause, supported by Oath or affirmation, and particularly describing the place to be searched, and the persons or things to be seized.

Amendment V [1791]

No person shall be held to answer for a capital, or otherwise infamous crime, unless on a presentment or indictment of a Grand Jury, except in cases arising in the land or naval forces, or in the Militia, when in actual service in time of War or public danger; nor shall any person be subject for the same offence to be twice put in jeopardy of life or limb; nor shall be compelled in any criminal case to be a witness against himself, nor be deprived of life, liberty, or property, without due process of law; nor shall private property be taken for public use, without just compensation.

Amendment VI [1791]

In all criminal prosecutions, the accused shall enjoy the right to a speedy and public trial, by an impartial jury of the State and district wherein the crime shall have been committed, which district shall have been previously ascertained by law, and to be informed of the nature and cause of the accusation; to be confronted with the witnesses against him; to have compulsory process for obtaining witnesses in his favor, and to have the Assistance of Counsel for his defence.

Amendment XIV [1868]

Section 1. All persons born or naturalized in the United States, and subject to the jurisdiction thereof, are citizens of the United States and of the State wherein they reside. No State shall make or enforce any law which shall abridge the privileges or immunities of citizens of the United States; nor shall any State deprive any person of life, liberty, or property, without due process of law; nor deny to any person within its jurisdiction the equal protection of the laws.

ADMINISTRATIVE PROCEDURE ACT

NOTE ON THE STRUCTURE OF THE APA

Since its original enactment in 1946, the Administrative Procedure Act has been amended and recodified several times. Some legal materials, particularly the older judicial decisions, may cite to the sections of the bill originally enacted (sections 2 through 12), which have been substantially rearranged in the current codification. To convert these citations into the current sections of Title 5, consult the conversion table at the end of this Appendix.

Several of the amendments to the APA have added major provisions to the Act, and these additions are often cited by their short titles or popular names. The following are the principal later statutes, which have been incorporated into the APA:

Statute	5 USCA Sections	Appendix Pages
Freedom of Information Act	552	335–46
Privacy Act	552a	346–65
Government in the Sunshine Act	552b	365–75
Regulatory Flexibility Act	601–11	388–99

UNITED STATES CODE, TITLE 5

Chapter 5—Administrative Procedure

§ 551. Definitions

For the purpose of this subchapter—

(1) "agency" means each authority of the Government of the United States, whether or not it is within or subject to review by another agency, but does not include—

(A) the Congress;

(B) the courts of the United States;

(C) the governments of the territories or possessions of the United States;

(D) the government of the District of Columbia;

or except as to the requirements of section 552 of this title—

(E) agencies composed of representatives of the parties or of representatives of organizations of the parties to the disputes determined by them;

(F) courts martial and military commissions;

(G) military authority exercised in the field in time of war or in occupied territory; or

(H) functions conferred by sections 1738, 1739, 1743, and 1744 of title 12; chapter 2 of title 41; or sections 1622, 1884, 1891–1902, and former section 1641(b)(2), of title 50, appendix;

(2) "person" includes an individual, partnership, corporation, association, or public or private organization other than an agency;

(3) "party" includes a person or agency named or admitted as a party, or properly seeking and entitled as of right to be admitted as a party, in an agency proceeding, and a person or agency admitted by an agency as a party for limited purposes;

(4) "rule" means the whole or a part of an agency statement of general or particular applicability and future effect designed to implement, interpret, or prescribe law or policy or describing the organization, procedure, or practice requirements of an agency and

includes the approval or prescription for the future of rates, wages, corporate or financial structures or reorganizations thereof, prices, facilities, appliances, services or allowances therefor or of valuations, costs, or accounting, or practices bearing on any of the foregoing;

(5) "rule making" means agency process for formulating, amending, or repealing a rule;

(6) "order" means the whole or a part of a final disposition, whether affirmative, negative, injunctive, or declaratory in form, of an agency in a matter other than rule making but including licensing;

(7) "adjudication" means agency process for the formulation of an order;

(8) "license" includes the whole or a part of an agency permit, certificate, approval, registration, charter, membership, statutory exemption or other form of permission;

(9) "licensing" includes agency process respecting the grant, renewal, denial, revocation, suspension, annulment, withdrawal, limitation, amendment, modification, or conditioning of a license;

(10) "sanction" includes the whole or a part of an agency—

 (A) prohibition, requirement, limitation, or other condition affecting the freedom of a person;

 (B) withholding of relief;

 (C) imposition of penalty or fine;

 (D) destruction, taking, seizure, or withholding of property;

(E) assessment of damages, reimbursement, restitution, compensation, costs, charges, or fees;

(F) requirement, revocation, or suspension of a license; or

(G) taking other compulsory or restrictive action;

(11) "relief" includes the whole or a part of an agency—

(A) grant of money, assistance, license, authority, exemption, exception, privilege, or remedy;

(B) recognition of a claim, right, immunity, privilege, exemption, or exception; or

(C) taking of other action on the application or petition of, and beneficial to, a person;

(12) "agency proceeding" means an agency process as defined by paragraphs (5), (7), and (9) of this section;

(13) "agency action" includes the whole or a part of an agency rule, order, license, sanction, relief, or the equivalent or denial thereof, or failure to act; and

(14) "ex parte communication" means an oral or written communication not on the public record with respect to which reasonable prior notice to all parties is not given, but it shall not include requests for status reports on any matter or proceeding covered by this subchapter.

§ 552. Public information; agency rules, opinions, orders, records, and proceedings

(a) Each agency shall make available to the public information as follows:

(1) Each agency shall separately state and currently publish in the Federal Register for the guidance of the public—

>(A) descriptions of its central and field organization and the established places at which, the employees (and in the case of a uniformed service, the members) from whom, and the methods whereby, the public may obtain information, make submittals or requests, or obtain decisions;

>(B) statements of the general course and method by which its functions are channeled and determined, including the nature and requirements of all formal and informal procedures available;

>(C) rules of procedure, descriptions of forms available or the places at which forms may be obtained, and instructions as to the scope and contents of all papers, reports, or examinations;

>(D) substantive rules of general applicability adopted as authorized by law, and statements of general policy or interpretations of general applicability formulated and adopted by the agency; and

>(E) each amendment, revision, or repeal of the foregoing.

Except to the extent that a person has actual and timely notice of the terms thereof, a person may not in any manner be required to resort to, or be adversely affected by, a matter required to be published in the Federal Register and not so published. For the purpose of this paragraph, matter reasonably available to the class of persons affected thereby is deemed published in the Federal Register when incorporated by reference therein with the approval of the Director of the Federal Register.

(2) Each agency, in accordance with published rules, shall make available for public inspection and copying—

   (A) final opinions, including concurring and dissenting opinions, as well as orders, made in the adjudication of cases;

   (B) those statements of policy and interpretations which have been adopted by the agency and are not published in the Federal Register; and

   (C) administrative staff manuals and instructions to staff that affect a member of the public;

unless the materials are promptly published and copies offered for sale. To the extent required to prevent a clearly unwarranted invasion of personal privacy, an agency may delete identifying details when it makes available or publishes an opinion, statement of policy, interpretation, or staff manual or instruction. However, in each case the justification for the deletion shall be explained fully in writing. Each agency shall also maintain and make available for public inspection and copying current indexes providing identifying information for the public as to any matter issued, adopted, or promulgated after July 4, 1967, and required by this paragraph to be made available or published. Each agency shall promptly publish, quarterly or more frequently, and distribute (by sale or otherwise) copies of each index or supplements thereto unless it determines by order published in the Federal Register that the publication would be unnecessary and impracticable, in which case the agency shall nonetheless provide copies of such index on request at a cost not to exceed the direct cost of duplication. A final order, opinion, statement of policy, interpretation, or staff manual or instruction that affects a member of the public may be relied on, used, or cited as precedent by an agency against a party other than an agency only if—

(i) it has been indexed and either made available or published as provided by this paragraph; or

(ii) the party has actual and timely notice of the terms thereof.

(3) Except with respect to the records made available under paragraphs (1) and (2) of this subsection, each agency, upon any request for records which (A) reasonably describes such records and (B) is made in accordance with published rules stating the time, place, fees (if any), and procedures to be followed, shall make the records promptly available to any person.

(4)(A) In order to carry out the provisions of this section, each agency shall promulgate regulations, pursuant to notice and receipt of public comment, specifying a uniform schedule of fees applicable to all constituent units of such agency. Such fees shall be limited to reasonable standard charges for document search and duplication and provide for recovery of only the direct costs of such search and duplication. Documents shall be furnished without charge or at a reduced charge where the agency determines that waiver or reduction of the fee is in the public interest because furnishing the information can be considered as primarily benefiting the general public.

(B) On complaint, the district court of the United States in the district in which the complainant resides, or has his principal place of business, or in which the agency records are situated, or in the District of Columbia, has jurisdiction to enjoin the agency from withholding agency records and to order the production of any agency records improperly withheld from the complainant. In such a case the court shall determine the matter de novo, and may examine the contents of such agency records in camera to determine whether such records or any part thereof shall be withheld under any of the exemptions set forth in subsection (b) of this section, and the burden is on the agency to sustain its action.

(C) Notwithstanding any other provision of law, the defendant shall serve an answer or otherwise plead to any complaint made under this subsection within thirty days after service upon the defendant of the pleading in which such complaint is made, unless the court otherwise directs for good cause shown.

(D) Except as to cases the court considers of greater importance, proceedings before the district court, as authorized by this subsection, and appeals therefrom, take precedence on the docket over all cases and shall be assigned for hearing and trial or for argument at the earliest practicable date and expedited in every way.

(E) The court may assess against the United States reasonable attorney fees and other litigation costs reasonably incurred in any case under this section in which the complainant has substantially prevailed.

(F) Whenever the court orders the production of any agency records improperly withheld from the complainant and assesses against the United States reasonable attorney fees and other litigation costs, and the court additionally issues a written finding that the circumstances surrounding the withholding raise questions whether agency personnel acted arbitrarily or capriciously with respect to the withholding, the Special Counsel shall promptly initiate a proceeding to determine whether disciplinary action is warranted against the officer or employee who was primarily responsible for the withholding. The Special Counsel, after investigation and consideration of the evidence submitted, shall submit his findings and recommendations to the administrative authority of the agency concerned and shall send copies of the findings and recommendations to the officer or employee or his representative. The administrative authority shall take the corrective action that the Special Counsel recommends.

(G) In the event of noncompliance with the order of the court, the district court may punish for contempt the responsible employee, and in the case of a uniformed service, the responsible member.

(5) Each agency having more than one member shall maintain and make available for public inspection a record of the final votes of each member in every agency proceeding.

(6)(A) Each agency, upon any request for records made under paragraph (1), (2), or (3) of this subsection, shall—

(i) determine within ten days (excepting Saturdays, Sundays and legal public holidays) after the receipt of any such request whether to comply with such request and shall immediately notify the person making such request of such determination and the reasons therefor, and of the right of such person to appeal to the head of the agency any adverse determination; and

(ii) make a determination with respect to any appeal within twenty days (excepting Saturdays, Sundays, and legal public holidays) after the receipt of such appeal. If on appeal the denial of the request for records is in whole or in part upheld, the agency shall notify the person making such request of the provisions for judicial review of that determination under paragraph (4) of this subsection.

(B) In unusual circumstances as specified in this subparagraph, the time limits prescribed in either clause (i) or clause (ii) of subparagraph (A) may be extended by written notice to the person making such request setting forth the reasons for such extension and the date on which a determination is expected to be dispatched. No such notice shall specify a date that would result in an extension for more than ten working days. As used in this subparagraph, "unusual circumstances" means, but only to the extent reasonably necessary to the proper processing of the particular request—

(i) the need to search for and collect the requested records from field facilities or other establishments that are separate from the office processing the request;

(ii) the need to search for, collect, and appropriately examine a voluminous amount of separate and distinct records which are demanded in a single request; or

(iii) the need for consultation, which shall be conducted with all practicable speed, with another agency having a substantial interest in the determination of the request or among two or more components of the agency having substantial subject-matter interest therein.

(C) Any person making a request to any agency for records under paragraph (1), (2), or (3) of this subsection shall be deemed to have exhausted his administrative remedies with respect to such request if the agency fails to comply with the applicable time limit provisions of this paragraph. If the Government can show exceptional circumstances exist and that the agency is exercising due diligence in responding to the request, the court may retain jurisdiction and allow the agency additional time to complete its review of the records. Upon any determination by an agency to comply with a request for records, the records shall be made promptly available to such person making such request. Any notification of denial of any request for records under this subsection shall set forth the names and titles or positions of each person responsible for the denial of such request.

(b) This section does not apply to matters that are—

(1)(A) specifically authorized under criteria established by an Executive order to be kept secret in the interest of national defense or foreign policy and (B) are in fact properly classified pursuant to such Executive order;

(2) related solely to the internal personnel rules and practices of an agency;

(3) specifically exempted from disclosure by statute (other than section 552b of this title), provided that such statute (A) requires that the matters be withheld from the public in such a manner as to leave no discretion on the issue, or (B) establishes particular criteria for withholding or refers to particular types of matters to be withheld;

(4) trade secrets and commercial or financial information obtained from a person and privileged or confidential;

(5) inter-agency or intra-agency memorandums or letters which would not be available by law to a party other than an agency in litigation with the agency;

(6) personnel and medical files and similar files the disclosure of which would constitute a clearly unwarranted invasion of personal privacy;

(7) investigatory records compiled for law enforcement purposes, but only to the extent that the production of such records would (A) interfere with enforcement proceedings, (B) deprive a person of a right to a fair trial or an impartial adjudication, (C) constitute an unwarranted invasion of personal privacy, (D) disclose the identity of a confidential source and, in the case of a record compiled by a criminal law enforcement authority in the course of a criminal investigation, or by an agency conducting a lawful national security intelligence investigation, confidential information furnished only by the confidential source, (E) disclose investigative techniques and procedures, or (F) endanger the life or physical safety of law enforcement personnel;

(8) contained in or related to examination, operating, or condition reports prepared by, on behalf of, or for the use of an agency responsible for the regulation or supervision of financial institutions; or

(9) geological and geophysical information and data, including maps, concerning wells.

Any reasonably segregable portion of a record shall be provided to any person requesting such record after deletion of the portions which are exempt under this subsection.

(c) This section does not authorize withholding of information or limit the availability of records to the public, except as specifically stated in this section. This section is not authority to withhold information from Congress.

(d) On or before March 1 of each calendar year, each agency shall submit a report covering the preceding calendar year to the Speaker of the House of Representatives and President of the Senate for referral to the appropriate committees of the Congress. The report shall include—

(1) the number of determinations made by such agency not to comply with requests for records made to such agency under subsection (a) and the reasons for each such determination;

(2) the number of appeals made by persons under subsection (a)(6), the result of such appeals, and the reason for the action upon each appeal that results in a denial of information;

(3) the names and titles or positions of each person responsible for the denial of records requested under this section, and the number of instances of participation for each;

(4) the results of each proceeding conducted pursuant to subsection (a)(4)(F), including a report of the disciplinary action taken against the officer or employee who was primarily responsible for improperly withholding records or an explanation of why disciplinary action was not taken;

(5) a copy of every rule made by such agency regarding this section;

(6) a copy of the fee schedule and the total amount of fees collected by the agency for making records available under this section; and

(7) such other information as indicates efforts to administer fully this section.

The Attorney General shall submit an annual report on or before March 1 of each calendar year which shall include for the prior calendar year a listing of the number of cases arising under this section, the exemption involved in each case, the disposition of such case, and the cost, fees, and penalties assessed under subsections (a)(4)(E), (F), and (G). Such report shall also include a description of the efforts undertaken by the Department of Justice to encourage agency compliance with this section.

(e) For purposes of this section, the term "agency" as defined in section 551(1) of this title includes any executive department, military department, Government corporation, Government controlled corporation, or other establishment in the executive branch of the Government (including the Executive Office of the President), or any independent regulatory agency.

§ 552a. Records maintained on individuals

(a) Definitions.—For purposes of this section—

(1) the term "agency" means agency as defined in section 552(e) of this title;

(2) the term "individual" means a citizen of the United States or an alien lawfully admitted for permanent residence;

(3) the term "maintain" includes maintain, collect, use, or disseminate;

(4) the term "record" means any item, collection, or grouping of information about an individual that is maintained by an agency, including, but not limited to, his education, financial transactions, medical history, and criminal or employment history and that contains his name, or the identifying number, symbol, or other identifying particular assigned to the indi-

vidual, such as a finger or voice print or a photograph;

(5) the term "system of records" means a group of any records under the control of any agency from which information is retrieved by the name of the individual or by some identifying number, symbol, or other identifying particular assigned to the individual;

(6) the term "statistical record" means a record in a system of records maintained for statistical research or reporting purposes only and not used in whole or in part in making any determination about an identifiable individual, except as provided by section 8 of title 13; and

(7) the term "routine use" means, with respect to the disclosure of a record, the use of such record for a purpose which is compatible with the purpose for which it was collected.

(b) Conditions of disclosure.—No agency shall disclose any record which is contained in a system of records by any means of communication to any person, or to another agency, except pursuant to a written request by, or with the prior written consent of, the individual to whom the record pertains, unless disclosure of the record would be—

(1) to those officers and employees of the agency which maintains the record who have a need for the record in the performance of their duties;

(2) required under section 552 of this title;

(3) for a routine use as defined in subsection (a)(7) of this section and described under subsection (e)(4)(D) of this section;

(4) to the Bureau of the Census for purposes of planning or carrying out a census or survey or related activity pursuant to the provisions of title 13;

(5) to a recipient who has provided the agency with advance adequate written assurance that the record will be used solely as a statistical research or reporting record, and the record is to be transferred in a form that is not individually identifiable;

(6) to the National Archives of the United States as a record which has sufficient historical or other value to warrant its continued preservation by the United States Government, or for evaluation by the Administrator of General Services or his designee to determine whether the record has such value;

(7) to another agency or to an instrumentality of any governmental jurisdiction within or under the control of the United States for a civil or criminal law enforcement activity if the activity is authorized by law, and if the head of the agency or instrumentality has made a written request to the agency which maintains the record specifying the particular portion desired and the law enforcement activity for which the record is sought;

(8) to a person pursuant to a showing of compelling circumstances affecting the health or safety of an individual if upon such disclosure notification is transmitted to the last known address of such individual;

(9) to either House of Congress, or, to the extent of matter within its jurisdiction, any committee or subcommittee thereof, any joint committee of Congress or subcommittee of any such joint committee;

(10) to the Comptroller General, or any of his authorized representatives, in the course of the performance of the duties of the General Accounting Office; or

(11) pursuant to the order of a court of competent jurisdiction.

(c) Accounting of Certain Disclosures.—Each agency, with respect to each system of records under its control, shall—

(1) except for disclosures made under subsections (b)(1) or (b)(2) of this section, keep an accurate accounting of—

(A) the date, nature, and purpose of each disclosure of a record to any person or to another agency made under subsection (b) of this section; and

(B) the name and address of the person or agency to whom the disclosure is made;

(2) retain the accounting made under paragraph (1) of this subsection for at least five years or the life of the record, whichever is longer, after the disclosure for which the accounting is made;

(3) except for disclosures made under subsection (b)(7) of this section, make the accounting made under paragraph (1) of this subsection available to the individual named in the record at his request; and

(4) inform any person or other agency about any correction or notation of dispute made by the agency in accordance with subsection (d) of this section of

[*349*]

any record that has been disclosed to the person or agency if an accounting of the disclosure was made.

(d) Access to records.—Each agency that maintains a system of records shall—

(1) upon request by any individual to gain access to his record or to any information pertaining to him which is contained in the system, permit him and upon his request, a person of his own choosing to accompany him, to review the record and have a copy made of all or any portion thereof in a form comprehensible to him, except that the agency may require the individual to furnish a written statement authorizing discussion of that individual's record in the accompanying person's presence;

(2) permit the individual to request amendment of a record pertaining to him and—

(A) not later than 10 days (excluding Saturdays, Sundays, and legal public holidays) after the date of receipt of such request, acknowledge in writing such receipt; and

(B) promptly, either—

(i) make any correction of any portion thereof which the individual believes is not accurate, relevant, timely, or complete; or

(ii) inform the individual of its refusal to amend the record in accordance with his request, the reason for the refusal, the procedures established by the agency for the individual to request a review of that refusal by the head of the agency or an officer designated by the head of the agency, and the name and business address of that official;

(3) permit the individual who disagrees with the refusal of the agency to amend his record to request a review of such refusal, and not later than 30 days (excluding Saturdays, Sundays, and legal public holidays) from the date on which the individual requests such review, complete such review and make a final determination unless, for good cause shown, the head of the agency extends such 30-day period; and if, after his review, the reviewing official also refuses to amend the record in accordance with the request, permit the individual to file with the agency a concise statement setting forth the reasons for his disagreement with the refusal of the agency, and notify the individual of the provisions for judicial review of the reviewing official's determination under subsection (g)(1)(A) of this section;

(4) in any disclosure, containing information about which the individual has filed a statement of disagreement, occurring after the filing of the statement under paragraph (3) of this subsection, clearly note any portion of the record which is disputed and provide copies of the statement and, if the agency deems it appropriate, copies of a concise statement of the reasons of the agency for not making the amendments requested, to persons or other agencies to whom the disputed record has been disclosed; and

(5) nothing in this section shall allow an individual access to any information compiled in reasonable anticipation of a civil action or proceeding.

(e) Agency requirements.—Each agency that maintains a system of records shall—

(1) maintain in its records only such information about an individual as is relevant and necessary to accomplish a purpose of the agency required to be accomplished by statute or by executive order of the President;

(2) collect information to the greatest extent practicable directly from the subject individual when the information may result in adverse determinations about an individual's rights, benefits, and privileges under Federal programs;

(3) inform each individual whom it asks to supply information, on the form which it uses to collect the information or on a separate form that can be retained by the individual—

(A) the authority (whether granted by statute, or by executive order of the President) which authorizes the solicitation of the information and whether disclosure of such information is mandatory or voluntary;

(B) the principal purpose or purposes for which the information is intended to be used;

(C) the routine uses which may be made of the information, as published pursuant to paragraph (4)(D) of this subsection; and

(D) the effects on him, if any, of not providing all or any part of the requested information;

(4) subject to the provisions of paragraph (11) of this subsection, publish in the Federal Register at least

annually a notice of the existence and character of the system of records, which notice shall include—

(A) the name and location of the system;

(B) the categories of individuals on whom records are maintained in the system;

(C) the categories of records maintained in the system;

(D) each routine use of the records contained in the system, including the categories of users and the purpose of such use;

(E) the policies and practices of the agency regarding storage, retrievability, access controls, retention, and disposal of the records;

(F) the title and business address of the agency official who is responsible for the system of records;

(G) the agency procedures whereby an individual can be notified at his request if the system of records contains a record pertaining to him;

(H) the agency procedures whereby an individual can be notified at his request how he can gain access to any record pertaining to him contained in the system of records, and how he can contest its content; and

(I) the categories of sources of records in the system;

(5) maintain all records which are used by the agency in making any determination about any individual with such accuracy, relevance, timeliness, and

completeness as is reasonably necessary to assure fairness to the individual in the determination;

(6) prior to disseminating any record about an individual to any person other than an agency, unless the dissemination is made pursuant to subsection (b)(2) of this section, make reasonable efforts to assure that such records are accurate, complete, timely, and relevant for agency purposes;

(7) maintain no record describing how any individual exercises rights guaranteed by the First Amendment unless expressly authorized by statute or by the individual about whom the record is maintained or unless pertinent to and within the scope of an authorized law enforcement activity;

(8) make reasonable efforts to serve notice on an individual when any record on such individual is made available to any person under compulsory legal process when such process becomes a matter of public record;

(9) establish rules of conduct for persons involved in the design, development, operation, or maintenance of any system of records, or in maintaining any record, and instruct each such person with respect to such rules and the requirements of this section, including any other rules and procedures adopted pursuant to this section and the penalties for noncompliance;

(10) establish appropriate administrative, technical, and physical safeguards to insure the security and confidentiality of records and to protect against any anticipated threats or hazards to their security or

integrity which could result in substantial harm, embarrassment, inconvenience, or unfairness to any individual on whom information is maintained; and

(11) at least 30 days prior to publication of information under paragraph (4)(D) of this subsection, publish in the Federal Register notice of any new use or intended use of the information in the system, and provide an opportunity for interested persons to submit written data, views, or arguments to the agency.

(f) Agency rules.—In order to carry out the provisions of this section, each agency that maintains a system of records shall promulgate rules, in accordance with the requirements (including general notice) of section 553 of this title, which shall—

(1) establish procedures whereby an individual can be notified in response to his request if any system of records named by the individual contains a record pertaining to him;

(2) define reasonable times, places, and requirements for identifying an individual who requests his record or information pertaining to him before the agency shall make the record or information available to the individual;

(3) establish procedures for the disclosure to an individual upon his request of his record or information pertaining to him, including special procedure, if deemed necessary, for the disclosure to an individual of medical records, including psychological records, pertaining to him;

(4) establish procedures for reviewing a request from an individual concerning the amendment of any record or information pertaining to the individual, for making a determination on the request, for an appeal within the agency of an initial adverse agency determination, and for whatever additional means may be necessary for each individual to be able to exercise fully his rights under this section; and

(5) establish fees to be charged, if any, to any individual for making copies of his record, excluding the cost of any search for and review of the record.

The Office of the Federal Register shall annually compile and publish the rules promulgated under this subsection and agency notices published under subsection (e)(4) of this section in a form available to the public at low cost.

(g)(1) Civil remedies.—Whenever any agency

(A) makes a determination under subsection (d)(3) of this section not to amend an individual's record in accordance with his request, or fails to make such review in conformity with that subsection;

(B) refuses to comply with an individual request under subsection (d)(1) of this section;

(C) fails to maintain any record concerning any individual with such accuracy, relevance, timeliness, and completeness as is necessary to assure fairness in any determination relating to the qualifications, character, rights, or opportunities of, or benefits to the individual that may be made on the basis of such record, and consequently a determination is made which is adverse to the individual; or

(D) fails to comply with any other provision of this section, or any rule promulgated thereunder, in such a way as to have an adverse effect on an individual,

the individual may bring a civil action against the agency, and the district courts of the United States shall have jurisdiction in the matters under the provisions of this subsection.

(2)(A) In any suit brought under the provisions of subsection (g)(1)(A) of this section, the court may order the agency to amend the individual's record in accordance with his request or in such other way as the court may direct. In such a case the court shall determine the matter de novo.

(B) The court may assess against the United States reasonable attorney fees and other litigation costs reasonably incurred in any case under this paragraph in which the complainant has substantially prevailed.

(3)(A) In any suit brought under the provisions of subsection (g)(1)(B) of this section, the court may enjoin the agency from withholding the records and order the production to the complainant of any agency records improperly withheld from him. In such a case the court shall determine the matter de novo, and may examine the contents of any agency records in camera to determine whether the records or any portion thereof may be withheld under any of the exemptions set forth in subsection (k) of this section, and the burden is on the agency to sustain its action.

(B) The court may assess against the United States reasonable attorney fees and other litigation costs reasonably incurred in any case under this paragraph in which the complainant has substantially prevailed.

(4) In any suit brought under the provisions of subsection (g)(1)(C) or (D) of this section in which the court determines that the agency acted in a manner which was intentional or willful, the United States shall be liable to the individual in an amount equal to the sum of—

(A) actual damages sustained by the individual as a result of the refusal or failure, but in no case shall a person entitled to recovery receive less than the sum of $1,000; and

(B) the costs of the action together with reasonable attorney fees as determined by the court.

(5) An action to enforce any liability created under this section may be brought in the district court of the United States in the district in which the complainant resides, or has his principal place of business, or in which the agency records are situated, or in the District of Columbia, without regard to the amount in controversy, within two years from the date on which the cause of action arises, except that where an agency has materially and willfully misrepresented any information required under this section to be disclosed to an individual and the information so misrepresented is material to establishment of the liability of the agency to the individual under this section, the action may be brought at any time within two years after discovery by the individual of the misrepresentation. Nothing in this section shall be construed to authorize any civil action by reason of any injury sustained as the result of a disclosure of a record prior to September 27, 1975.

(h) Rights of legal guardians.—For the purposes of this section, the parent of any minor, or the legal guardian of any individual who has been declared to be incompetent due to physical or mental incapacity or age by a court of competent jurisdiction, may act on behalf of the individual.

(i)(1) Criminal penalties.—Any officer or employee of an agency, who by virtue of his employment or official position, has possession of, or access to, agency records which contain individually identifiable information the disclosure of which is prohibited by this section or by rules or regulations established thereunder, and who knowing that disclosure of the specific material is so prohibited, willfully discloses the material in any manner to any person or agency not entitled to receive it, shall be guilty of a misdemeanor and fined not more than $5,000.

(2) Any officer or employee of any agency who willfully maintains a system of records without meeting the notice requirements of subsection (e)(4) of this section shall be guilty of a misdemeanor and fined not more than $5,000.

(3) Any person who knowingly and willfully requests or obtains any record concerning an individual from an agency under false pretenses shall be guilty of a misdemeanor and fined not more than $5,000.

(j) General exemptions.—The head of any agency may promulgate rules, in accordance with the requirements (including general notice) of sections 553(b)(1), (2), and (3), (c), and (e) of this title, to exempt any system of records within the agency from any part of this section except subsections (b), (c)(1) and (2), (e)(4)(A) through (F), (e)(6), (7), (9), (10), and (11), and (i) if the system of records is—

(1) maintained by the Central Intelligence Agency; or

(2) maintained by an agency or component thereof which performs as its principal function any activity pertaining to the enforcement of criminal laws, including police efforts to prevent, control, or reduce crime or to apprehend criminals, and the activities of prosecutors, courts, correctional, probation, pardon, or parole authorities, and which consists of (A) information compiled for the purpose of identifying individual criminal offenders and alleged offenders and consisting only of identifying data and notations of arrests, the nature and disposition of criminal charges, sentencing, confinement, release, and parole and probation status; (B) information compiled for the purpose of a criminal investigation, including reports of informants and investigators, and associated with an identifiable individual; or (C) reports identifiable to an individual compiled at any stage of the process of enforcement of the criminal laws from arrest or indictment through release from supervision.

At the time rules are adopted under this subsection, the agency shall include in the statement required under section 553(c) of this title, the reasons why the system of records is to be exempted from a provision of this section.

(k) Specific exemptions.—The head of any agency may promulgate rules, in accordance with the requirements (including general notice) of sections 553(b)(1), (2), and (3), (c), and (e) of this title, to exempt any system of records within the agency from subsections (c)(3), (d), (e)(1), (e)(4)(G), (H), and (I) and (f) of this section if the system of records is—

(1) subject to the provisions of section 552(b)(1) of this title;

(2) investigatory material compiled for law enforcement purposes, other than material within the scope of subsection (j)(2) of this section: *Provided, however,* That if any individual is denied any right, privilege, or benefit that he would otherwise be entitled by Federal law, or for which he would otherwise be eligible, as a result of the maintenance of such material, such material shall be provided to such individual, except to the extent that the disclosure of such material would reveal the identity of a source who furnished information to the Government under an express promise that the identity of the source would be held in confidence, or, prior to the effective date of this section, under an implied promise that the identity of the source would be held in confidence;

(3) maintained in connection with providing protective services to the President of the United States or other individuals pursuant to section 3056 of title 18;

(4) required by statute to be maintained and used solely as statistical records;

(5) investigatory material compiled solely for the purpose of determining suitability, eligibility, or qualifications for Federal civilian employment, military service, Federal contracts, or access to classified information, but only to the extent that the

disclosure of such material would reveal the identity of a source who furnished information to the Government under an express promise that the identity of the source would be held in confidence, or prior to the effective date of this section, under an implied promise that the identity of the source would be held in confidence;

(6) testing or examination material used solely to determine individual qualifications for appointment or promotion in the Federal service the disclosure of which would compromise the objectivity or fairness of the testing or examination process; or

(7) evaluation material used to determine potential for promotion in the armed services, but only to the extent that the disclosure of such material would reveal the identity of a source who furnished information to the Government under an express promise that the identity of the source would be held in confidence, or, prior to the effective date of this section, under an implied promise that the identity of the source would be held in confidence.

At the time rules are adopted under this subsection, the agency shall include in the statement required under section 553(c) of this title, the reasons why the system of records is to be exempted from a provision of this section.

(*l*)(1) Archival records.—Each agency record which is accepted by the Administrator of General Services for storage, processing, and servicing in accordance with section 3103 of title 44 shall, for the purposes of this section, be considered to be maintained by the agency which deposited the record and shall be subject to the provisions of this section. The Administrator of General Services shall not disclose the record except to the agency which maintains the record, or under rules established by that agency which are not inconsistent with the provisions of this section.

(2) Each agency record pertaining to an identifiable individual which was transferred to the National Archives of the United States as a record which has sufficient historical or other value to warrant its continued preservation by the United States Government, prior to the effective date of this section, shall, for the purposes of this section, be considered to be maintained by the National Archives and shall not be subject to the provisions of this section, except that a statement generally describing such records (modeled after the requirements relating to records subject to subsections (e)(4)(A) through (G) of this section) shall be published in the Federal Register.

(3) Each agency record pertaining to an identifiable individual which is transferred to the National Archives of the United States as a record which has sufficient historical or other value to warrant its continued preservation by the United States Government, on or after the effective date of this section, shall, for the purposes of this section, be considered to be maintained by the National Archives and shall be exempt from the requirements of this section except subsections (e)(4)(A) through (G) and (e)(9) of this section.

(m) Government contractors.—When an agency provides by a contract for the operation by or on behalf of the agency of a system of records to accomplish an agency function, the agency shall, consistent with its authority, cause the requirements of this section to be applied to such system. For purposes of subsection (i) of this section any such contractor and any employee of such contractor, if such contract is agreed to on or after the effective date of this section, shall be considered to be an employee of an agency.

(n) Mailing lists.—An individual's name and address may not be sold or rented by an agency unless such action is specifically authorized by law. This provision shall not be construed to require the withholding of names and addresses otherwise permitted to be made public.

(o) Report on new systems.—Each agency shall provide adequate advance notice to Congress and the Office of Management and Budget of any proposal to establish or alter any system of records in order to permit an evaluation of the probable or potential effect of such proposal on the privacy and other personal or property rights of individuals or the disclosure of information relating to such individuals, and its effect on the preservation of the constitutional principles of federalism and separation of powers.

(p) Annual report.—The President shall submit to the Speaker of the House and the President of the Senate, by June 30 of each calendar year, a consolidated report, separately listing for each Federal agency the number of records contained in any system of records which were exempted from the application of this section under the provisions of subsections (j) and (k) of this section during the preceding calendar year, and the reasons for the exemptions, and such other information as indicates efforts to administer fully this section.

(q) Effect of other laws.—No agency shall rely on any exemption contained in section 552 of this title to withhold from an individual any record which is otherwise accessible to such individual under the provisions of this section.

§ 552b. Open meetings

(a) For purposes of this section—

(1) the term "agency" means any agency, as defined in section 552(e) of this title, headed by a collegial body composed of two or more individual members, a majority of whom are appointed to such position by the President with the advice and consent of the Senate, and any subdivision thereof authorized to act on behalf of the agency;

(2) the term "meeting" means the deliberations of at least the number of individual agency members required to take action on behalf of the agency where such deliberations determine or result in the joint conduct or disposition of official agency business, but does not include deliberations required or permitted by subsection (d) or (e); and

(3) the term "member" means an individual who belongs to a collegial body heading an agency.

(b) Members shall not jointly conduct or dispose of agency business other than in accordance with this section. Except as provided in subsection (c), every portion of every meeting of an agency shall be open to public observation.

(c) Except in a case where the agency finds that the public interest requires otherwise, the second sentence of subsection (b) shall not apply to any portion of an agency meeting, and the requirements of subsections (d) and (e) shall not apply to any information pertaining to such meeting otherwise required by this section to be disclosed to the public, where the agency properly determines that such portion or portions of its meeting or the disclosure of such information is likely to—

(1) disclose matters that are (A) specifically authorized under criteria established by an Executive order to be kept secret in the interests of national defense or foreign policy and (B) in fact properly classified pursuant to such Executive order;

(2) relate solely to the internal personnel rules and practices of an agency;

(3) disclose matters specifically exempted from disclosure by statute (other than section 552 of this title), provided that such statute (A) requires that the matters be withheld from the public in such a manner as to leave no discretion on the issue, or (B) establishes particular criteria for withholding or refers to particular types of matters to be withheld;

(4) disclose trade secrets and commercial or financial information obtained from a person and privileged or confidential;

(5) involve accusing any person of a crime, or formally censuring any person;

(6) disclose information of a personal nature where disclosure would constitute a clearly unwarranted invasion of personal privacy;

(7) disclose investigatory records compiled for law enforcement purposes, or information which if written

would be contained in such records, but only to the extent that the production of such records or information would (A) interfere with enforcement proceedings, (B) deprive a person of a right to a fair trial or an impartial adjudication, (C) constitute an unwarranted invasion of personal privacy, (D) disclose the identity of a confidential source and, in the case of a record compiled by a criminal law enforcement authority in the course of a criminal investigation, or by an agency conducting a lawful national security intelligence investigation, confidential information furnished only by the confidential source, (E) disclose investigative techniques and procedures, or (F) endanger the life or physical safety of law enforcement personnel;

(8) disclose information contained in or related to examination, operating, or condition reports prepared by, on behalf of, or for the use of an agency responsible for the regulation or supervision of financial institutions;

(9) disclose information the premature disclosure of which would—

(A) in the case of an agency which regulates currencies, securities, commodities, or financial institutions, be likely to (i) lead to significant financial speculation in currencies, securities, or commodities, or (ii) significantly endanger the stability of any financial institution; or

(B) in the case of any agency, be likely to significantly frustrate implementation of a proposed agency action, except that subparagraph (B) shall not apply in any instance where the agency has already disclosed to the public the content or nature of its proposed action, or where the agency is required by law to make such disclosure on its own initiative prior to taking final agency action on such proposal; or

(10) specifically concern the agency's issuance of a subpena, or the agency's participation in a civil action or proceeding, an action in a foreign court or international tribunal, or an arbitration, or the initiation, conduct, or disposition by the agency of a particular case of formal agency adjudication pursuant to the procedures in section 554 of this title or otherwise involving a determination on the record after opportunity for a hearing.

(d)(1) Action under subsection (c) shall be taken only when a majority of the entire membership of the agency (as defined in subsection (a)(1)) votes to take such action. A separate vote of the agency members shall be taken with respect to each agency meeting a portion or portions of which are proposed to be closed to the public pursuant to subsection (c), or with respect to any information which is proposed to be withheld under subsection (c). A single vote may be taken with respect to a series of meetings, a portion or portions of which are proposed to be closed to the public, or with respect to any information concerning such series of meetings, so long as each meeting in such series involves the same particular matters and is scheduled to be held no more than thirty days after the initial meeting in such series. The vote of each agency member participating in such vote shall be recorded and no proxies shall be allowed.

(2) Whenever any person whose interests may be directly affected by a portion of a meeting requests that the agency close such portion to the public for any of the reasons referred to in paragraph (5), (6), or (7) of subsection (c), the agency, upon request of any one of its members, shall vote by recorded vote whether to close such meeting.

(3) Within one day of any vote taken pursuant to paragraph (1) or (2), the agency shall make publicly available a written copy of such vote reflecting the vote of each member on the question. If a portion of a meeting is to be closed to the public, the agency shall, within one day of the vote taken pursuant to paragraph (1) or (2) of this subsection, make publicly available a full written explanation of its action closing the portion together with a list of all persons expected to attend the meeting and their affiliation.

(4) Any agency, a majority of whose meetings may properly be closed to the public pursuant to paragraph (4), (8), (9)(A), or (10) of subsection (c), or any combination thereof, may provide by regulation for the closing of such meetings or portions thereof in the event that a majority of the members of the agency votes by recorded vote at the beginning of such meeting, or portion thereof, to close the exempt portion or portions of the meeting, and a copy of such vote, reflecting the vote of each member on the question, is made available to the public. The provisions of paragraphs (1), (2), and (3) of this subsection and subsection (e) shall not apply to any portion of a meeting to which such regulations apply: *Provided,* That the agency shall, except to the extent that such information is exempt from disclosure under the provisions of subsection (c),

provide the public with public announcement of the time, place, and subject matter of the meeting and of each portion thereof at the earliest practicable time.

(e)(1) In the case of each meeting, the agency shall make public announcement, at least one week before the meeting, of the time, place, and subject matter of the meeting, whether it is to be open or closed to the public, and the name and phone number of the official designated by the agency to respond to requests for information about the meeting. Such announcement shall be made unless a majority of the members of the agency determines by a recorded vote that agency business requires that such meeting be called at an earlier date, in which case the agency shall make public announcement of the time, place, and subject matter of such meeting, and whether open or closed to the public, at the earliest practicable time.

(2) The time or place of a meeting may be changed following the public announcement required by paragraph (1) only if the agency publicly announces such change at the earliest practicable time. The subject matter of a meeting, or the determination of the agency to open or close a meeting, or portion of a meeting, to the public, may be changed following the public announcement required by this subsection only if (A) a majority of the entire membership of the agency determines by a recorded vote that agency business so requires and that no earlier announcement of the change was possible, and (B) the agency publicly announces such change and the vote of each member upon such change at the earliest practicable time.

(3) Immediately following each public announcement required by this subsection, notice of the time, place, and

subject matter of a meeting, whether the meeting is open or closed, any change in one of the preceding, and the name and phone number of the official designated by the agency to respond to requests for information about the meeting, shall also be submitted for publication in the Federal Register.

(f)(1) For every meeting closed pursuant to paragraphs (1) through (10) of subsection (c), the General Counsel or chief legal officer of the agency shall publicly certify that, in his or her opinion, the meeting may be closed to the public and shall state each relevant exemptive provision. A copy of such certification, together with a statement from the presiding officer of the meeting setting forth the time and place of the meeting, and the persons present, shall be retained by the agency. The agency shall maintain a complete transcript or electronic recording adequate to record fully the proceedings of each meeting, or portion of a meeting, closed to the public, except that in the case of a meeting, or portion of a meeting, closed to the public pursuant to paragraph (8), (9)(A), or (10) of subsection (c), the agency shall maintain either such a transcript or recording, or a set of minutes. Such minutes shall fully and clearly describe all matters discussed and shall provide a full and accurate summary of any actions taken, and the reasons therefor, including a description of each of the views expressed on any item and the record of any rollcall vote (reflecting the vote of each member on the question). All documents considered in connection with any action shall be identified in such minutes.

(2) The agency shall make promptly available to the public, in a place easily accessible to the public, the transcript, electronic recording, or minutes (as required by

paragraph (1)) of the discussion of any item on the agenda, or of any item of the testimony of any witness received at the meeting, except for such item or items of such discussion or testimony as the agency determines to contain information which may be withheld under subsection (c). Copies of such transcript, or minutes, or a transcription of such recording disclosing the identity of each speaker, shall be furnished to any person at the actual cost of duplication or transcription. The agency shall maintain a complete verbatim copy of the transcript, a complete copy of the minutes, or a complete electronic recording of each meeting, or portion of a meeting, closed to the public, for a period of at least two years after such meeting, or until one year after the conclusion of any agency proceeding with respect to which the meeting or portion was held, whichever occurs later.

(g) Each agency subject to the requirements of this section shall, within 180 days after the date of enactment of this section, following consultation with the Office of the Chairman of the Administrative Conference of the United States and published notice in the Federal Register of at least thirty days and opportunity for written comment by any person, promulgate regulations to implement the requirements of subsections (b) through (f) of this section. Any person may bring a proceeding in the United States District Court for the District of Columbia to require an agency to promulgate such regulations if such agency has not promulgated such regulations within the time period specified herein. Subject to any limitations of time provided by law, any person may bring a proceeding in the United States Court of Appeals for the District of Columbia to set aside agency regulations issued pursuant to this subsection that are not in accord with the requirements of subsections (b) through (f) of this section and to require the promulgation of regulations that are in accord with such subsections.

(h)(1) The district courts of the United States shall have jurisdiction to enforce the requirements of subsections (b) through (f) of this section by declaratory judgment, injunctive relief, or other relief as may be appropriate. Such actions may be brought by any person against an agency prior to, or within sixty days after, the meeting out of which the violation of this section arises, except that if public announcement of such meeting is not initially provided by the agency in accordance with the requirements of this section, such action may be instituted pursuant to this section at any time prior to sixty days after any public announcement of such meeting. Such actions may be brought in the district court of the United States for the district in which the agency meeting is held or in which the agency in question has its headquarters, or in the District Court for the District of Columbia. In such actions a defendant shall serve his answer within thirty days after the service of the complaint. The burden is on the defendant to sustain his action. In deciding such cases the court may examine in camera any portion of the transcript, electronic recording, or minutes of a meeting closed to the public, and may take such additional evidence as it deems necessary. The court, having due regard for orderly administration and the public interest, as well as the interests of the parties, may grant such equitable relief as it deems appropriate, including granting an injunction against future violations of this section or ordering the agency to make available to the public such portion of the transcript, recording, or minutes of a meeting as is not authorized to be withheld under subsection (c) of this section.

(2) Any Federal court otherwise authorized by law to review agency action may, at the application of any person properly participating in the proceeding pursuant to other applicable law, inquire into violations by the agency of the requirements of this section and afford such relief as it deems appropriate. Nothing in this section authorizes any Federal court having jurisdiction solely on the basis of paragraph (1) to set aside, enjoin, or invalidate any agency action (other than an action to close a meeting or to withhold information under this section) taken or discussed at any agency meeting out of which the violation of this section arose.

(i) The court may assess against any party reasonable attorney fees and other litigation costs reasonably incurred by any other party who substantially prevails in any action brought in accordance with the provisions of subsection (g) or (h) of this section, except that costs may be assessed against the plaintiff only where the court finds that the suit was initiated by the plaintiff primarily for frivolous or dilatory purposes. In the case of assessment of costs against an agency, the costs may be assessed by the court against the United States.

(j) Each agency subject to the requirements of this section shall annually report to Congress regarding its compliance with such requirements, including a tabulation of the total number of agency meetings open to the public, the total number of meetings closed to the public, the reasons for closing such meetings, and a description of any litigation brought against the agency under this section, including any costs assessed against the agency in such litigation (whether or not paid by the agency).

(k) Nothing herein expands or limits the present rights of any person under section 552 of this title, except that the exemptions set forth in subsection (c) of this section shall govern in the case of any request made pursuant to section 552 to copy or inspect the transcripts, recordings, or minutes described in subsection (f) of this section. The requirements of chapter 33 of title 44, United States Code, shall not apply to the transcripts, recordings, and minutes described in subsection (f) of this section.

(*l*) This section does not constitute authority to withhold any information from Congress, and does not authorize the closing of any agency meeting or portion thereof required by any other provision of law to be open.

(m) Nothing in this section authorizes any agency to withhold from any individual any record, including transcripts, recordings, or minutes required by this section, which is otherwise accessible to such individual under Section 552a of this title.

§ 553.   Rule making

(a) This section applies, according to the provisions thereof, except to the extent that there is involved—

(1) a military or foreign affairs function of the United States; or

(2) a matter relating to agency management or personnel or to public property, loans, grants, benefits, or contracts.

(b) General notice of proposed rule making shall be published in the Federal Register, unless persons subject thereto are named and either personally served or otherwise have actual notice thereof in accordance with law. The notice shall include—

(1) a statement of the time, place, and nature of public rule making proceedings;

(2) reference to the legal authority under which the rule is proposed; and

(3) either the terms or substance of the proposed rule or a description of the subjects and issues involved.

Except when notice or hearing is required by statute, this subsection does not apply—

(A) to interpretative rules, general statements of policy, or rules of agency organization, procedure, or practice; or

(B) when the agency for good cause finds (and incorporates the finding and a brief statement of reasons therefor in the rules issued) that notice and public procedure thereon are impracticable, unnecessary, or contrary to the public interest.

(c) After notice required by this section, the agency shall give interested persons an opportunity to participate in the rule making through submission of written data, views, or arguments with or without opportunity for oral presentation. After consideration of the relevant matter presented, the agency shall incorporate in the rules adopted a concise general statement of their basis and purpose. When rules are required by statute to be made on the record after opportunity for an agency hearing, sections 556 and 557 of this title apply instead of this subsection.

(d) The required publication or service of a substantive rule shall be made not less than 30 days before its effective date, except—

(1) a substantive rule which grants or recognizes an exemption or relieves a restriction;

(2) interpretative rules and statements of policy; or

(3) as otherwise provided by the agency for good cause found and published with the rule.

(e) Each agency shall give an interested person the right to petition for the issuance, amendent, or repeal of a rule.

§ 554. Adjudications

(a) This section applies, according to the provisions thereof, in every case of adjudication required by statute to be determined on the record after opportunity for an agency hearing, except to the extent that there is involved—

(1) a matter subject to a subsequent trial of the law and the facts de novo in a court;

(2) the selection or tenure of an employee, except a hearing examiner appointed under section 3105 of this title;

(3) proceedings in which decisions rest solely on inspections, tests, or elections;

(4) the conduct of military or foreign affairs functions;

(5) cases in which an agency is acting as an agent for a court; or

(6) the certification of worker representatives.

(b) Persons entitled to notice of an agency hearing shall be timely informed of—

(1) the time, place, and nature of the hearing;

(2) the legal authority and jurisdiction under which the hearing is to be held; and

(3) the matters of fact and law asserted.

When private persons are the moving parties, other parties to the proceeding shall give prompt notice of issues controverted in fact or law; and in other instances agencies may by rule require responsive pleading. In fixing the time and place for hearings, due regard shall be had for the convenience and necessity of the parties or their representatives.

(c) The agency shall give all interested parties opportunity for—

(1) the submission and consideration of facts, arguments, offers of settlement, or proposals of adjustment when time, the nature of the proceeding, and the public interest permit; and

(2) to the extent that the parties are unable so to determine a controversy by consent, hearing and decision on notice and in accordance with sections 556 and 557 of this title.

(d) The employee who presides at the reception of evidence pursuant to section 556 of this title shall make the recommended decision or initial decision required by section 557 of this title, unless he becomes unavailable to the agency. Except to the extent required for the disposition of ex parte matters as authorized by law, such an employee may not—

(1) consult a person or party on a fact in issue, unless on notice and opportunity for all parties to participate; or

(2) be responsible to or subject to the supervision or direction of an employee or agent engaged in the performance of investigative or prosecuting functions for an agency.

An employee or agent engaged in the performance of investigative or prosecuting functions for an agency in a case may not, in that or a factually related case, participate or advise in the decision, recommended decision, or agency review pursuant to section 557 of this title, except as witness or counsel in public proceedings. This subsection does not apply—

(A) in determining applications for initial licenses;

(B) to proceedings involving the validity or application of rates, facilities, or practices of public utilities or carriers; or

(C) to the agency or a member or members of the body comprising the agency.

(e) The agency, with like effect as in the case of other orders, and in its sound discretion, may issue a declaratory order to terminate a controversy or remove uncertainty.

§ 555. Ancillary matters

(a) This section applies, according to the provisions thereof, except as otherwise provided by this subchapter;

(b) A person compelled to appear in person before an agency or representative thereof is entitled to be accompanied, represented, and advised by counsel or, if permitted by the agency, by other qualified representative. A party is entitled to appear in person or by or with counsel or other duly qualified representative in an agency proceeding. So far as the orderly conduct of public business permits, an interested person may appear before an agency or its responsible employees for the presentation, adjustment, or determination of an issue, request, or controversy in a proceeding, whether interlocutory, summary, or otherwise, or in connection with an agency function. With due regard for the convenience and necessity of the parties or their representatives and within a reasonable time, each agency shall proceed to conclude a matter presented to it. This subsection does not grant or deny a person who is not a lawyer the right to appear for or represent others before an agency or in an agency proceeding.

(c) Process, requirement of a report, inspection, or other investigative act or demand may not be issued, made, or enforced except as authorized by law. A person compelled to submit data or evidence is entitled to retain or, on payment of lawfully prescribed costs, procure a copy or transcript thereof, except that in a non-public investigatory proceeding the witness may for good cause be limited to inspection of the official transcript of his testimony.

(d) Agency subpenas authorized by law shall be issued to a party on request and, when required by rules of procedure, on a statement or showing of general relevance and reasonable scope of the evidence sought. On contest, the court shall sustain the subpena or similar process or demand to the extent that it is found to be in accordance with law. In a proceeding for enforcement, the court shall issue an order requiring the appearance of the witness or the production of the evidence or data within a reasonable time under penalty of punishment for contempt in cases of contumacious failure to comply.

(e) Prompt notice shall be given of the denial in whole or in part of a written application, petition, or other request of an interested person made in connection with any agency proceeding. Except in affirming a prior denial or when the denial is self-explanatory, the notice shall be accompanied by a brief statement of the grounds for denial.

§ 556. Hearings; presiding employees; powers and duties; burden of proof; evidence; record as basis of decision

(a) This section applies, according to the provisions thereof, to hearings required by section 553 or 554 of this title to be conducted in accordance with this section.

(b) There shall preside at the taking of evidence—

(1) the agency;

(2) one or more members of the body which comprises the agency; or

(3) one or more hearing examiners appointed under section 3105 of this title.

This subchapter does not supersede the conduct of specified classes of proceedings, in whole or in part, by or before boards or other employees specially provided for by or designated under statute. The functions of presiding employees and of employees participating in decisions in accordance with section 557 of this title shall be conducted in an impartial manner. A presiding or participating employee may at any time disqualify himself. On the filing in good faith of a timely and sufficient affidavit of personal bias or other disqualification of a presiding or participating employee, the agency shall determine the matters as a part of the record and decision in the case.

(c) Subject to published rules of the agency and within its powers, employees presiding at hearings may—

(1) administer oaths and affirmations;

(2) issue subpenas authorized by law;

(3) rule on offers of proof and receive relevant evidence;

(4) take depositions or have depositions taken when the ends of justice would be served;

(5) regulate the course of the hearing;

(6) hold conferences for the settlement or simplification of the issues by consent of the parties;

(7) dispose of procedural requests or similar matters;

(8) make or recommend decisions in accordance with section 557 of this title; and

(9) take other action authorized by agency rule consistent with this subchapter.

(d) Except as otherwise provided by statute, the proponent of a rule or order has the burden of proof. Any oral or documentary evidence may be received, but the agency as a matter of policy shall provide for the exclusion of irrelevant, immaterial, or unduly repetitious evidence. A sanction may not be imposed or rule or order issued except on consideration of the whole record or those parts thereof cited by a party and supported by and in accordance with the reliable, probative, and substantial evidence. The agency may, to the extent consistent with the interests of justice and the policy of the underlying statutes administered by the agency, consider a violation of section 557(d) of this title sufficient grounds for a decision adverse to a party who has knowingly committed such violation or knowingly caused such violation to occur. A party is entitled to present his case or defense by oral or documentary evidence, to submit rebuttal evidence, and to conduct such cross-examination as may be required for a full and true disclosure of the facts. In rule making or determining claims for money or benefits or applications for initial licenses an agency may, when a party will not be prejudiced thereby, adopt procedures for the submission of all or part of the evidence in written form.

(e) The transcript of testimony and exhibits, together with all papers and requests filed in the proceeding, constitutes the exclusive record for decision in accordance with section 557 of this title and, on payment of lawfully prescribed costs, shall be made available to the parties. When an agency decision rests on official notice of a material fact not appearing in the evidence in the record, a party is entitled, on timely request, to an opportunity to show the contrary.

§ 557. Initial decisions; conclusiveness; review by agency; submissions by parties; contents of decisions; record

(a) This section applies, according to the provisions thereof, when a hearing is required to be conducted in accordance with section 556 of this title.

(b) When the agency did not preside at the reception of the evidence, the presiding employee or, in cases not subject to section 554(d) of this title, an employee qualified to preside at hearings pursuant to section 556 of this title, shall initially decide the case unless the agency requires, either in specific cases or by general rule, the entire record to be certified to it for decision. When the presiding employee makes an initial decision, that decision then becomes the decision of the agency without further proceedings unless there is an appeal to, or review on motion of, the agency within time provided by rule. On appeal from or review of the intitial decision, the agency has all the powers which it would have in making the initial decision except as it may limit the issues on notice or by rule. When the agency makes the decision without having presided at the reception of the evidence, the presiding employee or an employee qualified to preside at hearings pursuant to section 556 of this title shall first recommend a decision, except that in rule making or determining application for initial licenses—

(1) instead thereof the agency may issue a tentative decision or one of its responsible employees may recommend a decision; or

(2) this procedure may be omitted in a case in which the agency finds on the record that due and timely execution of its functions imperatively and unavoidably so requires.

(c) Before a recommended, initial, or tentative decision, or a decision on agency review of the decision of subordinate employees, the parties are entitled to a reasonable opportunity to submit for the consideration of the employees participating in the decisions—

(1) proposed findings and conclusions; or

(2) exceptions to the decisions or recommended decisions of subordinate employees or to tentative agency decisions; and

(3) supporting reasons for the exceptions or proposed findings or conclusions.

The record shall show the ruling on each finding, conclusion, or exception presented. All decisions, including initial, recommended, and tentative decisions, are a part of the record and shall include a statement of—

(A) findings and conclusions, and the reasons or basis therefor, on all the material issues of fact, law, or discretion presented on the record; and

(B) the appropriate rule, order, sanction, relief, or denial thereof.

(d)(1) In any agency proceeding which is subject to subsection (a) of this section, except to the extent required for the disposition of ex parte matters as authorized by law—

(A) no interested person outside the agency shall make or knowingly cause to be made to any member of the body comprising the agency, administrative law judge, or other employee who is or may reasonably be expected to be involved in the decisional process of the proceeding, an ex parte communication relevant to the merits of the proceeding;

(B) no member of the body comprising the agency, administrative law judge, or other employee who is or may reasonably be expected to be involved in the decisional process of the proceeding, shall make or knowingly cause to be made to any interested person

[*385*]

outside the agency an ex parte communication relevant to the merits of the proceeding;

(C) a member of the body comprising the agency, administrative law judge, or other employee who is or may reasonably be expected to be involved in the decisional process of such proceeding who receives, or who makes or knowingly causes to be made, a communication prohibited by this subsection shall place on the public record of the proceeding:

(i) all such written communications;

(ii) memoranda stating the substance of all such oral communications; and

(iii) all written responses, and memoranda stating the substance of all oral responses, to the materials described in clauses (i) and (ii) of this subparagraph;

(D) upon receipt of a communication knowingly made or knowingly caused to be made by a party in violation of this subsection, the agency, administrative law judge, or other employee presiding at the hearing may, to the extent consistent with the interests of justice and the policy of the underlying statutes, require the party to show cause why his claim or interest in the proceeding should not be dismissed, denied, disregarded, or otherwise adversely affected on account of such violation; and

(E) the prohibitions of this subsection shall apply beginning at such time as the agency may designate, but in no case shall they begin to apply later than the time at which a proceeding is noticed for hearing unless the person responsible for the communication has knowledge that it will be noticed, in which case the prohibitions shall apply beginning at the time of his acquisition of such knowledge.

(2) This subsection does not constitute authority to withhold information from Congress.

§ 558. Imposition of sanctions; determination of applications for licenses; suspension, revocation, and expiration of licenses

(a) This section applies, according to the provisions thereof, to the exercise of a power or authority.

(b) A sanction may not be imposed or a substantive rule or order issued except within jurisdiction delegated to the agency and as authorized by law.

(c) When application is made for a license required by law, the agency, with due regard for the rights and privileges of all the interested parties or adversely affected persons and within a reasonable time, shall set and complete proceedings required to be conducted in accordance with sections 556 and 557 of this title or other proceedings required by law and shall make its decision. Except in cases of willfulness or those in which public health, interest, or safety requires otherwise, the withdrawal, suspension, revocation, or annulment of a license is lawful only if, before the institution of agency proceedings therefor, the licensee has been given—

(1) notice by the agency in writing of the facts or conduct which may warrant the action; and

(2) opportunity to demonstrate or achieve compliance with all lawful requirements.

When the licensee has made timely and sufficient application for a renewal or a new license in accordance with agency rules, a license with reference to an activity of a continuing nature does not expire until the application has been finally determined by the agency.

§ 559. Effect on other laws; effect of subsequent statute

This subchapter, chapter 7, and sections 1305, 3105, 3344, 4301(2)(E), 5362, and 7521, and the provisions of section 5335(a)(B) of this title that relate to hearing examiners, do not limit or repeal additional requirements imposed by statute or otherwise recognized by law. Except as otherwise required by law, requirements or privileges relating to evidence or procedure apply equally to agencies and persons. Each agency is granted the authority necessary to comply with the requirements of this subchapter through the issuance of rules or otherwise. Subsequent statute may not be held to supersede or modify this subchapter, chapter 7, sections 1305, 3105, 3344, 4301(2)(E), 5362, or 7521, or the provisions of section 5335(a)(B) of this title that relate to hearing examiners, except to the extent that it does so expressly.

CHAPTER 6—THE ANALYSIS OF REGULATORY FUNCTIONS

§ 601. Definitions

For purposes of this chapter—

(1) the term 'agency' means an agency as defined in section 551(1) of this title;

(2) the term 'rule' means any rule for which the agency publishes a general notice of proposed

rulemaking pursuant to section 553(b) of this title, or any other law, including any rule of general applicability governing Federal grants to State and local governments for which the agency provides an opportunity for notice and public comment, except that the term 'rule' does not include a rule of particular applicability relating to rates, wages, corporate or financial structures or reorganizations thereof, prices, facilities, appliances, services, or allowances therefor or to valuations, costs or accounting, or practices relating to such rates, wages, structures, prices, appliances, services, or allowances;

(3) the term 'small business' has the same meaning as the term 'small business concern' under section 3 of the Small Business Act, unless an agency, after consultation with the Office of Advocacy of the Small Business Administration and after opportunity for public comment, establishes one or more definitions of such term which are appropriate to the activities of the agency and publishes such definition(s) in the Federal Register;

(4) the term 'small organization' means any not-for-profit enterprise which is independently owned and operated and is not dominant in its field, unless an agency establishes, after opportunity for public comment, one or more definitions of such term which are appropriate to the activities of the agency and publishes such definition(s) in the Federal Register;

(5) the term 'small governmental jurisdiction' means governments of cities, counties, towns, townships, villages, school districts, or special districts, with a

population of less than fifty thousand, unless an agency establishes, after opportunity for public comment, one or more definitions of such term which are appropriate to the activities of the agency and which are based on such factors as location in rural or sparsely populated areas or limited revenues due to the population of such jurisdiction, and publishes such definition(s) in the Federal Register; and

(6) the term 'small entity' shall have the same meaning as the terms 'small business', 'small organization' and 'small governmental jurisdiction' defined in paragraphs (3), (4) and (5) of this section.

§ 602. Regulatory agenda

(a) During the months of October and April of each year, each agency shall publish in the Federal Register a regulatory flexibility agenda which shall contain—

(1) a brief description of the subject area of any rule which the agency expects to propose or promulgate which is likely to have a significant economic impact on a substantial number of small entities;

(2) a summary of the nature of any such rule under consideration for each subject area listed in the agenda pursuant to paragraph (1), the objectives and legal basis for the issuance of the rule, and an approximate schedule for completing action on any rule for which the agency has issued a general notice of proposed rulemaking, and

(3) the name and telephone number of an agency official knowledgeable concerning the items listed in paragraph (1).

(b) Each regulatory flexibility agenda shall be transmitted to the Chief Counsel for Advocacy of the Small Business Administration for comment, if any.

(c) Each agency shall endeavor to provide notice of each regulatory flexibility agenda to small entities or their representatives through direct notification or publication of the agenda in publications likely to be obtained by such small entities and shall invite comments upon each subject area on the agenda.

(d) Nothing in this section precludes an agency from considering or acting on any matter not included in a regulatory flexibility agenda, or requires an agency to consider or act on any matter listed in such agenda.

§ 603. Initial regulatory flexibility analysis

(a) Whenever an agency is required by section 553 of this title, or any other law, to publish general notice of proposed rulemaking for any proposed rule, the agency shall prepare and make available for public comment an initial regulatory flexibility analysis. Such analysis shall describe the impact of the proposed rule on small entities. The initial regulatory flexibility analysis or a summary shall be published in the Federal Register at the time of the publication of general notice of proposed rulemaking for the rule. The agency shall transmit a copy of the initial regulatory flexibility analysis to the Chief Counsel for Advocacy of the Small Business Administration.

(b) Each initial regulatory flexibility analysis required under this section shall contain—

(1) a description of the reasons why action by the agency is being considered;

(2) a succinct statement of the objectives of, and legal basis for the proposed rule;

(3) a description of and, where feasible, an estimate of the number of small entities to which the proposed rule will apply;

(4) a description of the projected reporting, record-keeping and other compliance requirements of the proposed rule, including an estimate of the classes of small entities which will be subject to the requirement and the type of professional skills necessary for preparation of the report or record;

(5) an identification, to the extent practicable, of all relevant Federal rules which may duplicate, overlap or conflict with the proposed rule.

(c) Each initial regulatory flexibility analysis shall also contain a description of any significant alternatives to the proposed rule which accomplish the stated objectives of applicable statutes and which minimize any significant economic impact of the proposed rule on small entities. Consistent with the stated objectives of applicable statutes, the analysis shall discuss significant alternatives such as—

(1) the establishment of differing compliance or reporting requirements or timetables that take into account the resources available to small entities;

(2) the clarification, consolidation, or simplification of compliance and reporting requirements under the rule for such small entities;

(3) the use of preformance rather than design standards; and

(4) an exemption from coverage of the rule, or any part thereof, for such small entities.

§ 604. Final regulatory flexibility analysis

(a) When an agency promulgates a final rule under section 553 of this title, after being required by that section or any other law to publish a general notice of proposed rulemaking, the agency shall prepare a final regulatory flexibility analysis. Each final regulatory flexibility analysis shall contain—

(1) a succinct statement of the need for, and the objectives of, the rule;

(2) a summary of the issues raised by the public comments in response to the initial regulatory flexibility analysis, a summary of the assessment of the agency of such issues, and a statement of any changes made in the proposed rule as a result of such comments; and

(3) a description of each of the significant alternatives to the rule consistent with the stated objectives of applicable statutes and designed to minimize any significant economic impact of the rule on small entities which was considered by the agency, and a statement of the reasons why each one of such alternatives was rejected.

(b) The agency shall make copies of the final regulatory flexibility analysis available to members of the public and shall publish in the Federal Register at the time of publication of the final rule under section 553 of this title a statement describing how the public may obtain such copies.

§ 605. Avoidance of duplicative or unnecessary analyses

(a) Any Federal agency may perform the analyses required by sections 602, 603, and 604 of this title in conjunction with or as a part of any other agenda or analysis required by any other law if such other analysis satisfies the provisions of such sections.

(b) Sections 603 and 604 of this title shall not apply to any proposed or final rule if the head of the agency certifies that the rule will not, if promulgated, have a significant economic impact on a substantial number of small entities. If the head of the agency makes a certification under the preceding sentence, the agency shall publish such certification in the Federal Register, at the time of publication of general notice of proposed rulemaking for the rule or at the time of publication of the final rule, along with a succinct statement explaining the reasons for such certification, and provide such certification and statement to the Chief Counsel for Advocacy of the Small Business Administration.

(c) In order to avoid duplicative action, an agency may consider a series of closely related rules as one rule for the purposes of sections 602, 603, 604 and 610 of this title.

§ 606. Effect on other law

The requirements of sections 603 and 604 of this title do not alter in any manner standards otherwise applicable by law to agency action.

§ 607. Preparation of analyses

In complying with the provisions of sections 603 and 604 of this title, an agency may provide either a quantifiable or numerical description of the effects of a proposed rule or alternatives to the proposed rule, or more general descriptive statements if quantification is not practicable or reliable.

§ 608. Procedure for waiver or delay of completion

(a) An agency head may waive or delay the completion of some or all of the requirements of section 603 of this title by publishing in the Federal Register, not later than the date of publication of the final rule, a written finding, with reasons therefor, that the final rule is being promulgated in response to an emergency that makes compliance or timely compliance with the provisions of section 603 of this title impracticable.

(b) Except as provided in section 605(b), an agency head may not waive the requirements of section 604 of this title. An agency head may delay the completion of the requirements of section 604 of this title for a period of not more than one hundred and eighty days after the date of publication in the Federal Register of a final rule by publishing in the Federal Register, not later than such date of publication, a written finding, with reasons therefor, that the final rule is being promulgated in response to an emergency that makes timely compliance with the provisions of section 604 of this title impracticable. If the agency has not prepared a final regulatory analysis pursuant to section 604 of this title within one hundred and eighty days from the date of publication of the final rule, such rule shall lapse and have no effect. Such rule shall not be repromulgated until a final regulatory flexibility analysis has been completed by the agency.

§ 609. Procedures for gathering comments

When any rule is promulgated which will have a significant economic impact on a substantial number of small entities, the head of the agency promulgating the rule or the official of the agency with statutory responsibility for the promulgation of the rule shall assure that small entities have been given an opportunity to participate in the rulemaking for the rule through techniques such as—

(1) the inclusion in an advanced notice of proposed rulemaking, if issued, of a statement that the proposed rule may have a significant economic effect on a substantial number of small entities;

(2) the publication of general notice of proposed rulemaking in publications likely to be obtained by small entities;

(3) the direct notification of interested small entities;

(4) the conduct of open conferences or public hearings concerning the rule for small entities; and

(5) the adoption or modification of agency procedural rules to reduce the cost or complexity of participation in the rulemaking by small entities.

§ 610. Periodic review of rules

(a) Within one hundred and eighty days after the effective date of this chapter, each agency shall publish in the Federal Register a plan for the periodic review of the rules issued by the agency which have or will have a significant economic impact upon a substantial number of small entities.   Such plan may be amended by the agency at any time by publishing the revision in the Federal Register. The purpose of the review shall be to determine whether such rules should be continued without change, or should be amended or rescinded, consistent with the stated objectives of applicable statutes, to minimize any significant economic impact of the rules upon a substantial number of such small entities. The plan shall provide for the review of all such agency rules existing on the effective date of this chapter within ten years of that date and for the review of such rules adopted after the effective date of this chapter within ten years of the publication of such rules as the final rule. If the head of the agency determines that completion of the review of existing rules is not feasible by the established date, he shall so certify in a statement published in the Federal Register and may extend the completion date by one year at a time for a total of not more than five years.

(b) In reviewing rules to minimize any significant economic impact of the rule on a substantial number of small entities in a manner consistent with the stated objectives of applicable statutes, the agency shall consider the following factors—

(1) the continued need for the rule;

(2) the nature of complaints or comments received concerning the rule from the public;

(3) the complexity of the rule;

(4) the extent to which the rule overlaps, duplicates or conflicts with other Federal rules, and, to the extent feasible, with State and local governmental rules; and

(5) the length of time since the rule has been evaluated or the degree to which technology, economic conditions, or other factors have changed in the area affected by the rule.

(c) Each year, each agency shall publish in the Federal Register a list of the rules which have a significant economic impact on a substantial number of small entities, which are to be reviewed pursuant to this section during the succeeding twelve months. The list shall include a brief description of each rule and the need for and legal basis of such rule and shall invite public comment upon the rule.

§ 611. Judicial review

(a) Except as otherwise provided in subsection (b), any determination by an agency concerning the applicability of any of the provisions of this chapter to any action of the agency shall not be subject to judicial review.

(b) Any regulatory flexibility analysis prepared under sections 603 and 604 of this title and the compliance or noncompliance of the agency with the provisions of this chapter shall not be subject to judicial review. When an action for judicial review of a rule is instituted, any regulatory flexibility analysis for such rule shall constitute part of the whole record of agency action in connection with the review.

(c) Nothing in this section bars judicial review of any other impact statement or similar analysis required by any other law if judicial review of such statement or analysis is otherwise provided by law.

§ 612. Reports and intervention rights

(a) The Chief Counsel for Advocacy of the Small Business Administration shall monitor agency compliance with this chapter and shall report at least annually thereon to the President and to the Committees on the Judiciary of the Senate and House of Representatives, the Select Committee on Small Business of the Senate, and the Committee on Small Business of the House of Representatives.

(b) The Chief Counsel for Advocacy of the Small Business Administration is authorized to appear as amicus curiae in any action brought in a court of the United States to review a rule. In any such action, the Chief Counsel is authorized to present his views with respect to the effect of the rule on small entities.

(c) A court of the United States shall grant the application of the Chief Counsel for Advocacy of the Small Business Administration to appear in any such action for the purposes described in subsection (b).

Chapter 7—Judicial Review

§ 701. Application; definitions

(a) This chapter applies, according to the provisions thereof, except to the extent that—

   (1) statutes preclude judicial review; or

   (2) agency action is committed to agency discretion by law.

(b) For the purpose of this chapter—

   (1) "agency" means each authority of the Government of the United States, whether or not it is

within or subject to review by another agency, but does not include—

(A) the Congress;

(B) the courts of the United States;

(C) the governments of the territories or possessions of the United States;

(D) the government of the District of Columbia;

(E) agencies composed of representatives of the parties or of representatives of organizations of the parties to the disputes determined by them;

(F) courts martial and military commissions;

(G) military authority exercised in the field in time of war or in occupied territory; or

(H) functions conferred by sections 1738, 1739, 1743, and 1744 of title 12; chapter 2 of title 41; or sections 1622, 1884, 1891–1902, and former section 1641(b)(2), of title 50, appendix; and

(2) "person", "rule", "order", "license", "sanction", "relief", and "agency action" have the meanings given them by section 551 of this title.

§ 702. Right of review

A person suffering legal wrong because of agency action, or adversely affected or aggrieved by agency action within the meaning of a relevant statute, is entitled to judicial review thereof. An action in a court of the United States seeking relief other than money damages and stating a claim that an agency or an officer or employee thereof acted or failed to act in an official capacity or under color of legal authority shall not be dismissed nor relief therein be denied on the ground that it is against the United States or that the United States is an indispensable party. The United States may be named as a defendant in any such action, and a judgment or decree may be entered against the United States: *Provided,* That any mandatory or injunctive decree shall specify the Federal officer or officers (by name or by title), and their successors in office, personally responsible for compliance. Nothing herein (1) affects other limitations on judicial review or the power or duty of the court to dismiss any action or deny relief on any other appropriate legal or equitable ground; or (2) confers authority to grant relief if any other statute that grants consent to suit expressly or impliedly forbids the relief which is sought.

§ 703. Form and venue of proceeding

The form of proceeding for judicial review is the special statutory review proceeding relevant to the subject matter in a court specified by statute or, in the absence or inadequacy thereof, any applicable form of legal action, including actions for declaratory judgments or writs of prohibitory or mandatory injunction or habeas corpus, in a court of competent jurisdiction. If no special statutory review proceeding is applicable, the action for judicial review may be brought against the United States, the agency by its official title, or the appropriate officer. Except to the extent that prior, adequate, and exclusive opportunity for judicial review is provided by law, agency action is subject to judicial review in civil or criminal proceedings for judicial enforcement.

§ 704. Actions reviewable

Agency action made reviewable by statute and final agency action for which there is no adequate remedy in a court are subject to judicial review. A preliminary, procedural, or intermediate agency action or ruling not directly reviewable is subject to review on the review of the final agency action. Except as otherwise expressly required by statute, agency action otherwise final is final for the purposes of this section whether or not there has been presented or determined an application for a declaratory order, for any form of reconsideration, or, unless the agency otherwise requires by rule and provides that the action meanwhile is inoperative, for an appeal to superior agency authority.

§ 705. Relief pending review

When an agency finds that justice so requires, it may postpone the effective date of action taken by it, pending judicial review. On such conditions as may be required and to the extent necessary to prevent irreparable injury, the reviewing court, including the court to which a case may be taken on appeal from or on application for certiorari or other writ to a reviewing court, may issue all necessary and appropriate process to postpone the effective date of an agency action or to preserve status or rights pending conclusion of the review proceedings.

§ 706. Scope of review

To the extent necessary to decision and when presented, the reviewing court shall decide all relevant questions of law, interpret constitutional and statutory provisions, and determine the meaning or applicability of the terms of an agency action. The reviewing court shall—

    (1) compel agency action unlawfully withheld or unreasonably delayed; and

    (2) hold unlawful and set aside agency action, findings, and conclusions found to be—

        (A) arbitrary, capricious, an abuse of discretion, or otherwise not in accordance with law;

        (B) contrary to constitutional right, power, privilege, or immunity;

        (C) in excess of statutory jurisdiction, authority, or limitations, or short of statutory right;

        (D) without observance of procedure required by law;

        (E) unsupported by substantial evidence in a case subject to section 556 and 557 of this title or otherwise reviewed on the record of an agency hearing provided by statute; or

        (F) unwarranted by the facts to the extent that the facts are subject to trial de novo by the reviewing court.

In making the foregoing determinations, the court shall review the whole record or those parts of it cited by a party, and due account shall be taken of the rule of prejudicial error.

ADMINISTRATIVE LAW JUDGES

§ 3105. Appointment of administrative law judges

Each agency shall appoint as many administrative law judges as are necessary for proceedings required to be conducted in accordance with sections 556 and 557 of this title. Administrative law judges shall be assigned to cases in rotation so far as practicable, and may not perform duties inconsistent with their duties and responsibilities as administrative law judges.

§ 7521. Actions against administrative law judges

(a) An action may be taken against an administrative law judge appointed under section 3105 of this title by the agency in which the administrative law judge is employed only for good cause established and determined by the Merit Systems Protection Board on the record after opportunity for hearing before the Board. . . . [Actions covered include removal, suspension, and reduction in grade or pay.]

§ 5372. Administrative law judges

Administrative law judges appointed under section 3105 of this title are entitled to pay prescribed by the Office of Personnel Management independently of agency recommendations or ratings and in accordance with subchapter III of this chapter and chapter 51 of this title.

§ 3344. Details; administrative law judges

An agency as defined by section 551 of this title which occasionally or temporarily is insufficiently staffed with administrative law judges appointed under section 3105 of this title may use administrative law judges selected by the Office of Personnel Management from and with the consent of other agencies.

§ 1305. Administrative law judges

For the purpose of sections 3105, 3344, 4301(2)(D), and 5372 of this title and the provisions of section 5335(a)(B) of this title that relate to administrative law judges, the Office of Personnel Management may, and for the purpose of section 7521 of this title, the Merit Systems Protection Board may investigate, require reports by agencies, issue reports, including an annual report to Congress, prescribe regulations, appoint advisory committees as necessary, recommend legislation, subpena witnesses and records, and pay witness fees as established for the courts of the United States.

Table Correlating the 1946 Administrative Procedure Act With Parallel Sections Codified in 5 U.S.C.A.

Parallel Section 1946 Administrative Procedure Act	5 U.S.C.A.
Sec. 2(a)	§ 551(1)
Sec. 2(b)	§ 551(2), (3)
Sec. 2(c)	§ 551(4), (5)
Sec. 2(d)	§ 551(6), (7)
Sec. 2(e)	§ 551(8), (9)
Sec. 2(f)	§ 551(10), (11)
Sec. 2(g)	§ 551(12), (13)
Sec. 3	§ 552(a)-(e)
Sec. 4	§ 533(a)
Sec. 4(a)	§ 553(b)
Sec. 4(b)	§ 553(c)
Sec. 4(c)	§ 553(d)
Sec. 4(d)	§ 553(e)

APPENDIX I

Parallel Section 1946 Administrative Procedure Act	5 U.S.C.A.
Sec. 10(e)	§ 706(1), (2)
Sec. 11 (1st sentence)	§ 3105
Sec. 11 (2d sentence)	§ 7521
Sec. 11 (3d sentence)	§ 5362
Sec. 11 (4th sentence)	§ 3344
Sec. 11 (5th sentence)	§ 1305

APPENDIX II

THE FEDERAL ALPHABET SOUP: A GUIDE TO COMMON ABBREVIATIONS AND ACRONYMS

A common source of confusion is the tendency of courts, commentators and administrators themselves to refer to agencies by their initials. This Appendix provides a translation of some of these acronyms into their English equivalents. General information about the functions and organization of each federal agency can be found in the current edition of the Government Manual.

ACUS	Administrative Conference of the United States
AEC	Atomic Energy Commission (superseded; functions now divided between Nuclear Regulatory Commission and Department of Energy)
CAB	Civil Aeronautics Board
CBO	Congressional Budget Office
CFTC	Commodity Futures Trading Commission
CIA	Central Intelligence Agency
CPSC	Consumer Product Safety Commission
CSC	Civil Service Commission (superseded; functions transferred to OPM, MSPB)
DHHS	Department of Health and Human Services (formerly HEW)
DOD	Department of Defense
DOJ	Department of Justice

DOT ...... Department of Transportation

EEOC ..... Equal Employment Opportunity Commission

EPA ...... Environmental Protection Agency

FAA ...... Federal Aviation Administration

FBI ...... Federal Bureau of Investigation

FCC ...... Federal Communications Commission

FDA ...... Food and Drug Administration

FERC ..... Federal Energy Regulatory Commission (formerly FPC)

FPC ...... Federal Power Commission (superseded; functions assumed by FERC)

FRB ...... Federal Reserve Board

FTC ...... Federal Trade Commission

GAO ...... General Accounting Office

HEW ...... Department of Health, Education, and Welfare (superseded; functions divided between DHHS and Department of Education)

HUD ...... Department of Housing and Urban Development

ICC ...... Interstate Commerce Commission

INS ...... Immigration and Naturalization Service

IRS ...... Internal Revenue Service

MSPB ..... Merit Systems Protection Board (formerly part of CSC)

NHTSA .... National Highway Traffic Safety Administration

NIRA ..... National Industrial Recovery Administration (terminated)

NLRB ..... National Labor Relations Board

NMB ...... National Mediation Board

NRC ...... Nuclear Regulatory Commission
NSC .... National Security Council
OMB ...... Office of Management and Budget
OPA .... Office of Price Administration (terminated after World War II)
OPM ...... Office of Personnel Management (formerly part of CSC)
OSHA ..... Occupational Safety and Health Administration
OSHRC .... Occupational Safety and Health Review Commission
OTA .... Office of Technology Assessment
RARG ..... Regulatory Analysis Review Group
SEC .... Securities Exchange Commission
SSA .... Social Security Administration
TVA ...... Tennessee Valley Authority
USDA ..... Department of Agriculture
VA .... Veterans' Administration

APPENDIX III

NOTES ON USING THE APA

The Administrative Procedure Act is a fairly complex statute, and the interrelationships between the APA and the agencies' organic statutes create further problems of analysis. This Appendix suggests a strategy for applying the APA to unfamiliar fact situations. The four general questions set out below are derived from the grounds for judicial reversal of agency decisions contained in Section 706 of the APA. In answering these questions, the normal aids for statutory construction should be used: analysis of the language and structure of the relevant statutory provisions, any available legislative history, judicial decisions interpreting the statutes in question, and functional or policy arguments.

1. *What are the Substantive Standards or Limits Which the Legislature has Imposed on this Type of Decision*? Logically, the first step of the analysis is to get a clear idea of what the Congress has told the agency to do in making the particular kind of decision which is under consideration. The APA has several provisions which empower reviewing courts to set aside an agency decision which exceeds these bounds. If the agency tries to regulate persons or subjects that fall outside the scope of authority delegated by the legislature, its decision will be reversible as "in excess of statutory jurisdiction, authority, or limitations" under section 706(2)(C). Similarly, if the agency fails to consider factors which the legislature has directed it to

take into account, or if it considers irrelevant factors, or if it fails to give the proper weight to relevant factors, its decision may be "an abuse of discretion or otherwise not in accordance with law" within the meaning of section 706(2)(A). The agency's own standards may also impose substantive limits, since a failure to obey its own rules or to follow precedents without a reasonable explanation may be an abuse of discretion. See generally pp. 68–80 supra.

2. *What Procedure is the Agency Required to use in Making this Kind of Decision?* Section 706(2)(D) provides for reversal of agency actions taken "without observance of procedure required by law." Statutory limits on agency procedure may be found either in the particular statutes granting authority to the agency, or in the APA, or in both places. Statutes enacted subsequent to the APA may, of course, contain their own procedural requirements which wholly supersede the APA, and section 551(1) of the Act contains some exceptions to its coverage. More commonly, however, the particular agency statutes must be read together with the APA in order to determine what procedures are required.

Since the APA divides agency decisions into adjudication and rulemaking, the first step is to determine whether the agency action you are concerned with is a "rule" or an adjudicative "order" within the meaning of APA section 551(4), (6). See generally pp. 180–82, 240–41 supra.

If the decision is a rule (which will normally mean that it is of general applicability and future effect), then it must be determined whether the proceeding is formal or informal rulemaking under the APA, or a special "hybrid" proceeding. Formal rulemaking, involving a full trial-type hearing, must be triggered by a requirement in the particular statute that the rule "be made on the record after an opportunity for an agency hearing," 5 U.S.C.A. § 553(c). When such a requirement exists, then the characteristics of the trial-type hearing are specified by sections 556 and 557. However, because formal rulemaking can be extremely cumbersome, there is a strong presumption against it and the congressional intent to require formal rulemaking must be plain. See generally pp. 251–55 supra. When there is no requirement of formal rulemaking in the particular statute, then the informal or notice-and-comment rulemaking procedures of section 553 will apply. This section generally imposes only three procedural requirements: the agency must publish a notice of rulemaking in the Federal Register, it must allow interested persons an opportunity to submit written comments, and it must issue a concise general statement of basis and purpose with the final rule. Note that section 553 contains several broad exceptions from those public participation requirements, including the issuance of interpretative or procedural rules.

When the particular statutes authorizing rulemaking direct the agencies to use some procedures beyond the minimal notice-and-comment requirements, but stop short of the full trial-type hearing of formal rulemaking, the process is generally described as "hybrid rulemaking." See pp. 255–65 supra. In this situation, section 553 and the particular statute are read cumulatively to define the procedural requirements.

[*413*]

If the agency action is adjudication rather than rulemaking, the APA will govern the procedures only if it is a formal adjudication—that is, one in which the agency is required to conduct a formal trial-type hearing. The test for formal adjudication is essentially the same as the test for formal rulemaking: is the decision "required by statute to be determined on the record after opportunity for an agency hearing," 5 U.S.C.A. § 554(a). However, since trial-type hearings are more suitable for adjudication than for rulemaking, there is generally not a strong presumption against formal proceedings in adjudication as there is in rulemaking. This is particularly true when the party requesting a hearing is the holder of a substantial property interest, or "quasi property" like a license. As with rulemaking, the requirement for an on-the-record hearing usually must be found outside the APA—most commonly, in the statute giving the agency the power to make the kind of decision in question.

When neither the APA, nor the particular statute, nor the agency's own rules of practice confer the desired right to a hearing, the injured party may still be able to establish some right to participate in the decisionmaking process by challenging the agency's procedures as a denial of procedural due process. Section 706(2)(B) of the APA directs a reviewing court to set aside agency action which is "contrary to constitutional right, power, privilege, or immunity." However, to prevail on due process grounds the challenging party must establish that he holds a protected liberty or property interest which is threatened by the agency action, and that the particular procedural rights he is seeking are justified when compared with their costs. See generally pp. 139–79 supra. If the proceeding is rulemaking involving general rather than specific facts, he will probably not be able to meet the constitutional tests. See pp. 256–57 supra.

3. *How much Factual Support is Necessary to Uphold the Agency's Decision?* In enacting a particular regulatory program, Congress is of course free to specify the kind of evidence that is needed to support a decision (e. g., "the best available scientific data") and the amount of evidence. When Congress does not specify the amount or type, then the APA generally permits the agency to rely upon any available evidence, and it provides three standards under which reviewing courts can assess the quantum or weight of factual support. The first of these is the "unwarranted by the facts" standard of section 706(2)(F), which permits the court to conduct its own trial of the facts, without deference to agency findings. This is a rare form of review, applicable only when the agency has conducted an adjudication with completely inadequate factfinding proceedings. Citizens to Preserve Overton Park, Inc. v. Volpe, 401 U.S. 402, 415 (1971).[1] More commonly, the choice will be between the "arbitrary and capricious" standard of section 706(2)(A), or the "substantial evidence" test of section 706(2)(E). The APA makes the choice between these two fact review provisions depend upon the kind of procedures which the agency has used in making its decisions. If the procedure is formal adjudication or formal rulemaking—in other words, if the

---

1. Independent judicial factfinding is also available when issues not before the agency are raised in a proceeding to enforce nonadjudicative agency actions. Id.

agency was required to hold a full trial-type hearing—then the substantial evidence test will apply; otherwise, the arbitrary and capricious standard is applicable. For discussion of the meaning and application of these two tests, see pages 233–36, 265–74 supra.

4. *Is Judicial Review Available*? To enforce the rights created by the APA and other statutes, a party must first be able to present his claims to a court which is empowered to consider the merits. The APA does not by itself give the courts jurisdiction to review agency decisions; it merely tells the court what to do once it has obtained jurisdiction. Normally, a party seeking review would look first for a "special statutory review" provision—one in the statutes relating to the particular agency or function, authorizing the courts to hear challenges to the validity of agency action. If there is no such special statutory review, then the challenging party would seek to bring his claim within one of the general jurisdictional statutes such as the federal question provision or the Mandamus and Venue Act; paradoxically, this is called "nonstatutory" review. See pp. 286–300 supra.

After having found a jurisdictional basis for his claim, the party seeking review would be concerned with whether there was some practical or technical reason for the court to avoid reaching the merits of his claim. There is a presumption of reviewability, but it can be overcome in appropriate cases. Two of these technical grounds for denying review are enumerated in section 701(a) of the APA. If Congress has clearly indicated its intention to bar review (again, usually in the particular statute granting power to the agency), then there may be a statutory preclusion of review within the meaning of section 701(a)(1). Alternatively, if the statute gives the agency such broad discretion that a reviewing court has essentially no law to apply, or there are other practical reasons to avoid even limited judicial review, then the action may be "committed to agency discretion" within the meaning of section 701(a)(2). If the challenging party can avoid these doctrines, he still must be concerned with whether he is a proper party to invoke the judicial process (whether he has standing to seek review), and whether this is the proper time to review the agency's decision (whether the controversy is ripe and the plaintiff has exhausted his administrative remedies). These doctrines are partly based on the language of sections 702–04, but for the most part they arise from common law "prudential" considerations and the constitutional limit of the judicial power to cases or controversies. See generally pp. 300–21 supra.

*

INDEX

References are to Pages

INDEX

INDEX

References are to Pages

INDEX

INDEX

INDEX

INDEX

INDEX

FINALITY

FINDINGS AND CONCLUSIONS

FOREIGN AFFAIRS

FORMAL ADJUDICATIONS

INDEX

INDEX
References are to Pages

INDEX

[432]

INDEX
References are to Pages

INDEX

INDEX
References are to Pages

INDEX

[*438*]

INDEX

INDEX

INDEX

INDEX

INDEX

[443]

INDEX

INDEX

†